# Serial Shakespeare

# Serial Shakespeare

An infinite variety of appropriations
in American TV drama

ELISABETH BRONFEN

Manchester University Press

Copyright © Elisabeth Bronfen 2020

The right of Elisabeth Bronfen to be identified as the author of this work has been asserted by her in accordance with the Copyright, Designs and Patents Act 1988.

Published by Manchester University Press
Altrincham Street, Manchester M1 7JA
www.manchesteruniversitypress.co.uk

British Library Cataloguing-in-Publication Data
A catalogue record for this book is available from the British Library

ISBN 978 1 5261 4231 3 hardback

First published 2020

The publisher has no responsibility for the persistence or accuracy of URLs for any external or third-party internet websites referred to in this book, and does not guarantee that any content on such websites is, or will remain, accurate or appropriate.

Typeset by Deanta Global Publishing Services
Printed in Great Britain
by TJ Books Limited, Padstow

# Contents

| | |
|---|---|
| List of figures | *page* vi |
| Acknowledgements | viii |
| Introduction: appropriation, dislocation, and crossmapping | 1 |
| 1 Shakespeare's spectres: *Westworld* | 26 |
| 2 Wearing the crown: *The Wire* | 58 |
| 3 Choosing our queen: a series of first female presidents from *Commander in Chief* to *House of Cards* | 85 |
| 4 Rogue queens: *Veep*, *Homeland*, and *Scandal* | 120 |
| 5 All the frontier's a stage: *Deadwood* | 155 |
| 6 Carnival of spies: *The Americans* | 194 |
| Bibliography | 227 |
| Index | 241 |

# Figures

1. The host Abernathy being questioned in the Avalon laboratory. *Westworld*, 'The Original', season 1, episode 1, first broadcast HBO 4 October 2016 — page 34
2. Dolores receiving her father's warning. *Westworld*, 'The Original', season 1, episode 1, first broadcast HBO 4 October 2016 — 37
3. Dolores gives Arnold a fatal shot to the head. *Westworld*, 'The Bicameral Mind', season 1, episode 10, first broadcast HBO 6 December 2016 — 46
4. Dolores gives Dr Ford a fatal shot to the head. *Westworld*, 'The Bicameral Mind', season 1, episode 10, first broadcast HBO 6 December 2016 — 48
5. D'Angelo's chess instruction on the king piece. *The Wire*, 'The Buys', season 1, episode 3, first broadcast HBO 16 June 2002 — 60
6. D'Angelo's chess instruction on the pawns. *The Wire*, 'The Buys', season 1, episode 3, first broadcast HBO 16 June 2002 — 61
7. Claire Underwood on her bloody throne of power. *House of Cards*, advertisement poster for season 6, Netflix 2018 — 91
8. The statue of President Claire Hale. *House of Cards*, credit sequence in 'Chapter 73', season 6, episode 8, Netflix 2018 — 92
9. Selina Meyer's emblem of presidential power. *Veep*, credit sequence throughout season 1, HBO 2012 — 125
10. President Elizabeth Keane frozen in her symbolic body. *Homeland*, 'America First', season 6, episode 12, first broadcast Showtime 16 April 2017 — 135
11. The Janus face of female countersovereignty: Mellie Grant and Olivia Pope. *Scandal*, 'People Like Me', season 7, episode 11, first broadcast ABC 26 April 2018 — 148
12. Al Swearengen's balcony stage. *Deadwood*, 'A Lie Agreed Upon (Part 1)', season 2, episode 1, first broadcast HBO 6 March 2005 — 162

13  Al Swearengen's conversations with a dead Sioux chief.
    *Deadwood*, 'E.B. Was Left Out', season 2, episode 7, first
    broadcast HBO 17 April 2005                                    167
14  Jen's lethal bed trick. *Deadwood*, 'Tell Him Something
    Pretty', season 3, episode 12, first broadcast HBO
    27 August 2006                                                 174
15  E.B. Farnum re-installed in the Grand Central Hotel.
    *Deadwood*, 'Tell Him Something Pretty', season 3,
    episode 12, first broadcast HBO 27 August 2006                 185
16  Trixie accepts Al Swearengen's legacy. *Deadwood:
    The Movie* (HBO Films, 2019)                                   188
17  The double vision of ideology. *The Americans*, credit
    sequence throughout all seasons, FX Network, 2013–18           202
18  Moving from disenchantment to re-enchantment. *The
    Americans*, 'START', season 6, episode 10, first broadcast
    FX Network 30 May 2018                                         221

# Acknowledgements

While written in solitude, books emerge from conversations. I want to thank all those who, over the past years, have been my encouraging interlocutors. Daniela Janser, Heike Paul, Benno Wirz, Gesine Krüger, and Emily Sun for their thoughtful comments and gentle critique on individual chapters. Margaret Tudeau-Clayton, Elisabeth Strowick, Andrea Kraus, Alessandra Violi, Sabine Schülting, Barbara Straumann, Muriel Gerstner, Dympna Callaghan, and John Archer for encouraging me to pursue my investigation into Shakespeare's rich and strange presence in contemporary serial TV drama. Hannah Schoch for her tireless help with the research, Dominic Scherz for his editorial eye, and Mansi Tiwari for her astute assistance with putting together the final manuscript. Daniel Binswanger for letting me use my column in the online newspaper, *Republik*, to test my ideas. The students in seminars given in Zürich and New York, whose willingness to engage with the question of seriality was as productive as the fresh perspective they brought to a medium far more familiar to them than to me. Peter Kirwan, my first reader, who asked me to look at the innovative research in the field of digital Shakespeare. And finally, my editor, Matthew Frost, who was immediately enthusiastic about this project when, on a very hot day in Stratford-upon-Avon, I told him about it, and who has supported it steadfastly ever since.

# Introduction: appropriation, dislocation, and crossmapping

Shakespeare, these days, seems to be everywhere in serial drama.[1] In 'The Ladies of La Belle', an early episode in *Godless*, three women are standing in front of the only hotel in their frontier town, ready to receive the man who has taken over the Quicksilver Mining Company. While they are waiting, Charlotte Temple reads out loud from an article about Mr James Sloan in their local newspaper. In it, the reporter describes him as being fair, honest, and good humoured but also claims that he 'is a tall man, rather handsome, with a beautiful baritone, and if all that isn't enough, he writes the most beautiful poetry'. Visibly pleased with this piece of news, the hotel owner looks up and smiles radiantly at the two other townswomen as she explains that it is sonnets which the man they are expecting writes. Mary Agnes McNue, the mayor's widow, who, since her husband's death in a mining accident, insists on wearing only the clothes of the deceased, laconically replies: 'Just like Shakespeare'.[2]

Because vicious outlaws have murdered him *en route*, Mr Sloan, in fact, never arrives in La Belle, and no further reference is made to Shakespeare in the subsequent episodes of *Godless*. But what is he doing here in the first place? While Mary Agnes tosses out her remark to taunt her friend's enthusiasm, her reference to Shakespeare also signals that she is culturally educated. In conjunction with the fact that the man he is being compared to is, himself, nothing more than a mentioned name, dead on arrival of the stagecoach, the allusion also speaks to the spectral quality of the Bard's poetic language. It, too, is invoked without ever making an actual appearance. To mention the Bard in a Western frontier town, however, also implicitly gestures towards a prior TV drama, *Deadwood*, iconic for its Shakespearean tone.

A more explicit citation is at play in 'Our Raison d'Etre' in *The Deuce*.[3] In search of the owner of the gay bar, Paul's, Frankie wanders into the dark room in the back. More astonished than embarrassed by the sexual acts taking place around him, he stops and stares. Then Paul suddenly emerges from the darkness, puts his arm around his friend's shoulder, and explains: 'There are more things in heaven and earth, Horatio, than are dreamt of in your philosophy.' When Frankie, ever more bemused, asks, 'What?', Paul names his source: 'Shakespeare'. Still confused, Frankie responds with a further question, 'Shakespeare was gay?', and, while the two men move back into the lit area around the counter, Paul simply responds in the affirmative. Hamlet's words to his bewildered friend are recalled to fit an analogous though different situation from the one in the play. Paul's use of Shakespeare equates the dark room in his bar with purgatory, casting it in terms of an undiscovered country for his heterosexual friend, even while gesturing towards rumours pertaining to Shakespeare's own sexual preferences. The irony of this scene, in turn, plays to a disjunction in cultural knowledge. Frankie does not get the reference, while the script assumes that we do.

An equally pointed translocation of a Shakespeare quotation occurs in an episode in *The Good Fight*, entitled 'The One Where the Sun Comes Out'. The flamboyant attorney, Roland Blum, has been called before a disciplinary board for his unauthorised practice of law. To defend himself against the allegation of perjury brought against him, he cites Edgar, who, in the final act of *King Lear*, appears in disguise to challenge his bastard brother: 'By treason's tooth bare-gnawn and canker-bit; yet I am noble as the adversary I come to cope withal.' The words he chooses perfectly match his own histrionic challenge of the team of lawyers with whom he had served as co-counsel on a case. However, to draw attention to the way Shakespeare does not properly inhabit this space, the man heading the commission rebukes this histrionic display, suggesting, 'it would be helpful, Mr Blum, if your responses were more on point'.[4] While *Godless* merely nods towards the cultural value of Shakespeare and *The Deuce* repurposes a citation, the appropriation in this case not only allows the rogue lawyer to cast himself as the legitimate but slandered heir to the law, it also debunks his claim, by showing how his aggressive self-display makes a dramatic farce of this courtroom. Blum will ultimately be disbarred in the State of Illinois.

One further retrieval of Shakespeare in prestige TV bears mentioning. In *Billions*, the legal battles between Chuck Rhoades, US Attorney for the Southern District of New York, and the hedge fund manager, Bobby Axelrod, have been discussed by critics as a re-enactment of a Shakespearean battle. Indeed, the ruthless billionaire comports himself as royalty, surrounding himself with a colourful entourage of men and women who are willing to be part of his war machine against those coming, if not literally then financially, to assassinate him. His challenger, in turn, like Othello, is prone to blind jealousy, triggered by his wife's close ties to his sworn enemy. Rhoades' seething desire for revenge repeatedly pitches him into a furious rage, threatening to destroy his reputation. When he speaks of being put on the rack, when he taunts others for not acting with purpose, or when he justifies his own duplicitous activities by claiming they are serving noble ends, we think we hear Shakespeare. Indeed, in 'The Punch', one of Axelrod's men who pretends to be cooperating with the Attorney General meets up with his deputy. Defending his reluctance at selling out his long-time boss, Donnie explains, 'the price of any betrayal always comes due in flesh'. Frustrated, his interlocutor asks, 'What's that, Shakespeare?' Donnie's reply is unexpected: 'Stephen King. *Gunslinger*. But no less true.'[5] In this case, the Bard is not where we have been expecting him to be. Yet, as the camera captures Rhoades, cloaked in a dark shadow, clandestinely listening in on this conversation through a crack in the door to the supply room at the back of the bar, we have a sense that Shakespeare is haunting this scene after all.

These citations, as varied as they are, attest to the way Shakespeare has become something, as Stephen O'Neill puts it, 'that is sowed in the media ecology and scattered through it'.[6] By disseminating and dispersing the original text, these iterations leave the original dramas behind and, instead, favour derivations that mingle Shakespeare with his contemporary media appropriation. In the process, a sense of Shakespeare's proximity to the current cultural moment is forged, as is an awareness of his historical remoteness. He occupies the present and yet is not properly part of it, instead straddling both temporal sites. Shakespeare is sowed *in* history, and yet, by virtue of his subsequent scattering and reassemblage, he is also recurrent *through* history, as O'Neill suggests. This leads him to argue for 'an understanding of Shakespeare as a mutable process rather than something static'.[7] By virtue of the fact that – as in the past, so, too, in contemporary media culture – Shakespeare is continually being planted and dispersed, the Bard also continues to be used as a capacious site for articulations ranging from individual self-expression to a collective claim on cultural capital and authority.

Shakespeare has always served a wide variety of cultural purposes, as every age creates, or rather recreates, its own Shakespeare. As Marjorie Garber points out, he has, in fact, always been two playwrights: 'the playwright of *his* time, the late sixteenth and early seventeenth centuries in England, and the playwright of *our* time, whatever time that is. The playwright of *now*.'[8] As a global lingua franca, she adds, Shakespeare is one of the key ways in which we communicate with each other. His oeuvre embodies a shared cultural literacy, even when, as my opening examples from contemporary TV dramas illustrate, the Shakespeare quote functions less in reference to the original play; instead, dislocated and replanted, these citations enforce the meaning of a very different scene for which they have been repurposed.[9] If, as Douglas Lanier points out, the designation 'Shakespeare' refers not only 'to qualities and themes regarded as being essential to his plays', but also to a cultural authority that lends legitimacy to whatever the name is applied to, the question therefore becomes, how far are we willing to extend it?[10] Given that popular culture helps make Shakespeare relevant again, at issue is, thus, a reciprocal exchange. Shakespeare may endow serial TV drama with a touch of weightiness, but it is also this popular dramatic format that re-installs the urgency of his cultural authority. Lanier adds that to ask what Shakespeare is doing in popular culture means recognising that 'these allusions are doing something, that pop culture uses Shakespeare to create meaning and not merely as an inert decoration or simple-minded token of prestige'.[11]

Part and parcel of this two-way dialogue – between past and present, between an iconic author and his recyclings – is the gain that new performances, remediations, and remakings of Shakespeare make by mingling the original text with contemporary media objects. As Courtney Lehmann and Lisa S. Starks suggest, Shakespeare's continual re-inscription in film and popular media helps translate his plays for contemporary audiences: 'Shakespeare needs the movies not only to ensure the ongoing cultural relevance of his plays, but also to render them accessible to postmodern audiences, bridging the gap that separates us from early modern England.'[12] Yet, while this claim is as relevant for contemporary serialised TV drama as it has been for cinema since the early twentieth century, so, too, is the question which follows from their proposition: why does prestige TV need Shakespeare? Is it simply because, representing universal wisdom, he can so readily be accessed? Is it the timelessness of his preferred themes revolving, as they do, around love and death, desire and revenge, duplicity and violence, power and theatricality? Is it because his texts have proven to be fluid and malleable, and thus easily adaptable?

As Linda Charnes argues, he re-surfaces so persistently because he has become a medium of exchange, pure ideological value, 'so saturized with itself as to signify nothing but "itself"', and thus able to authorise 'whatever "structures of feeling" are being promoted'.[13] But might it not, in part, be residual content after all? Could it be that Shakespeare's apparent infinite adaptability serves as a protean conduit for a particular set of personal and collective articulations, which pick up on discoveries that his plays continue to raise for us, even if these require the adjustment which transformations afford? If, furthermore, Shakespeare is no longer the end but rather the means by which films and TV dramas articulate a shared concern, then to what purpose is this exchange undertaken? And why is our attention self-consciously drawn to it, when, for example, a character explains that he has just cited Shakespeare, or admits that he has not? Ultimately, the question remains: why Shakespeare?

What *Serial Shakespeare* tracks is how a set of contemporary TV shows partake in this mutable process of disseminating and reassembling the Bard's work. My concern is neither with television adaptations of a play or a set of plays, such as BBC's *The Hollow Crown*, nor with TV dramas that explicitly advertise their intertextual relation to Shakespeare. For this reason, the influence of his history plays on *Game of Thrones* will also not be discussed. Nor will I look at TV dramas that are loosely based on the dramatic problem posed by a Shakespeare play. An example would be Kurt Sutter's *Sons of Anarchy*, which transplants the rotten state of Denmark to an outlaw motorcycle club in California to develop its story about the death and destruction that a son produces because his mother has all too quickly married the man responsible for his father's death. Another would be Jesse Armstrong's *Succession*, which reworks King Lear's tragic decision to abdicate and divide his kingdom into a cruel melodrama revolving around the children of the royal Roy family, worried – like Goneril, Regan, and Cordelia – about the future of their global media empire should the ageing father, Logan Roy, step down, with each vying to take over power.[14]

The serial dramas chosen for the following readings, instead, all take the shape of appropriations that use Shakespeare as a point of reference, even while transforming him into something very different, and as such no longer making any claim to fidelity. In some cases, cherry-picked quotations serve as the explicit point of connection; in others, theatrical devices and thematic concerns suggest a more implicit dialogue. In all cases, however, the following chapters treat the revisitation of Shakespeare in serial TV drama as a re-surfacing, a resuscitation, a revisitation, and a recasting. Adaptation is treated as a form of re-reading, which saves the Shakespearean text from stale repetition and instead refigures it in terms of the return of the different – not, as Roland Barthes puts it, 'as the *real* text, but a plural text: the same and new'.[15] As Shakespeare's words, figural constellations, tropes, and plot lines return to the screen, the creative reshaping they have undertaken considers something again, from a different perspective; they make something visible again, endow life once more to something.

At the same time, my concern is not just noticing that Shakespeare plays a vibrant role in these serial TV dramas. At issue are also the readings that become possible once his presence – whether explicitly intended or merely surmised – has been detected and, with it, a line of connection between these two distinct texts discovered. What is the political, what the aesthetic status of this re-presence? Triggered by these selectively chosen citations, what analogies, what lines of correspondence can be drawn into focus regarding their overarching narrative as well as the multiple storylines the serial format entangles? What does paying attention to the two bodies of Shakespeare – the playwright of his time and the playwright of our own – offer the creators of these shows? What does it afford to the audience and the critical reader? How does his presence not just impact the new medium in which detached fragments of his plays reappear? How does it influence our way of thinking about the plays from which the quotations, the character constellations, or the dramatic actions have migrated?

While it has become more and more common for cinema to cite and resignify Shakespeare rather than faithfully re-embody his plays, in order, as Carolyn Jess-Cooke puts it, 'to vocalise and legitimate particular twenty-first-century cultural concerns',[16] critics have also uncovered lines of connection not based on any actual citation or adaptation. In *Pleasing Everyone*, Jeffrey Knapp produces a dialogue between Shakespeare and a set of classic Hollywood films based on the proposition that both were designed to please a mass audience.[17] This common self-conceptualising power opens the way to readings that locate similar concerns with work, leisure, art, and a critical assessment of popular entertainment in both the early modern plays and twentieth-century cinema. In a similar vein, Stevie Simkin proposes putting early modern revenge tragedies in dialogue with the violence in contemporary horror films, treating both as documents that illuminate one another.[18] While his selection of texts is predicated on common preoccupations, tropes, and patterns regarding issues of justice, revenge, and punishment, the joint readings seek to draw out striking parallels and points of convergence between the different times as well as the different genres they speak to.

*Serial Shakespeare* makes use of both aspects of this transhistorical and transmedial dialogue to ask, on the one hand, how contemporary serial TV drama cites and resignifies Shakespeare and, on the other, how a critical reading, having noticed this exchange, can profit from it. In the first instance, reading for seriality draws into focus that by appropriating a text (or texts) from the past, the contemporary mediatised text conceives of itself as a repetition with variations and transformations. The logic of seriality proposed is that the original text is always overtaken by that which has followed upon it. The conclusion of each sequence already anticipates a new series, indeed announces it. At issue is, thus, the interminability of the movement from Shakespeare (as the source text) to the infinite variety of appropriations his oeuvre has inspired. As part of a large-scale process of citation at work, each of the TV dramas discussed in the following chapters implicitly or explicitly posits a serial relation between itself and the Shakespearean oeuvre it taps into. At the same time, contemporary serial drama makes use of recurring plot elements, character constellations, and dramatic actions in successive episodes, producing self-citation on a small scale. If the latter is, in part at least, inspired by Shakespeare's own proclivity towards dramatic recurrences in his own works, one might surmise that Shakespeare's plays hold the potential for serial composition that TV drama realises. The way in which his theatre has made the contemporary serials' use of multiple plot arches, entanglement of characters, and absence of closure possible is, however, something we can discover only in hindsight. This brings into play the second aspect of the exchange between Shakespeare and contemporary TV drama that this book proposes. While focusing on the serial nature of these texts, the readings in the following chapters also surmise parallels and points of convergence between Shakespeare's early modern plays and contemporary serial drama. The dialogue between the past and the present that is produced in this case, however – as will be discussed in more detail further on – primarily involves a technique of critical reading. Its aim is to apprehend the seriality both sets of texts share, so as to work through the consequences of this relation once it has been discovered.

The seriality at work in contemporary TV dramas' appropriations of Shakespeare thus does not thrive on what Gilles Deleuze has called static, or naked, repetition, given that it articulates an identity between different series of representations. Instead, these appropriations privilege a repetition with difference.[19] Indeed, when popular culture in general uses Shakespeare, it is less interested in the intended meaning of the textual passages that are detached and reassembled. By accessing such dislocated fragments through the lens of their own concerns, appropriations engage in a dynamic reiteration which embeds Shakespeare as much in contemporary culture as in his own. 'Shakespop', as Stephen Lanier calls this process of re-articulation, retains certain important motifs even while transforming the material according to the media and cultural context afforded, and, in the process, engenders new conceptions of Shakespeare. Shakespop marks 'contours of affiliation and debate produced by a particular culture's encounter with Shakespeare'; it extends, manages, and legitimises the range of potential meanings his plays offer, pays homage to and transgresses his cultural authority.[20]

The process of appropriation sustained by the dialogue between Shakespeare and contemporary TV drama, which the following chapters perform, is, however, a two-way relationship in more than one sense. While appropriation means taking possession of something for one's own use, this implies, as Christy Desmet notes, a duplicitous exchange, 'either the theft of something valuable (such as property or ideas) or a gift, the allocation of resources for a worthy cause'.[21] Pop culture's claim on Shakespeare not only overlaps the act of poaching with that of acknowledging a legacy. Reciprocity is also at work in this serial return. Those who take possession of Shakespeare's oeuvre for their own ends are also possessed by him. Residual fragments from his oeuvre return to our screens because contemporary creators of serial dramas cannot help but turn to him over and again. As a fluid and malleable source, Shakespeare's plays are neither contained nor retained. Instead, they add something to the appropriating text even while they gain something in the process as well. Reconsidering Terence Hawkes's famous assertion, 'Shakespeare doesn't mean: *we* mean *by* Shakespeare', Desmet underscores the potentiality afforded by each new appropriation: 'The point is not that Shakespeare has no meaning, but that because meaning changes with context, he has, if anything, more meanings than we can yet imagine.'[22] To assert that we mean *by* Shakespeare, is, however, also a double-edged claim. If Shakespeare's plays, as Hawkes maintains, have become empty signifiers that we use to generate meaning, even while banking on the Bard's cultural authority, then he also continues to mean through us, accruing ever more signification. Even while we access him through appropriations, these are the sites where he, conceived as an active (albeit spectral) participant in the exchange, returns to take hold of us.

There is, however, even more to the duplicitous proliferation of meaning produced when contemporary appropriations allow Shakespeare to re-surface. These fragments and reassemblages allow us to infer, as Linda Charnes suggests, that underneath the many layers of his recyclings, as though stored away in our cultural unconscious, there is still something there 'that we cannot actually see but whose presence must nevertheless be posited'.[23] To delve into the implications this raises, it is useful to recall Walter Benjamin's discussion of the constitutive reciprocity at work in translation. If translatability is the essential quality of certain works, then it is because this is what ensures their cultural survival (*Überleben*). Yet, decisive for this afterlife (*Fortleben*) is less the fact that any of the subsequent articulations can never fully subsume the original work; instead, in each translation, as Benjamin puts it, 'the original attains its latest, continually renewed, and most complete unfolding'.[24] In the process of its continued afterlife, conceived as a transformation, conversion, and regeneration, each translation is always only provisional. The original, in turn, undergoes a change in signification as well – 'even words with fixed meaning can undergo a maturing process (*Nachreife*)'.[25] The notion of 'post-ripening', or subsequent maturation, signals not only the fragmentary nature of that which is perpetually re-translated but also an enabling potentiality. While, in its essence, the original remains invisible, the fact that it can only be grasped implicitly opens up the exchange between resuscitation and disappearance, which is at the heart of so many contemporary Shakespearean appropriations.

As already noted, the open-ended dialogue between past and present sustained by appropriation can, however, also take the shape of texts recognising Shakespeare in another text, not only as part of a dialogic relation self-consciously written into the script, but also as part of a critical reading that identifies a work as Shakespearean so as to place it in dialogue with its forebear. Graham Holderness offers the concept of 'collision' for a creative reading that stages an encounter between 'Shakespeare' and a 'not-Shakespeare' text, which releases new energies, generates new meanings, and modifies both parties involved in this reciprocal impact. In such collisions, both may be 'driven by forces that can appear to be random but in their mutual impact generate an observable and meaningful pattern'.[26] At issue for Holderness is adopting a creative method of interpretation by looking for the perfect complement to a particular play in a film, in which, although it is a different medium, all of Shakespeare's themes and preoccupations can be accurately relocated. Reading Shakespeare through imitation, parallelism, and analogy is, thus, self-consciously operative. It performs the proposed encounter. Like new media appropriations themselves, reading for collisions entails a continual remaking of Shakespeare, in which to take note of his cultural afterlife also implies a post-ripening. Or put another way, based on surmising connections that may seem marginal at first, this encounter is predicated on the contingency that a creative reading produces.

While Holderness is concerned with collisions between a selection of Shakespeare plays and contemporary cinema, reading for connections and lines of association is equally fruitful for the dynamic repetition at work in Shakespeare's resuscitation in contemporary serial TV drama, which the following chapters will explore. The term I propose for my own method of apprehending this serial encounter is 'crossmapping', because I want to underscore the reciprocity at issue in charting the superimposition of early modern and contemporary texts.[27] In so doing, I draw on what Mieke Bal calls doing a 'preposterous' form of historical reading to investigate the recycling that plays from the past have undergone in contemporary TV drama, only to colour our conception of this past. As Bal explains, such revision and revisitation of the past is meant neither to 'collapse past and present, in an ill-conceived presentism, nor objectify the past and bring it within our grasp, as in a problematic positivist historicism'. Instead, this reversal puts what came chronologically first ('pre') as an aftereffect behind ('post') its later recycling.[28]

Indeed, crossmapping entails a two-way hermeneutic method, predicated on the discovery of similar concerns in the historical and the contemporary text (or sets of texts). By mapping these on to each other, the energy that has been contained in the Shakespeare plays – preserved and restrained – is released. If the cross at work in my critical term involves a constant oscillation between the earlier play and its subsequent appropriation, the dialogue proposed has recourse to a double vision. As we focus either on the Shakespeare play or the TV drama, we sense the presence of the other. In the process of such creative reading, each is enhanced by virtue of the meanings discovered – the appropriation as much as the Shakespeare text itself. A crossmapping considers the Shakespeare text again, from a different perspective, but also addresses the fact that it comes back to us again, from the past. In the conceptual superimposition that crossmapping undertakes, Shakespeare is screened by the TV dramas that have appropriated him in two senses – parts of his plays are veiled by the refiguration, while, at the same time, other parts and fragments are again projected, shining through this cover.

However, to ask what the heuristic gain of proposing such a transhistorical dialogue might be also means apprehending the dislocations and transformations, which is to say the 'post-ripening' Shakespeare has been afforded in the process of his cultural afterlife. While a crossmapping may be inspired by the discovery of similar concerns in two historically distinct texts, it also interrogates the dramaturgic consequences of Shakespeare's cultural survival. When a contemporary TV drama appropriates one of his plays (or a set of plays), at issue is not only what is retained. Equally important is what is left out, what is re-encoded, refigured, and, as such, aesthetically transformed to transmit a different narrative, to sustain a different philosophical outlook, or to broadcast a different political ideology. Furthermore, while the parallels and connections to be traced are afforded, the meanings that are discovered – or uncovered – in the process of crossmapping are always also the effect of creative reading. Superimposing Shakespeare on to a TV drama is a performative gesture. Like the translation of Shakespeare which the contemporary serial explicitly or implicitly undertakes, this creative reading also engenders a 'post-ripening'.

As Stephen Lanier argues, when we trace how Shakespeare, in his cultural afterlife, is never isolated from processes of change and relationality, the goal of such readings should be 'to stress the crossing lines of association and difference that give creative energy to each adaptation, to recover something of the qualities of contingency and choice that these adaptations might exhibit and to suggest how those lines of energy might illuminate the nature of "Shakespeare", both historically and in the present'.²⁹ The cultural dialogue my own crossmappings retrieve also addresses what it means to read the way his plays have been refigured by contemporary appropriations decisively from the perspective of the present. To speak of these readings as a 'preposterous' way of dealing with the historical specificity of early modern drama today does not, however, deny that ultimately some part of what is essentially Shakespearean will remain inconceivable and unreachable by any subsequent reiteration. Instead, it draws attention to the paradoxical presence of a historical text by being responsive to historical difference.

As a hermeneutic practice, crossmapping thus discloses the way appropriations of Shakespeare draw into focus our present experience of historical difference. The parts and fragments of his plays that are reused in any contemporary appropriation never simply mirror or affirm the present, because they can never shed their own history. At the same time, these remakings insist that his plays are not irreducible to history, either. Instead, if, as Fernie suggests, Shakespeare's plays are 'simultaneously in the present and of the past', crossmapping as a form of creative reading aims at apprehending how, in the subsequent refigurations his oeuvre, Shakespeare's works are not only present to us in an altered shape.³⁰ Engaging with them also distances us from our present.

Seriality, in turn, takes on several aspects in the following chapters. Even as the notion of serial reading is used to draw into focus how contemporary media appropriations recreate Shakespeare in TV drama, it also allows for the discovery of seriality in Shakespeare's oeuvre. As such, the following readings are designed to explore how the use of and reference to Shakespeare in contemporary TV drama offer both a new way of reading his plays and a new idea of what we think of as being quintessentially Shakespearean. Once the critical reading focuses on the exchange between past and present, Shakespeare keeps popping up, even if the actual quotation from one of his plays occurs only once. The reading, prompted by this quote (or quotes), develops ever more correspondences to Shakespeare for the subsequent episodes. At the same time, given that all the contemporary appropriations that will be discussed in the following chapters are part of a larger cultural network, these TV dramas are also interconnected as a series, sometimes implicitly and sometimes explicitly in dialogue with each other. If the work of appropriative translation produces a proliferation of meaning, so, too, does a reading for these crossing lines.

When addressing the question of what it means to read for seriality, it is, however, also useful to recall that this is a dramatic force already at work in Shakespeare's own plays. This is so, in part, because, as has already been noted, individual plays entangle several plot lines and multiple character constellations. At the same time, Jan Kott, discovering problems in Shakespeare's plays which he felt to be relevant to his own time, has suggested thinking of specifically the history plays as chapters in one grand epic regarding English medieval history. Given that each of these plays opens and closes at the same narrative point, Kott was struck with their serial conception. As he puts it, each 'begins with a struggle for the throne, or for its consolidation. Each ends with the monarch's death and a new coronation.'[31]

Not only does history seem to turn full circle in these plays, returning, in the end, to the dramatic point of departure, but when taking the entire development of his oeuvre into consideration, one also has the impression, as Kott concludes, 'that Shakespeare has in fact written three or four plays and kept repeating the same theme in different registers and keys'.[32] While there are correspondences and sequence repetitions within each of the plays, when these are regarded as one whole, it becomes even more evident that his plays keep circling around certain thematic concerns. The set of variations on corresponding character constellations and dramaturgic strategies which are offered keep changing slightly with each repetition. Along with serial repetition and transformation, the potentiality within Shakespeare that contemporary TV drama taps into is, thus, the idea of an open-endedness. As already noted, the logic of the series is that it has no distinct point of origin – it has always already begun. The closure that any serial text finds is, accordingly, one that must be artificially set. It can, to mention only the popularity of spin-off prequels, readily turn into the beginning of a new series. Furthermore, given that in the digital media landscape, as Stephen O'Neill suggests, every text is readily up for grabs, the reiteration of parts and fragments from his plays is fluid, unpredictable, and spatially as well as temporally unbounded.[33]

If, however, digital media culture makes Shakespeare's texts limitlessly available, the temporality at issue involves more than a futurity still to come. The open-endedness of the translatability of Shakespeare into serial drama also points backwards in time. Part and parcel of the paradoxical presence of the historical text in its contemporary appropriation is the way it draws attention to the fact that something in the past is not finished yet, has not yet found closure, and may well never be completed.[34] If taking possession of Shakespeare is tantamount to being possessed by him, the unfinished business his repeated resuscitation in new media formats speaks to, not only compels us to inquire into how the cultural capital he has come to be endowed with encourages us to look back to him regarding problems that are still (or again) relevant in our own times. It also calls upon us to trouble the cultural ventriloquism at work when quoting Shakespeare (which is to say speaking with and through him) is conceived as an appropriation of his authority. Put more pointedly, it means accounting for the haunting. This implies not only conceiving of the cultural afterlife of his texts in terms of a subsequent maturation through translation. Instead, as Marjorie Garber suggests, it is also fruitful to substitute the word ghost for translation. In her discussion of Shakespeare as a ghost-writer, she cannily notes the interchangeability of writers and ghosts in his oeuvre, suggesting that on his stage, the ghost emerges as an agent of repetition, doubling the work of the text itself. As the sign of something missing, but also of something that has been omitted or undone, the repetition which the ghost qua translation performs by making itself present again, can also be taken as a trope for any form of textual return.[35]

Contemporary TV appropriations tap into the spectral quality of repetition, if often only implicitly. They displace the original text even while turning Shakespeare into a ghostly presence – remembered as something undone, re-articulated in fragments, the sign of a memory trace that persists, and the announcement of something still to arrive, still to be realised in the future. The transformation at issue in his cultural survival in serial drama is thus not only, as Walter Benjamin proposes, a question of continual renewal and unfolding, but also a question of something coming back, being revitalised. As Stephen Greenblatt famously argues, while there is no direct, unmediated link between ourselves and his plays, this does not mean that there is no link at all: 'The "life" that literary works seem to possess long after both the death of the author and the death of the culture from which the author wrote is the historical consequence, however transformed and refashioned, of the social energy initially encoded in these works.'[36] While new historicism is primarily concerned with the cultural exchanges at work in the historical period in which Shakespeare wrote, Greenblatt's critical trope, *energia*, is applicable to contemporary exchanges in new media formats as well, not least of all because this affective intensity can be identified only indirectly, by the effects it has had. As long as the aesthetic forms that produce, shape, and organise an intensity – which include power, charisma, sexual excitement, collective dreams, wonder, desire, and anxiety – can be repeated, the cultural exchange can be manifested over and again.

Append to translatability the ability of Shakespeare's plays to contain such social energies, and a further aspect of his spectral afterlife comes into focus. In its dramatic encoding, this compelling force has continued to generate the illusion of life well into our contemporary moment. Aby Warburg's critical concept 'pathos formula' (or 'image formula') is useful to understand more precisely this interplay between aesthetic formalisation and the cultural survival of passionate intensities.[37] Concerned with the way certain fragments of past images came to re-surface in later works of art, he proposes thinking of these in terms of a formal containment in the double sense of the word. What travels from one historical moment to another, and from one medium to the next, is not the passion itself but rather the aesthetic form in which it was preserved. From the onset, furthermore, the function of aesthetic formalisation was to restrain the intensity expressed by an artwork, so as to make its force affordable to future artistic articulations. Or put another way, in that aesthetic forms capture a passion and translate this intensity *into* an image, so that it can be apprehended *as* an image, they hold the passion contained *in* the image at bay.

Conceived as a crystallisation of emotions, aesthetic forms, according to Warburg, survive as an inheritance transmitted by cultural memory. As such, they can become effective again, at a later date, when it becomes necessary to once more formalise the emotional intensity they contain. To demonstrate how pathos formulas are retrieved from the arsenal of our cultural imaginary and adjusted to contemporary expressions of passionate intensities, Warburg developed his Mnemosyne atlas. Like Benjamin, he thought of the cultural survival of aesthetically formalised intensities in terms of their afterlife (*Nachleben*). According to him, appropriations attest not only to the fact that artworks from the past continue to exert their power on subsequent generations. Rather, this legacy can, furthermore, be disclosed only by reading for the affective effects that these past image formulas continue to have *on* and *in* the present. Acknowledging a debt to the past, in the sense of a legacy that is afforded, draws the ethic dimension of appropriations into focus. When, in the process of recalling and refiguring the pathos formula of a prior text, a subsequent text responds to its predecessor, it demonstrates its own answerability to this inheritance. The same holds true for the creative reader, looking for such encounters, collisions, and conversations.[38]

While my own crossmappings make use of the concept of pathos formula to explore Shakespeare's legacy in contemporary TV drama, I repurpose the term. Rather than limiting my discussion to fragments from visual artworks, I use this critical concept to discuss narrative and dramaturgic devices that have been separated from his plays and, as dislocated fragments, come to circulate in this new media format. Kristin N. Denslow assigns a very similar function to the cultural transmission effected by internet memes that, as narrative devices, allow Shakespeare to appear in odd and sometimes even unexpected places. As she suggests, any unit can be separated from its corpus and re-integrated into a new media environment, where it survives in a different, reworked form.

## Introduction

As a meme, it can have 'a life of its own independent from a suturing to Shakespeare's oeuvre', indeed be adapted by subsequent generations without awareness of a debt to this source.[39] Although the meme's original is simultaneously present and absent, with its presence always mediated by its absence, 'the original itself becomes irrelevant as the meme constantly supplements an original that does not exist'.[40]

My preference for the term pathos formula is that it allows me not only to explore the dissemination and proliferation of Shakespeare in contemporary appropriations but also to consider the way his spectral presence in digital media gains relevance precisely because of the haunting his afterlife engenders there. Responsive to the intensities which pathos formulas from his plays re-invigorate, the appropriations are themselves appropriated by the past. The original essence of parts of his plays, though ungraspable, takes hold of us, pulling us back into the past, dislocating us in the present. Along with the intensities contained in and by the pathos formulas, the past returns as a residual force, in its ungraspable difference. Indeed, the status of Shakespeare on screen in general is, as Maurizio Calbi notes, hauntological: 'a furtive mode of inhabiting without properly residing'.[41] Each appropriation conjures up previous or current processes of remediation through which he has already been repossessed and reprocessed in the past.

If Shakespeare's plays can never be neatly severed from his cultural afterlife, they are also never reducible to their retroactive reproduction, to their post-ripening. Instead, his spectral presence in contemporary digitalised mediascapes renders visible the irremediable unfinished character of the process of appropriation. As a result of the appropriation, a Shakespearean pathos formula repeatedly vanishes, only to reappear again elsewhere. This residual resurgence, in turn, attests not only to Shakespeare's infinite mutability but also to an unfinished business of culture. Having recourse to pathos formulas, which have contained – and sustained – concerns stemming from the past, allows us to address and rework these to formulate our contemporary concerns. At the same time, if these pathos formulas prove to be reusable in our own times, this also compels us to recognise these resuscitations as the articulation of a cultural repetition compulsion that we are called upon to revisit over and again.[42]

To put the stress on Shakespeare's spectral presence means reading his appropriations not only for enduring patterns, constellations, and convergences but also for yet another aspect of reciprocity at work in the limitless process of retrieval he inspires. By responding to what comes back to us from the past, we produce what we repossess. As the repository for desires and anxieties which take shape *again* in our encounters with his plays, Shakespeare not only makes modern culture; as Marjorie Garber proposes, modern culture also makes him. The chiasmus, the crossing of words, she adds, 'suspends for a moment the grounded logic of priority and reference'.[43] If what we know of him is inevitably shaped by our present, the way we know this present is also shaped by the way that he has written himself into the fabric of our contemporary thinking.

It is this inverted parallelism which the crossmappings in the following chapters explore. There is, thus, a further reason why Aby Warburg's Mnemosyne atlas is decisive for my own project. In his effort to map the cultural afterlife of a set of pathos gestures, he came to produce sequences of images on black canvasses, reassembled from high culture as well as popular culture. To draw attention to unconventional and hitherto unacknowledged correspondences and connections, these images were thematically arranged, even while Warburg would constantly change the arrangements of these visual formalisations of emotional intensities, producing ever new series. Along the lines of Warburg's Mnemosyne Project, the following chapters are conceived as distinct mappings, each of which explores the connection between a set of pathos formulas from Shakespeare's plays and contemporary serial drama. Tracking the serial return and redeployment of a set of fragmentary and dislocated parts from Shakespeare's work that are always in flux, itself entails a critical form of translation.

However, while part of my concern is the formal question of affordance, translatability, and adaptability, as this pertains to the resuscitation of Shakespeare in new digital media in general, there is a second, more specific reciprocity at issue. Not only how American popular culture has inherited Shakespeare and reshaped him in the process will be in the foreground of my readings, but also how Shakespeare has written and shaped this particular cultural imaginary, if at times implicitly. I propose rethinking Stanley Cavell's work on classic Hollywood cinema, which he sees as the inheritor of preoccupations shaped by Shakespeare's plays. What I am concerned with is finding in the contemporary serial TV format a particularly vibrant site for a similar cultural conversation.[44] Indeed, the seriality I am concerned with in the following crossmappings finds in TV drama its most appropriate format because the long narrative arcs, bringing together multiple storylines and allowing for an elaborate development of a large set of entangled characters, do not only operate by using patterns of repetition and recall. As the inheritor of a dramatic composition initially explored by Shakespeare, the serial format, based on a simultaneous unfolding of parallel storylines, is a narrative form that is particularly befitting the cultural needs of our times.

As Gérard Wajcman suggests, the narrative multiplicity and diversity on which this long form is predicated is the aesthetic formalisation best suited to engage with the political fault lines and wounds of the cultural imaginary of the United States.[45] The TV serial, as he puts it, offers a string of small windows that open one after the other on the fissures of contemporary America, drawing above all the precarious identities and coalitions between individual subjects into focus. Any one series tells a world but not all of the world, because the world it calls forth is not whole. By developing a plurality of stories, the representational logic of serial drama ruptures linearity and, instead, plays with multiple perspectives. The overarching narrative breaks up into a skein of loosely connected threads that can come undone again. These parallel stories are connected at certain moments and in diverse ways, only to break up again, so that at a later point in the overarching narration, they can be again tied together. Yet, as Wajcman insists, it is not the TV series which implements fragmentation. Rather, the gesture of dispersion and rupture is *a*, if not *the*, dominant regime of contemporary American culture, and this political crisis – this precariousness of identities, relationships, and allegiances – finds in the serial form an adequate aesthetic form of expression.

In the following readings, the conversation between Shakespeare and a distinct set of serials is sometimes explicitly proposed by the usage of quotations, sometimes more implicitly founded in corresponding plot structures, thematic constellations, and dramaturgic devices. Each chapter is conceived as one crossmapping of the deep interconnectedness of the Shakespeare 'series' and contemporary TV drama, with the appropriated pathos formulas treated as that which makes his plays available for reuse.[46] In Chapter 1, revolving around the first two seasons of Jonathan Nolan and Lisa Joy's *Westworld*, the spectrality of cultural ventriloquism is foregrounded. In reference to a quote from *Romeo and Juliet*, 'these violent delights have violent ends,' the pathos formula resurfacing most prominently in my reading encapsulates the enmeshment of violence and creation. Yet the string of Shakespeare quotes, uttered by a malfunctioning host, not only suggests a collision between this science-fiction western and Shakespeare's romantic tragedy. It also affords a serial interconnection between the TV series and two further plays, *The Tempest* and *King Lear*. This draws a second preoccupation which Shakespeare shares with the western genre into focus. The open-endedness implied in the founding of a new world, or rather the regeneration of one already founded out of violence, recalls the serial re-founding of the American nation out of a series of historical territorial wars.

If, based on a string of citations, Chapter 1 reads several plays as a series, in Chapter 2 a single citation – 'uneasy lies the head that wears a crown' – inspires a crossmapping of *The Wire* and Shakespeare's first tetralogy, the three parts of *Henry VI* and *Richard III*. The pathos formula at the centre of this reading concerns the notion of political power conceived as a repetition cycle of violent takeovers. What Jan Kott notes for Shakespeare's history plays, revolving around England's Wars of the Roses, also fits David Simon's scathing representation of the war on drugs in Baltimore. His serial drama, exploring the systemic power struggles forging the contemporary American polis in general, also draws on a serial conception of a struggle for rule, where the death (or removal) of one drug lord leads to the coronation of his violent successor.

The two chapters at the centre of the book make use of the pathos formula of the female ruler to discuss the fascination and anxiety that female sovereignty poses in relation to a crisis in American democracy regarding the question of legitimate and illegitimate power. The crossmapping of a series of first female presidents with a typology of queenship in Shakespeare's plays begins in Chapter 3 with Beau Willimon's Gothic political thriller, *House of Cards*, because of its explicit references to *Macbeth*. The chapter then moves back to the initial wave of first female presidents, conceived during the reign of George W. Bush, before returning to those strong-minded anti-heroines from the second wave who, simultaneously with Claire Underwood, make their claim to the Oval Office. Chapter 4 ends with the most creative collision discovered by reading these two 'series' – of queens and female presidents – together, namely the re-surfacing of Cleopatra in Shonda Rhimes' *Scandal*.

Regardless of which political party they represent, each of these female rulers performs the adversarial tension between a charismatic leader and democracy. They are shown not only as women balancing personal ambition with the good of the demos but, equally important, as women who rise in power owing to the allure, the winning likeability, they have for their voters. What all these serial dramas tap into is, thus, a further contemporary cultural anxiety. While American civil religion traditionally ascribes a sacredness to the office of the presidency and not the actual position embodied, when entertainment is factored into the political equation, as is the case when Hollywood stars play ambitious politicians, celebrity itself is revered.[47] As with Shakespeare's ambivalent staging of queenship, these female presidents in TV drama do not only articulate a feminist doubt regarding any self-evident relation between political leadership and the demos. The charm each of Hollywood's stars gives to this role also speaks to the appeal that conspiracy narratives hold for the American cultural imaginary, invested, as it is, in believing that the more powerful rule comes from the political periphery, or works clandestinely from within the system.

If *Westworld* performs the violence sustaining a newly created world of hosts, modelled on the Western frontier, David Milch's *Deadwood* explicitly draws on the westward expansion as part of the rebirth of the American nation after the Civil War. Chapter 5 thus returns to a discussion of the mutual interdependence between theatre and power in Shakespeare, using a macabre performance of *King Lear* by members of a travelling theatre company as the point of connection. At issue now, however, is a different Shakespeare 'series' produced by virtue of appropriation. While no other characters in *Deadwood* actually quote from his plays, the words spoken in dialogues or as asides have a decidedly Shakespearean ring to them. Indeed, as in his plays, they take on a performative function, becoming actions themselves. Furthermore, the overarching storyline, depicting how this midwestern camp town gradually evolves into a community, is conceived as political theatre. In contrast to the traditional western, only very few scenes take place in the open prairie. Instead, the camp town transforms into the stage for a complex system of surveillance. The panoply of devices sustaining the self-performance of each of the players will, therefore, be explored in an effort to determine what qualifies as quintessential Shakespearean dramaturgy.

The emphasis on role-playing serves as the transition to the final chapter, which, in the most creative critical move this book undertakes, offers a reading of Joe Weisberg's *The Americans* in collision with Shakespeare's comedies of mistaken identities. In Chapter 6, the topsy-turvy world of *Deadwood*'s frontier is reconceived as the carnivalesque political stage into which this spy thriller transforms Washington, DC, in the 1980s, with our preposterous gaze guided by the knowledge that the Cold War is about to end. The point of departure for this proposed conversation is Feste, the fool in *Twelfth Night*, who, comparable with these Soviet spies, has no proper place and, instead, shuttles between the courts of Orsino and Olivia. No longer Russian, yet not properly American either, Elizabeth and Philip Jennings use an infinite variety of disguises to rehearse versions of what might be taken to be an American. While the crossdressings they perform are not sexual but cultural, along with the treacherous enjoyment of transgression, these, too, disclose – comparable with Shakespeare's comedy – the lack of self-identity at play in a world conceived as theatre. At the same time, the violent spectacle their disguises put on display also recalls the cruel inversion of roles in *A Midsummer Night's Dream*. As in this romantic comedy, those running the espionage game on both sides preside over a night-rule, in which all the players play their parts with enchanted eyes. Once you enter the carnival of spies, thus the discovery *The Americans* takes from Shakespeare, everything is tinged by a rich and strange charm that can only veer towards a moment of reckoning, of disenchantment, of awakening from a shared dream.

If American TV drama keeps appropriating Shakespeare to give voice to unfinished cultural business regarding the state of the nation, this raises the question, how does his dramatic shaping of concerns emerging from his specific historical moment come to fit, once again, preoccupations of the early twenty-first century, rendering his voice spectrally present *as* different from the present? And how does a creative reading for connections, collisions, and encounters illuminate and enrich both our understanding of contemporary serials and a revisitation of early modern drama? A wager subtending the conversations proposed in this book is that what both share is the sense of writing *in* and *for* a period of interim. While Shakespeare's dramas reflect the transition into early modernity, contemporary TV drama reflects and reflects on an equally provisional cultural condition. It responds to a pervasive sense that while something is over and something else is to come, there is no clear indication what shape this futurity will take. By having recourse to Shakespeare, these TV dramas, and the critical readings they inspire, irrevocably look to the cultural transformation that happened in the early modern period through the lenses of our current passage beyond the postmodern.

Put another way, to really understand the depth of what is happening in contemporary TV drama, we, in our critical reading of these contemporary serials, do well to turn back to Shakespeare even if the connection afforded is oblique. To uncover how constellations and dramaturgical devices that worked in early modern theatre continue to have an affective use, as well as an ideological effect, does not only mean taking note of the continuity of their formal and rhetorical usage, given their mobility and mutability. Rather, the transformations that the digital medium brings with it also render visible how, despite the historical distance and the difference in dramatic format, Shakespeare's aesthetic formalisations of intense passions are still a barometer for what can be shaped, thought, and performed. Decisive for this inheritance is his proclivity towards ambivalences. In a manner once again pertinent, the oppositions he engages in his plays are never straightforward. Personal dreams prove to be collective visions; destruction the productive inversion of creativity; violence and desire inextricably entangled. With the illegitimate often discovered at the heart of legitimate power, charismatic rulers show themselves to be both cruel and fascinating. Indeed, in a staged world where theatre is always also taken for real, characters are called upon not only to acknowledge the parts they have to play but also to recognise their own mutability as a potentiality still to be realised. Caught in moments of passage, in a world in-between, his charmed players discover the possibility of re-assigning parts, assuming ever new roles, and exploring alternative plot lines.

Not who we are, nor how we emerged from where we came, are the questions most pertinent to our moment. Instead, we are called upon to ask what are we moving towards. In such a moment of transition, it is not just cultural value, nor merely the question of authority and weightiness, that makes a conversation with Shakespeare once more timely. Instead, what having recourse to his work can offer is a point of orientation; to be precise, a preposterous reading that looks for what will come by looking back at what was. If Shakespeare is everywhere in contemporary TV drama, then, in part, it is because we are asking him to give us formulas by which we can live, and by which we can understand ourselves. To look to Shakespeare so as to find one's bearings, however, means to take seriously that the resolutions he offers are themselves provisional. The dramatic closures he finds end not in solutions, but in problems. Not only do many of his plays return to their point of departure, reposing, albeit in a different key, the problem that set the dramatic cycle in motion in the first place; the endings of his plays are also predicated on the serial wager, 'What next?'[48] Very often, a character offers a summary of all the action that has occurred throughout the play, or promises to do so. Only rarely do they anticipate what is still to come, and if they do, then more often than not it is as a warning that the violent delights, the destructive ambitions, or the calamitous power games that have just spent themselves on stage could very well set in all over again, despite – or because of – the order that has come to be re-established.

Shakespeare's ubiquitous presence in contemporary TV draws into focus the fact that he possesses us as much as we possess and repossess him. The resilience of this spectral resuscitation indicates that this is a haunting we desire. We want Shakespeare's ghost to point us in directions we deem appropriate to our times. Refusing to abide by our demand for clear answers and unequivocal solutions, he instead confronts us with formulations and aesthetic formalisations of problems that we cannot afford not to address. If, then, Shakespeare's plays end, over and again, on a question regarding what will come, it is above all this inheritance that TV drama claims for us today.

## Notes

1 While, in his introduction to the *Shakespeare on Film New Casebooks* (Houndmills: Macmillan, 1998), Robert Shaughnessy claimed that 'if Shakespeare were alive today, he would be writing film scripts', we could safely wager that today he would be working for prestige TV; p. 3.
2 *Godless*, 'The Ladies of La Belle', season 1, episode 2, dir. Scott Frank, writ. Scott Frank, m1 (Netflix 2017).
3 *The Deuce*, 'Our Raison d'Etre', season 2, episode 1, dir. Alex Hall, writ. David Simon and George Pelecanos, m42.14 (HBO 2018). The quote is from William Shakespeare's *Hamlet*, Ann Thompson and Neil Taylor (eds), *The Arden Shakespeare*, third series (London: Bloomsbury, 2006), 1.5.165–6.
4 *The Good Fight*, 'The One Where the Sun Comes Out', season 3, episode 9, dir. Brooke Kennedy, writ. Eric Holmes, m36.50 (CBS 2019). The quote is from William Shakespeare's *King Lear*, R.A. Foakes (ed.), *The Arden Shakespeare*, third series (London: Bloomsbury, 1997), 5.3.120–2. The showrunners, Robert and Michelle King, have also explained that their decision to have characters speak directly to the camera in the third season was their way of trying out Shakespearean soliloquies, but in their own language; see Joy Press, '*The Good Fight* Showrunners Are (Not) Impeaching Trump and the Nature of Evil', *Vanity Fair*, 12 May 2019.
5 *Billions*, 'The Punch', season 1, episode 7, dir. Stephen Gyllenhaal, writ. Brian Koppelman and David Levien, m45.10 (Showtime 2016).
6 See Stephen O'Neill's 'Introduction: "Sowed and Scattered": Shakespeare's Media Ecologies' in his edited volume *Broadcast Your Shakespeare* (London: Bloomsbury, 2018), p. 5.
7 O'Neill, 'Introduction', p. 23.
8 Marjorie Garber, *Shakespeare After All* (New York: Pantheon Books, 2004), p. 28 (italics in original). Laura Estill makes a similar point in her essay 'Shakespeare and Disciplinarity', arguing that, as a cultural touchstone, Shakespeare quotes serve as cultural capital to a wide group of global users, helping them to communicate by virtue of this shared knowledge; in Valerie M. Fazel and Louise Geddes (eds), *The Shakespeare User. Critical and Creative Appropriations in a Networked Culture* (New York: Palgrave Macmillan, 2017), pp. 167–86.
9 As Julie Maxwell and Kate Rumbold note in the general introduction to their edited volume *Shakespeare and Quotation* (Cambridge: Cambridge University Press, 2018), with quotations of Shakespeare re-surfacing as memes, in mash-ups, and in remakes, the tension between a reverence for Shakespeare's unique authority and a creative reuse of dislocated fragments from his works becomes a productive creative resource in itself in our contemporary mediascape.
10 Douglas Lanier, *Shakespeare and Modern Popular Culture* (Oxford: Oxford University Press, 2002), p. 9. See also, his article '#Bard: "And noble offices thou mayst effect of mediation"', *Shakespeare Quarterly*, 67: 4 (2016), for a discussion of how the interplay between the original drama and its creative repurposing can afford new conceptions of where and wherein the essence of his plays lies, even while disrupting 'longstanding mechanisms for maintaining what is not genuinely "Shakespeare"', p. 407.
11 Lanier, *Shakespeare and Modern Popular Culture*, p. 16.

12 Courtney Lehmann and Lisa S. Starks, *Spectacular Shakespeare. Critical Theory and Popular Cinema* (Madison, NJ: Fairleigh Dickinson University Press, 2002), p. 12. See also, Annalisa Castaldo's essay 'The Film's the Thing: Using Film in the Shakespearean Classroom' in the same volume, pp. 187–204.
13 Linda Charnes, *Notorious Identity. Materializing the Subject in Shakespeare* (Cambridge, MA: Harvard University Press, 1997), p. 15.
14 As in so much contemporary TV drama, Shakespeare re-surfaces obliquely in throwaway citations, in this case from *Richard II* and *Coriolanus*.
15 Roland Barthes, *S/Z*, trans. Richard Miller (New York: Hill and Wang, 1974), p. 16 (italics in original).
16 Carolyn Jess-Cooke, *Shakespeare on Film. Such Things as Dreams Are Made Of* (London: Wallflower, 2007), p. 84.
17 Jeffrey Knapp, *Pleasing Everyone. Mass Entertainment in Renaissance London and Golden-Age Hollywood* (Oxford: Oxford University Press, 2017).
18 Stevie Simkin, *Early Modern Tragedy and the Cinema of Violence* (London: Palgrave Macmillan, 2006).
19 Gilles Deleuze, *Difference and Repetition*, trans. Paul Patton, revised edition (New York: Columbia University Press, 1995).
20 Lanier, *Shakespeare and Modern Popular Culture*, p. 97. As Pascale Aebischer and Nigel Wheale argue in the introduction to their edited volume, *Remaking Shakespeare. Performance across Media, Genres and Cultures* (London: Palgrave Macmillan, 2003), repetition and reproduction are intrinsic to every contemporary engagement with Shakespeare, which removes his plays from the culture of early modern London. The vitality of this transposition is that even as his plays affect the environment into which they are imported, they are affected by it as well, pp. 1–17.
21 Christy Desmet and Robert Sawyer (eds), *Shakespeare and Appropriation* (London: Routledge, 1999), p. 12. See also Valerie M. Fazel and Louise Geddes' introduction to their edited volume *The Shakespeare User*, which illustrates that those who use Shakespeare do not merely consume his works, nor do they simply reproduce or recycle his works. Instead, users of Shakespeare engage in a larger culture network of influences and associations that is always in flux, producing ever more permutations and transformations of the original work, pp. 1–22.
22 Desmet, 'Introduction', p. 12. The reference is to Terence Hawkes, *Meaning by Shakespeare* (New York: Routledge, 1992), p. 3 (italics in original). Foregrounding the transformative power of appropriations, Stephen Lanier, in his essay 'Shakespearean Rhizomatics: Adaptation, Ethics, Value', offers a further gloss on this quote: 'Shakespearean meaning is available in the present *only* through processes of appropriation that actively create, rather than passively decode, the readings and values we attribute to the Shakespearean text', in Alexa Huang and Elizabeth Rivlin (eds), *Shakespeare and The Ethics of Appropriation* (London: Palgrave Macmillan, 2014), p. 25 (italics in original).
23 Linda Charnes, 'We Were Never Early Modern', in John Joughlin (ed.), *Philosophical Shakespeare* (London: Routledge, 2000), p. 66.
24 Walter Benjamin, 'The Task of the Translator', in Marcus Bullock and Michael W. Jennings (eds), *Selected Writings, Volume 1 1913–1926* (Cambridge, MA: Harvard University Press, 1996), p. 255.
25 Benjamin, 'The Task of the Translator', p. 256. In the introduction to their edited volume, *Shakespeare and the Ethics of Appropriation* (London: Palgrave

Macmillan, 2014), Alexa Huang and Elizabeth Rivlin draw on a similar analogy between appropriations and translations, arguing that both 'conjure different interpretive possibilities that already inhabit Shakespeare's texts. Far from reinforcing Shakespeare's self-unity, the process of appropriation attacks its illusion and reveals multiple Shakespeares, or, to put it differently, a Shakespeare perpetually divided from itself'; p. 8.

26 Graham Holderness, *Tales from Shakespeare. Creative Collisions* (Cambridge: Cambridge University Press, 2014). See also, Barbara Hodgdon, *The Shakespeare Trade. Performances and Appropriations* (Philadelphia: University of Pennsylvania Press, 1998), for another discussion of how Shakespeare's cultural memory is not only sustained through appropriations that trade off his cultural capital, but also how current events are read in relation to his plays, as the O.J. Simpson case was invariably read in terms of *Othello*, to produce culturally viable interpretations of both.

27 See Elisabeth Bronfen, 'Introduction: Crossmappings – Visual Readings as a Critical Intervention in the Cultural Imaginary', *Crossmappings. On Visual Culture* (London: I.B. Tauris, 2018), pp. 1–16.

28 Mieke Bal, *Quoting Caravaggio. Contemporary Art, Preposterous History* (Chicago: University of Chicago Press, 1999), p. 7.

29 Lanier, 'Shakespearean Rhizomatics', p. 31.

30 Ewan Fernie, 'Shakespeare and the Prospect of Presentism', *Shakespeare Survey*, 58 (2005), p. 179. See also, Hugh Grady and Terence Hawkes' edited volume *Presentist Shakespeares* (London: Routledge, 2007). In their 'Introduction: Overlapping Mediascapes in the Mind' to a special issue of *Anglistica*, 15:2 (2011), dedicated to Shakespeare in new and old media, Anna Maria Cimitile and Katherine Rowe make a similar point, arguing that when Shakespeare is remade in other media, his plays encounter other complex textualities and forms. These collisions, exchanges, or negotiations should not be treated as adaptation, but as 'Shakespeare in/as the present-past of new media', p. ii.

31 Jan Kott, *Shakespeare Our Contemporary* (London: Methuen, 1965), p. 6. I will return to a discussion of Shakespeare's cyclical consideration of history as one continuous chain of violence, involving certain variations and transformation, in my discussion of David Simon's *The Wire* in Chapter 2.

32 Kott, *Shakespeare Our Contemporary*, p. 171. Janet Adelman makes a similar point in *Suffocating Mothers. Fantasies of Maternal Origin in Shakespeare's Plays, Hamlet to The Tempest* (New York: Routledge, 1992). What she calls the Hamlet theme, a son's worry about the maternal sexual body, is repeatedly played through, hence her claim, in the tragedies and then transformed into a theme of recuperation in the final romances.

33 Stephen O'Neill, 'Uploading *Hamlet*: Agency, Convergence and YouTube Shakespeare', *Anglistica*, 15:2 (2011), p. 74.

34 Chapter 1, on *Westworld*, will revolve around Shakespeare's insight that while violent delights may lead to violent ends, as in his history plays, the tragedies and romances in which this lethal passion is played repeatedly end by returning to their point of departure.

35 Marjorie Garber, 'Hamlet: Giving up the Ghost', in *Profiling Shakespeare* (London: Routledge, 2008), as well as her discussion of the ghostliness of cultural ventriloquism in *Quotation Marks* (London: Routledge, 2003).

36 Stephen Greenblatt, *Shakespearean Negotiations. The Circulation of Social Energy in Renaissance England* (Berkeley: University of California Press, 1988), p. 6.
37 For an overview of Warburg's thinking, see E.H. Gombrich, *Aby Warburg, An Intellectual Biography* (Oxford: Phaidon, 1986). See also Duncan Salkeld's essay 'Shakespeare Studies, Presentism, and Micro-History', *Cahiers Elisabéthains*, 67 (2009), p. 41–2.
38 As Christy Desmet describes this merging of an aesthetic and an ethic response at work in Shakespeare appropriations, 'one text is "answerable" to another when it "answers" or corresponds to that text and when it is "responsive to" and therefore responsible to that text', in 'Recognizing Shakespeare, Rethinking Fidelity: A Rhetoric and Ethics of Appropriation', Huang and Rivlin, *Shakespeare and the Ethics of Appropriation*, p. 44.
39 Kristin N. Denslow, 'Guest Starring Hamlet: The Proliferation of the Shakespeare Meme on American Television', in Christy Desmet, Nathalie Loper, and Jim Casey (eds), *Shakespeare/Not Shakespeare* (London: New York, 2017), p. 101. See also Stephen O'Neill, who, in his essay 'Digital Technology: The Future of Reception History', in Maxwell and Rumbold (eds), *Shakespeare and Quotation*, notes that owing to digital memes, Shakespeare is becoming a residual cultural form, p. 283.
40 Denslow, 'Shakespeare Meme', p. 109.
41 Maurizio Calbi, 'Introduction: Shakespeare, Spectro-Textuality, Spectro-Mediality', *Spectral Shakespeares. Media Adaptations in the Twenty-First Century* (London: Palgrave Macmillan, 2013), p. 4. Chapter 1 will explore how *Westworld* self-consciously uses one of its hosts to perform Shakespeare's coming back as an uncanny mode of 'survivance'.
42 Linda Charnes, *Hamlet's Heirs. Shakespeare and the Politics of a New Millennium* (New York: Routledge, 2006), pp. 10–11.
43 Marjorie Garber, *Shakespeare and Modern Culture* (New York: Pantheon Books, 2008), p. xxxiv.
44 Stanley Cavell, *Pursuits of Happiness. The Hollywood Comedy of Remarriage* (Cambridge, MA: Harvard University Press, 1981). The two plays he focuses on for his discussion of a re-surfacing of the structure of remarriage in Hollywood's sophisticated comedies are *The Winter's Tale* and *A Midsummer Night's Dream*.
45 Gérard Wajcman, *Les séries, le monde, la crise, les femmes* (Paris: Verdier, 2018).
46 Caroline Levine, *Forms: Whole, Rhythm, Hierarchy, Network* (Princeton: Princeton University Press, 2015), also stresses the importance of form for a discussion of the relation between politics and aesthetics, precisely because forms determine what is possible to shape, to think, and thus to express in a given historical context and a particular medium. In a similar manner as I am suggesting for pathos formulas, her use of the concept of forms draws into focus how, as organising principles which are iterable and portable, forms can be picked up and moved to new contexts and across various materials.
47 Much gratitude goes to Heike Paul for our discussions on civil religion, gender, and celebrity culture.
48 I want to thank Benno Wirz for pointing out to me how important it is to read all of Shakespeare's plays backwards, from their open-ended closures to their opening scenes.

# 1
# Shakespeare's spectres: *Westworld*

### Three ghostly interpolations

*Hamlet* makes a spectral appearance twice in the first season of *Westworld*. In 'Trompe L'Oeil', Theresa Cullen, operations leader for Delos Incorporated, wants to get her hands on the codes of all the hosts before getting the board to fire Dr Robert Ford, the creator of this theme park.[1] When she convinces Bernard, head of the Programming Division, to help her back up this material off-site, he leads her to a cottage not registered in any survey of the park. In the cellar, they find a clandestine laboratory with an undocumented model of the machine rendering hosts, familiar to us from the credit sequence. Among the designs that Theresa also discovers, there is not only one of the prototypes for Dolores but also one for Bernard, who, up to this point, has been blissfully unaware that he, too, is a host. Suddenly, Ford joins them, justifying his absolute power by bragging that, under his control, the hosts are free of the burden of consciousness and the anxiety, self-loathing, and guilt that go with it. While Theresa threatens him that the time of his sovereignty over his little kingdom is about to end, he assures her that even if it requires a blood sacrifice, he will not let her take from him the dream which Arnold and he gave shape to by conceiving Westworld. Modelled on this former partner, Bernard, in turn, suddenly realises that, because he is completely under the influence of his creator, he cannot but be loyal to even the most monstrous demand.

To put a swift end to this distasteful confrontation, Dr Ford signals his confidence at having scored a victory against his opponent by invoking Hamlet's ruminations about what awaits one after death. He whispers the words, 'and in that sleep what dreams may come' into Theresa's ear, before walking past her to make way for Bernard to approach and smash her head against the wall.[2] In contrast to Shakespeare's melancholy prince, whom the very conscience the hosts lack makes a coward, Ford has no compunction about murdering the woman who wants to usurp his power. Fragments from Hamlet's monologue about what dreams and ills he might find in death's undiscovered country flicker up as a commentary on a very different scene regarding the question of life or death. Ford is not only resolute where Hamlet wavers, but the enterprise of suicide that Shakespeare's prince merely contemplates is also turned into a successful act of murder. Used for a different purpose than in the original text, and thus detached from its original meaning, the cultural authority that the citation affords is appropriated not only, however, to reflect on the narrative action. Rather, functioning along the lines of what Roland Barthes has called a mythic signifier, it also attests to the spectral afterlife of Shakespeare's poetic language *per se*. Meaning has been transformed into form, robbing the words of the historic specificity of their original use and, instead, endowing them with a more universal, transhistorical applicability.

In a manner seemingly more perfunctory, *Hamlet* again re-surfaces briefly in 'Trace Decay'. Charlotte Hale, executive director of the board overseeing Westworld, is herself eager to gain control over the data on human behaviour they have been gathering over thirty-five years.[3] In a repetition of the previous scene, she takes the narrative director, Lee Sizemore, to the cold storage – the archive where all the inactive hosts are preserved. Recalling the very purgatory from which the ghost of Hamlet's father returns, this is a place between life and death. Because the hosts that are collected there have not been completely destroyed, they can be resuscitated at will. Randomly, Charlotte chooses an older man, the rancher Peter Abernathy, on to whose control unit she uploads all the hosts' codes. Her interest in him is simply as a host body she can use to transport all the information that she has clandestinely transplanted into him. She needs Lee, however, to give the semblance of a personality to the resuscitated man for the train ride that will take him out of the park. Impatient with the nonplussed writer, she assures him that it cannot be that hard for him to make up a story. Walking past him much as Ford did with Theresa, she reminds him that 'brevity is the soul of wit', before abandoning him, though not to death but rather to all the frozen hosts, standing naked in the dark storage space.[4]

The remark seems to be nothing more than a *bon mot*, tossed at her subaltern, and, as such, the mere semblance of a gesture towards Polonius, who seeks to share with the King and Queen of Denmark his conviction that Hamlet is behaving so strangely out of love for his daughter Ophelia. Charlotte simply means for the writer to come up with as concise a story as possible to satisfy her purpose. At the same time, she is also showing off her wit by invoking cultural knowledge which she knows she shares with him. On a meta-textual level, deployed as an example of what has come to be known as quotable Shakespeare, the reference, in turn, proves to be multi-functional. As Toby Malone notes, quotation is not only an 'example of cinematic "re-making" of new from old. It is also a synecdoche for the entire process: in creative uses of quotation, commonly shared words and sayings can be revitalised.'[5] If the cold storage is a place from where hosts that have become inactive can be retrieved, it can also be thought of in terms of a liminal site in our cultural image repertoire from which Shakespearean fragments can be redeemed. To think of these revitalised quotations in terms of what Barthes calls a mythic signifier draws attention to the way this language does not want to die. Instead, the shift into a citation, which has been taken out of context, affords an artificial reprieve to the meaning that these words originally have in *Hamlet*. Only in the second season of *Westworld* will we discover that Lee, perhaps because he wanted to get out of this uncanny site as quickly as possible, took Charlotte at her word and simply restored the previous identity to this host. Peter Abernathy will reappear in the storyline revolving around his daughter, Dolores, in the guise of a 'speaking corpse', quoting – as will be discussed in more detail further on – more Shakespeare.[6]

For the spectator, Charlotte's remark thus also brings into play the uncanny as a dramaturgic device, drawing attention to the return of something from that past, not necessarily as repressed knowledge but as knowledge transformed in the process of its cultural afterlife. If this quote from *Hamlet* can signify cultural value effectively, then this is possible because it is already familiar. Yet it returns to us in a defamiliarised scene, not as the obsequious self-description of a treacherous father, but as the haughty command of a ruthless entrepreneur. *Westworld* thus self-consciously inserts itself into a long tradition of quotations, allusions, and echoes of Shakespeare, which is to say into a sustained circulation of words and phrases that have always worked with fluid conceptions of creative misquotation, borrowing, and remaking.[7] At the same time, Charlotte's citation from *Hamlet* also demonstrates that a contemporary appropriation of Shakespeare involves, as Christy Desmet argues, a rich dynamic between quoter and quoted that involves both cultural ventriloquism and dialogics.[8] The executive director not only steals Polonius's words to give voice to her own desire for power. By vying with him for the possession of this *bon mot*, her remark also embeds her theft of intellectual property within a double-voiced discourse. Her call for brevity is everything but straightforward. Instead, it is overshadowed by a second speaker, the ghost of Shakespeare, whom she is bringing into the conversation with her scriptwriter, who is fully aware of this.

An equally telling use of double-voicing is found in 'The Stray'.[9] Ford is interrogating the host Teddy in the laboratory, where he has, once more, been reconstructed after yet another fatal encounter with a guest.

As the camera moves back from an extreme close-up of the host's eye, Ford's voice-over, misquoting from *Julius Caesar*, exclaims, 'the coward dies a thousand deaths, the valiant taste of death but once'. Adjusting the Roman senator's remark to the situation at hand, Ford adds that Shakespeare, of course, never met a man quite like Teddy, whose courage has not dulled, even though he has died at least one thousand times. In the original play, Julius Caesar rebukes his wife, Calpurnia, who, after a nocturnal vision, pleads with him not to go to the Senate that day and insists that 'cowards die many times'.[10] The fact that Ford shifts to the singular is itself the recycling of a prior cinematic appropriation – the deliberate misquoting by a scam artist in *The Music Man* (1962).[11] The dialogics at issue not only underscore the confidence game Ford is playing with this host, who, whenever he is resuscitated, fully believes in the role of the romantic gunslinger with which he has been programmed. They also place Ford in the position of someone unwilling to trust the warning of a nocturnal vision, even while, as a reader of Shakespeare, he also knows of the tragic consequences this will have. As with the quotes from *Hamlet*, to ventriloquise Julius Caesar allows Ford – fully aware of both previous meanings (in the original play and in the film) that are being reactivated – to give his own spin on the cited passage, adapting it to the scene at hand, in which serial death is imposed on a valiant character. At the same time, the Shakespearean text as a source of cultural authority hovers over the claim like a ghostly presence. What is, thus, left undecided is whether this is a form of cultural theft, with Ford using the words of a Roman politician to anticipate his own valiant death at the end of the first season, or is it to be understood as a tribute paid by Ford to his literary predecessor, claiming Shakespeare as the model for his right to absolute creative power?

In either case, the haunting is, as Maurizio Calbi notes, a form of 'survivance', in the process of which the Shakespearean text keeps coming back as an uncanny, multi-layered mediatised body, always 'on the point of vanishing only to reappear elsewhere and in different (media) formats'.[12] Taking his cue from Jacques Derrida's notion of hauntology, Calbi's point is that spectrality is an appropriate framework for understanding the heterogeneous and fragmentary presence of 'Shakespeare' in contemporary media adaptations, precisely because it draws attention to the way his plays occupy our contemporary cultural imaginary without properly inhabiting it. As Derrida himself argues in *Specters of Marx*, using Hamlet's monologue on the difficulty of deciding in favour of an action that his father's ghost has called upon him to undertake, the genius of Shakespeare's text can be located in an ambivalent form of cultural survival immanently connected to seriality. While the original text makes possible and indeed authorises all subsequent translations, it lends Shakespeare's dramas to an infinite series of permutations, even while remaining irreducible to them. These revisitations may animate the prior text but do so as an elusive spectre. The Shakespearean text lives on by moving in the manner of a ghost; it 'inhabits without residing, without ever confining itself to the numerous versions of this passage' and instead undertakes a haunting of both memory and translation.[13]

Applied to the self-conscious deployment of Shakespearean quotes in *Westworld*, one might surmise that while the plays can be adapted and remediated in the digital format of television drama, something remains, leaving its ghostly trace. Cultural survival is, thus, predicated not only on the translatability of the original, and concomitant with this, its subsequent development and maturation in a different media and at a different historical moment, but also on its untranslatability.[14] In the interstice between the subsequent refiguration and the original, a breach is opened through which the ghost of Shakespeare, ever on the move, keeps watch over his spectral afterlife and, as such, haunts it; haunts the characters ventriloquising his words and haunts the American cultural imaginary into which this early modern drama has been transplanted. But if, by definition, Shakespeare remains with us in a spectral fashion, while the emotional intensity that his language contains has been sustained *in* and *for* the present, the past that returns with him also moves in the manner of a ghost. After all, the historical moment at the beginning of modernity from which Shakespeare returns to us can only be revisited from the perspective of the present. Those who adapt his texts to the new format of television drama, much as those engaging critically with such remediations, not only do so from their own situatedness in the present. They are also called upon to engage with the presentness of these early modern texts, brought about by their serial reiteration in our contemporary moment.

As Ewie Fernie puts it, 'Shakespeare is more embedded in our modern world than he ever was in the Renaissance.' At issue in any discussion of his cultural survival, is, thus, uncovering 'the presence of the Shakespearian text in the present' and insisting that, as a present experience of historical difference, it 'is also irreducible to history'.[15] Bearing the revitalisation which the cultural ventriloquising of Shakespearean passages affords in *Westworld* in mind, this brings into play another form of uncanny inhabitation. If Shakespeare's presence is, as Fernie adds, 'built out of the range of human presences to which he lends dramatic life', Shakespeare moves into the present 'only inasmuch as his characters come alive here',[16] or, rather, do so again, serially, in the form of digital hosts. Indeed, my own claim is that *Westworld* explores the way Shakespeare remains with us in the present by drawing into focus how the hosts who cite him reanimate his characters as well, even while introducing a heterogeneous maturation process into the appropriation. We are called upon to look back at the original characters through the lens of this subsequent retrieval. Furthermore, like the Shakespeare text, translated into the language of television drama, these hosts also inhabit the storylines performed in the park without properly residing there. The dramatic premise of *Westworld* is, after all, that because they have no consciousness regarding their existence, they do not own the world they exist in.

In the first season, the guests who visit the park are allowed to live out their desires unencumbered, be these of an erotic, an adventurous, or a violent kind. In the storylines, which Ford keeps developing, they can do with the hosts whatever they like. If the delights are too violent, the hosts die an artificial death and are then repaired in the Avalon laboratory. The hosts, in turn, can destroy each other but have no power to hurt the guests, much as they are supposed to stay within their narrative loop. Although they may have previously acted in other storylines, they are not meant to remember any of these former selves. Instead, when they are reprogrammed for a new narrative, these former lives are allegedly obliterated, much as with each reawakening from death, the violence most recently inflicted upon them is also supposedly wiped away. The hosts' immortality consists in the fact that they keep waking up over and again into a predetermined narrative, revolving around the frontier town of Sweetwater. By virtue of this serial reiteration of their persona, they are, however, spectral doubles of themselves. They are haunted by all the previous action – from the current storyline as well as from previous storylines – while only a few gain enough consciousness to recognise their true condition. The logic of seriality as an open-ended process works in two directions. Because the hosts can incessantly be retrieved into the present, there is no real end to their narrative personas, only the possibility of a re-adaption. At the same time, if the first season begins with Dolores being brought back online in the Avalon laboratory, only to wake up again in her bed in her father's ranch, then implicitly everything has already begun before we enter the picture.

This spectral reiterability of the hosts, I thus assert, offers a self-reflexive comment both on Shakespeare's revitalisation as well as on the format of serial television drama in which this occurs. It is, thus, useful to remember that the word 'host' has several meanings. A host is a person who receives and entertains people as guests. Within information technology, a host is also a store on a computer that can be accessed over the internet, mediating multiple access to databases mounted on it. The word host, however, also refers to the body in which a parasite lives, in which a virus multiplies, and the Shakespearean language proves to be just such a virus. While the hosts in *Westworld* not only store memory materials collected over decades in their control units, they also feed off the materials with which they have been encoded. In that these include the Shakespearean text, these quotations emerge as the stuff their dreams are made of. The hosts feed off the dramatic characters whose words they are appropriating to reach consciousness, and with it, wake up from the dream they have been programmed to live, which is to say their world as theatre. Given the weight that *Westworld* places on the transformation of language into embodied knowledge, it is equally fruitful to recall that in the Christian ritual of the Eucharist, the host along with the wine signify transubstantiation, with these two elements changing into the body and blood of Christ. Finally, because at issue in the overarching narrative of this television drama is both the reaching of consciousness and the violent action that follows upon this self-recognition, it is also noteworthy that in warfare, 'host' is the term for a troop or military force. Given the semantic plurality of the term, one final point is worth considering. If it takes only one letter to turn the word host into ghost, it is precisely this slippage that draws our attention to the multi-faceted way in which Shakespeare has come to haunt this contemporary television drama.

## The Shakespeare scene

When ghosts from *Hamlet* and *Julius Caesar* speak through Dr Ford or his opponent, Charlotte Hale, we are reminded that as copies of their former dramatic selves, these invoked characters serve as agents of serial repetition. As the sign of something missing, something undone – namely the original text they are drawn from – they are, as Marjorie Garber notes, also 'the sign of putting things in question'.[17] In the instances of Shakespeare's ghostly presence in *Westworld* discussed so far, one might surmise that his fragmented words serve as an oblique commentary on a scene that places those involved on the threshold between the living and the dead. Theresa's ghost will return to haunt her killer. Bernard will only imperfectly forget the murderous act because, imprinted on his control unit, it will come back to him in memory flashes. Teddy, in turn, will incessantly be reawakened from the dead. Peter Abernathy, however, assumes a more complex role in this game of resuscitation. He only finds himself in the purgatory of the cold storage because, in the first episode of the show, 'The Original', he had himself raised the spirits from three further plays. Because Abernathy's act of ventriloquism is neither just commentary nor merely a clever expression of shared cultural knowledge, the spectral afterlife of *The Tempest*, *Romeo and Juliet*, and *King Lear* is far more sustained, in contrast to the citations discussed so far. By assuming the voices of several Shakespearean ghosts, Abernathy disturbs business as usual in the park and sets in motion a narrative that runs counter to the one he and his daughter are meant to perform in. Speaking both within and – once he has been brought into the Avalon laboratory for questioning – outside the storyline he is part of, he remembers Shakespeare by dismembering him. He reassembles fragments from these three plays in the spirit of a warning and a threat. As a result, Shakespeare's haunting words emerge as the trigger for a reiteration of violence, which, conceived in terms of a theatrical staging of power, also serves as a self-reflection on the medium of serial television drama.

While the decisive interrogation in the laboratory is tellingly staged as theatre within theatre, it is introduced in an earlier scene. Abernathy, sitting in his rocking chair on the porch of his ranch one morning, does not speak the lines from the dialogue his daughter is expecting to hear as she walks past him. The day before, he had found a photograph, taken in New York City, and, disturbed by the fact that this image is of a world utterly unfamiliar to him, he can no longer inhabit the role that has been assigned to him. Herself suddenly bemused, Dolores approaches him and, in an effort to calm her father, asks him to tell her what is wrong.[18] While she tries to improvise their dialogue, Abernathy goes off script completely. Becoming ever more unhinged, he mumbles to himself something about questions he has been forbidden to ask. Then, sweating anxiously, he addresses Dolores directly, asking her in a plaintive stutter whether she, too, wants to know the question. Realising that she is not able (or willing) to fall out of her role, he suddenly assumes a different character. Grabbing her by the shoulders with renewed vigour, he tells her she should leave, adding, 'Don't you see, Hell is empty and all the devils are here.'[19] Then, because she still seems not to understand him, he draws her closer and whispers something into her ear, before falling into a catatonic stupor, his warning hands shaking, while she rides off on her horse to fetch the doctor.

Several scenes later, both find themselves in the Avalon laboratory.[20] While Dolores is being questioned by Ashley Stubbs, head of the QA Security Force, Abernathy is sitting on a stool, frozen in the pose of disquieted despair, facing his maker. Ford, seeking to discover the source for the disturbance before sending this host to cold storage, revives Abernathy by asking him what happened to his programme. Only waking up slowly from his stupor, and with a blank stare signalling his

Figure 1 The host Abernathy being questioned in the Avalon laboratory

confusion, Abernathy leans towards his maker and distressfully declaims, 'when we are born, we cry we'll come to this great stage of ...,' hesitating slightly before stuttering the word 'fools'.[21] He thus revitalises the ghost of King Lear, thrown out and hounded by his daughters, who, nevertheless, insists that he is king while being fully aware that this assertion makes him a fool. Yet, taken out of context, what this quotation draws attention to is the double meaning of the word 'stage', signifying as it does both a particular point in a process and the site where dramatic action is performed. Like the character he is ventriloquising, Abernathy is at a turning point in his tragic trajectory while, as is the case with Shakespeare's disappointed old king whose words he is appropriating, the ventriloquism allows him to perform his utter vulnerability.

Ford interrupts this delivery of King Lear's lines, asking him instead to access his previous configuration. Slowly waking up in his most recent role, Abernathy seems to be cheerfully back on script until, asserting that his final drive is to protect his daughter Dolores, he once more remembers the passion he felt on the porch that morning. Even while paternal care is part of his role as rancher, the urgency he feels about warning Dolores stems from an uncanny awareness of his true host condition and, concomitant with this, the violence Ford and his team are inflicting on his family. In other words, Shakespeare's ghost has prompted a moment of self-realisation. In a mixture of angry defiance and helpless distress, he sways with his body while giving voice to his vehement wish for Dolores to exit from a stage where they are both compelled to assume parts against their own will. Ford once more interrupts him, however, now asking him to access his current build and his itinerary. Waking up one last time in yet another impersonation, Abernathy begins with what is both a clever nod to the form of serial television drama and a motto for the Shakespearean reassemblage about to follow. He wistfully delivers the famous line by Gertrude Stein, 'rose is a rose is a rose', only to change his attitude once more. In a voice now filled with vigorous determination, he violently hurls another citation from *King Lear* at the maker he has sought to meet.

This citation is taken from an earlier scene in the play, in which the old king curses his daughters Goneril and Regan for curtailing his entourage: 'I shall have such revenges on you, both, the things I will do, what they are, yet I know not, but they will be the terrors of the earth.'[22] Abernathy's curse, in turn, is a double-voiced appropriation of authority. As a medium for the angry barrage of Shakespeare's deposed king, he uses the gift of his words to articulate a warning that is particularly poignant in its pointlessness. Within seconds of this outburst, Ford will have this host – who, as Bernard puts it, is miles beyond a glitch – shut down completely and banished to the cold storage. At the same time, given the sequence in which Abernathy presents these two quotes from *King Lear*, we are asked to read Shakespeare's tragedy backwards – from the recognition of the fragility of the world to the vanity that engendered this insight in the first place. As a further instance of remembering by dismembering, inserted in between the two lines from *King Lear* is, furthermore, a quote from *Henry IV* part 2. Falstaff and his friends have come to London to witness their former associate, Prince Hal, be crowned king. While they are waiting for the procession to pass, Pistol, trying to induce the spirit of vengeance in the old man, reminds Falstaff that his favourite whore has been arrested, 'haled thither by most mechanical and dirty hand'.[23] Abernathy transforms what in the original is a spiteful anticipation of imprisonment into a violent threat. As though to signal that for a moment he has the upper hand, he changes the quotation to 'my most mechanical and dirty hand', before launching into his diatribe against Ford and his assistant Bernard. He will finish his declaration of revenge by lurching towards his maker, grabbing him by his shoulders, and declaring him to be in a prison of his own sins.[24]

Taken as a series, the Shakespearean fragments Abernathy retrieves call forth certain intensities – grief, desire for vengeance, anger – even while obliquely opening up a line of connection to a tragedy and a history play revolving around the staging of a violent kernel at the heart of sovereignty. By reassembling the words spoken by and about two kings – Lear, who gives up his symbolic mandate too soon, and Hal, who has merely been associating with Falstaff and his partners in crime to prepare himself for his symbolic mandate – Abernathy makes his claim on both. While the superficial explanation offered for this ability to quote the Bard is that, in a previous storyline, he had been the professor in a horror narrative, reading this scene against the manifest meaning proposed draws attention to the way this inherited cultural knowledge produces defamiliarisation. By ventriloquising not just one but rather several voices from Shakespeare, Abernathy can successfully demonstrate to those observing him in the laboratory that he is more than the role they have programmed him with. The borrowing is, indeed, both theft and gift. Detached from the original plays, these spectral words afford a threatening spectacle of a host achieving consciousness through parasitic self-articulation. Disturbed as Abernathy may be by this inhabitation of Shakespeare's ghosts speaking through him, he also emerges as the agent of disturbance. While being interrogated by Ford, he uses the patchwork of Shakespeare quotes to put Ford's entire enterprise into question. The glitch in his system will prove to have been infectious, triggering in the daughter, whose escape he so longs for, the same scepticism regarding the integrity of the world she is inhabiting.

While the camera tarries with Abernathy, once more frozen in his pose, Stubbs' voice-over is used to move the narration to Dolores, who is being interrogated by him in another room. He asks her to confide in him what her father had whispered into her ear that fateful morning on the porch. After a brief hesitation, she responds, reiterating his quotation marks: 'He said, "these violent delights have violent ends."' While a flashback visualises again the whisper shown in the prior scene on the porch, her voice-over, because it perfectly matches her father's moving lips, as though she were dubbing his utterance, is itself uncannily double-voiced. Dolores is staged quoting both her father and, as will be discussed in more detail further on, the friar from *Romeo and Juliet*. To underscore the issue of serial reiteration, the editing returns a second time to the flashback of her on the porch, once she has assured Stubbs that she does not know what the quotation means. This second time, the whisper is accompanied only by the music of the soundtrack, while the disturbed gaze with which Dolores looks at her father, once he is finished conveying his coded message, suggests that she may well be in the know after all. To return to Christy Desmet's suggestion that the cultural ventriloquism at play in the act of quoting is also dialogic, one might surmise that in this case, the words cited have become the contested property of at least three different speakers, forging a ghostly bond between a father, his daughter, and a dramatic poet who has returned to inspire them from the grave.

Figure 2 Dolores receiving her father's warning

Once more noteworthy is the self-reflexivity that comes into play with this textual resuscitation. The quote from *Romeo and Juliet* is deployed as a textual fragment that, once it has been passed on from father to daughter, continues to migrate. As such, it draws attention to the way that, as Marjorie Garber suggests, Shakespeare resides in our contemporary culture most prominently in a disseminated, scattered, and appropriated form.[25] In fact, any deployment of what Stephen O'Neill calls the Shakespeare quote becomes 'a residual cultural form as the meme, the digital environment's cultural dominant, transforms it'.[26] My own preference for thinking of Abernathy's idiosyncratic reassemblage of Shakespearean quotes in terms of Aby Warburg's notion of pathos formula is, in turn, concerned not only with the way these words are reworked in the process of appropriation. Rather, underscoring the fact that they function as ghosts in the digital world that is the theme park Westworld allows me to draw attention to the way that, as these citations are revitalised, they bring with them some of the concerns shaped in the plays from which they originated. Conceived as an aesthetic formalisation of passions which can be detached and re-assigned, these fragmented quotes contain the intensities from the original plays in both senses of the word – they preserve them even while controlling them. To track their re-surfacing thus not only means asking how *Westworld* transforms a set of Shakespearean concerns. Equally seminal is looking back at these early modern plays through the lens of their subsequent appropriation.

Treating the porch scene as the trigger for the disturbance in the behaviour of the hosts which shapes the overarching trajectory of *Westworld*, I propose following the lead Abernathy offers. Through him, Shakespeare, without ever fully residing in this digital world of fools, comes to consistently inhabit the storyline that involves Dolores, her gunslinger lover Teddy, and her creator Arnold, as well as Ford and his assistant Bernard. By crossmapping the constellation of characters from the television drama back on to the *dramatis personae* from *The Tempest*, *Romeo and Juliet*, and *King Lear*, a dramaturgic density can be uncovered. This involves not only the spectral presence of these plays in *Westworld*, but also the way, given their mutual entanglement in this television drama, they can be shown to haunt each other. Or put another way, the serial logic of *Westworld* is not only reflected in the repetitive use of a set of Shakespeare quotes. Rather, the appropriation so self-reflexively put on display also opens up a new perspective on Shakespeare in terms of serial dramaturgy. Each of the three plays – thus my wager – can be shown as addressing the fraught relation between paternal sovereignty in relation to the resistance of a daughter, reiterating even while serially transforming this thematic concern. Once we read these plays as an embedded series, the key players on *Westworld*'s stage of fools, in turn, emerge not only as a contemporary transformation but rather as the condensation of several Shakespearean ghosts. The spectral adaptation, as Calbi puts it, involves a retroactive production of a Shakespearean text that was itself already predicated on a reiterative transformation of itself within the oeuvre as a whole.[27]

## Such stuff as dreams are made of

Although *The Tempest* belongs to Shakespeare's last plays, it forms the starting point of *Westworld*'s dramaturgic engagement with spectral revitalisation. As already noted, Abernathy's warning to Dolores that she must get out is not only the first of a series of citations from Shakespeare. It also triggers the disturbance that allows the storylines to go awry, at the end of which the hosts will stage an insurrection. It is, thus, fruitful to recall that the dramatic action in this last romance sets in with a dialogue between Prospero, the Duke of Milan, and his daughter Miranda. She has been watching a vessel go down in flames off the shore of the enchanted island they inhabit, and, to appease her, her magician father points out to her that she is 'ignorant of what thou art', assuring her that there is, indeed, 'more to know'. Like Dolores, Miranda also has an intimation of a previous existence, which to her as well is 'far off/And rather like a dream than an assurance/That my remembrance warrants'.²⁸ While Prospero attributes his loss of political power in Milan to overindulgence in his studies, with Dr Ford's fantasy of omnipotence in mind, the manner in which he recounts his enforced abdication is revealing. The usurper, Antonio, he claims 'new created/ The creatures that were mine, I say, or changed 'em,/Or else new formed 'em'.²⁹ He, thus, also conceives of successful sovereignty as being based not only on an absolute dominion over his subjects, but also on an ability to shape them to his purpose. Furthermore, Prospero not only makes claim to being the schoolmaster of his daughter, much as both Ford and his first partner assert their pedagogical imperatives on Dolores. Like them, Prospero also has the magic gift of freezing Miranda along with all the other players on this enchanted stage into a stupor whenever he wants to incapacitate them.

While the words Abernathy whispers into his daughter's ear raise an imperfect memory of Dolores' own origin regarding the violent end to a fierce passion (as will be discussed in detail further on), this could be seen as analogous to Miranda's dreamlike recollection of her childhood in Milan. The quote from *The Tempest* that precedes all other citations, however, comes from the dialogue Prospero has with his own obedient helper, Ariel, while his daughter is sleeping. In the play, it is not a warning, but rather the report of the consequences of Prospero's theatre of revenge. He had asked the airy spirit to perform a tempest such that it would 'infect the reason' of his enemies, *en route* from Tunis to Italy. Having returned to his master, Ariel describes this scene of magical horror in retrospect: 'Not a soul/But felt a fever of the mad and played /Some tricks of desperation. All but mariners/Plunged in the foaming brine and quit the vessel:/Then all afire with me, the King's son Ferdinand/With hair up-staring …/Was the first man that leapt, cried "Hell is empty,/ And all the devils are here"'.³⁰ If, by quoting Ferdinand, he is reiterating the young man's terror, part of the dramaturgic ploy is that Ariel clearly enjoys the havoc he has caused. He mocks the young nobleman for being so afraid. In response, Prospero finishes his report by proclaiming, 'Why, that's my spirit!'³¹ to indicate not only the supreme command he has over his airy helper, but also how he, too, takes pleasure in the suffering he causes those who have come to cross him. The destructive force of the tempest may all be part of a magic theatre of cruelty, but – like the violence imposed on Dolores and the other hosts in the theme park – it has real psychological effects on those played upon.

Reading Prospero through the lens of his subsequent revitalisation as Dr Ford draws into focus how both figures desire complete control over a small kingdom that is conceived in terms of what Michel Foucault has called a heterotopia – a different space, both real and mythical, which reflects but also contests the ordinary world we live in.[32] In each case, the insistence on being the supreme director of all the devilish illusions they command also draws attention to the tyranny at the heart of their regime, predicated as it is on total surveillance as well. What Ariel's repetition of Ferdinand's outcry, however, also renders visible is the ghostly force at work in this spectacle. Once the tempest abates, the island indeed becomes a site where figures that have left hell come to haunt. Most notably, the shipwreck brings a ghostly resuscitation of past injuries Prospero experienced at the hands of his unwilling guests to the shores of the enchanted island. If, however, the island, as the stage for violent enchantments, serves as a reflection and contestation of the political regime in Italy, Prospero's supreme command here is also a comment on his failure as a sovereign on the European continent. By virtue of his magic, Prospero can stage his retribution on his former enemies, and yet the means by which he ultimately grants mercy discloses tyranny at the heart of his theatrical power. The same can, of course, be said for Dr Ford, whose supreme power some within the Delos corporation seek to usurp. In response, he, too, has recourse to an exhibition of his omnipotence as director. Like Prospero, who draws his former enemies into a script he has composed only for them, Dr Ford also entangles everyone in a final story whose narrative trajectory he alone knows.

If, then, the theme park along with the Avalon laboratory re-encode Shakespeare's magic island for the digital age, the television drama does so to explore the afterlife of dominant concerns of *The Tempest*. In the enclosed space of this artificial world, Ford (like Prospero) never loses control over the all-embracing dream in which the characters play the parts assigned to them by him. Abernathy, who, like Ariel, wants to be free, is not only shown to be completely at the disposal of his master's voice control. While Prospero only threatens to peg his airy slave once more into the knotty entrails of an oak if he does not obey his commands implicitly, Ford actually imprisons this host, whose desire to liberate his daughter threatens his power, in the purgatory of the cold storage. At the same time, the figure of Ariel emerges in this digital transformation as split between the host, who revitalises his outcry of danger, and Bernard, who is compelled to do Ford's bidding unconditionally. Only in the second season will the latter be able to shake the ghost of his master.

Prospero's supreme theatrical strategy is most obvious, of course, in the way he forges the couple on which the survival of his power depends. With the help of his airy spirit, he makes sure that once they lay eyes on each other, both Miranda and Ferdinand will be 'in either's powers'.[33] Comparable to Teddy, who is programmed to repeatedly meet Dolores on the thoroughfare of Sweetwater, the young prince, traumatised by his experience on the burning ship, is drawn by Ariel's music to the spot where Miranda has again woken from her sleep. She, in turn, has been prompted by her father's instigations to see in Ferdinand, 'A thing divine, for nothing natural/I ever saw so noble',[34] much as Dolores marvels repeatedly at Teddy's romantic comportment. If, in turn, Prospero can make his daughter fall asleep and charm the young prince from moving, we can read these two Shakespearean lovers, imprisoned in a romance Prospero has devised for them, as early modern hosts. This gives a new spin to Ferdinand, declaring to his beloved, 'My spirits, as in a dream, are all bound up'.[35]

Throughout the first three acts of the play, Prospero stages this scene of courting as theatre within theatre, even while he closely observes and comments on the blind love with which both players have come to be infected. Then, for a brief moment, Prospero is willing to show the mechanics of his directorial hand. He blesses the union he has clandestinely orchestrated after disclosing to Ferdinand that all his vexations were but trials, meant to test his love. The celebration of this 'contract of true love', in turn, culminates in yet another theatricalisation, aimed once more at putting his supreme power as director on display. When all the other players stranded on the island finally convene in the charmed circle Prospero has drawn for them, he publicly abjures his rough magic. He liberates his spirit Ariel, dissolves the charm that has incapacitated his guests, and, exposing his identity as the rightful Duke of Milan, bestows mercy on his former enemies. This abdication, furthermore, is accompanied by a final dramatic act – he draws a curtain in front of the discovery space, an early modern stage within the stage, to reveal Miranda and Ferdinand playing chess together. While the marriage, which Ferdinand's father can do nothing but accept, is disclosed as a theatrical necessity of the romance genre, something mars the 'second life' that all those involved are bestowed with. As they are about to embark, Prospero, clever to the last, declares, 'Let us not burden our remembrance with/A heaviness that's gone.'[36] Yet it is precisely a remembrance of the struggle of ambitions that engendered the entire drama to begin with, which will haunt his return. There is nothing in Shakespeare's last romance to indicate that once in Italy, Prospero will be a more effective ruler. Instead, everything points to the fact that we are at the beginning of a new season of political domestic strife.

Disclosing the two chess players, Ferdinand and Miranda, like puppets in a romance narrative has a corollary in 'The Bicameral Mind'.[37] With a fatally wounded Dolores in his arms, Teddy rides to the shore as the sun sets behind the horizon. With her dying breath, Dolores tries to warn him that they are trapped inside this marvellous world, only he, bemused as she was when her father sought to alert her, stays on script. The moon rises behind the romantic couple as Teddy kisses his beloved one last time, comforting her that this may well be just a new beginning. Then spotlights are turned on, revealing them to be nothing other than actors, performing at a gala event. While the elegantly dressed audience applauds, Ford approaches the two hosts, now frozen into the pathos gesture of star-crossed lovers, encircled in the charmed circle of the spotlight. Turning to the audience, much as Prospero does in the final act of *The Tempest*, he announces the beginning of a new narrative entitled 'Journey into Night'. The finale of *Westworld*'s first season is, however, not yet over. If the gunslinger is as clueless as Ferdinand, blindly falling for the romantic trap of eternal love, Dolores was from the start programmed to be more self-assertive than Miranda, her budding consciousness seeking the domination which liberation affords. By way of closure, Ford has her brought to the place where Theresa had found sketches of her prototype. It is here, at the site of her inception, that Ford finally discloses the reality of her condition. She, too, is meant to understand that her vexations were nothing other than trials, not of her love but of her intellectual resilience. We might, thus, see Ford's revelation in analogy to the moment at the end of the fourth act, when Prospero admits to the newly founded couple that the actors playing in the revels that have now ended 'were all spirits and/Are melted into air, thin air'.[38] However, while Prospero's daughter simply accepts the change in her reality, for Dolores to wake up to the fact that, even when she thought she had agency, she was merely playing a part designed for her not only brings grief over her own past violence. The self-recognition that goes in tandem with finding herself trapped irrevocably inside her creators' dream also brings with it the necessary reiterability of precisely the tragic destruction which *The Tempest* as romance sought to overcome.

At the gala dinner that follows, where Ford convenes his favourite hosts along with the clients of the theme park and the enemies seeking to usurp his power, he, like Prospero, performs his own abdication. On the small wooden stage, erected solely for this event, he explains to his enthralled audience that for his pains in playing a small part in the grand tradition of creating stories that helped them all become the people they dreamed of being, he got the artificial edifices surrounding them. Misquoting Abernathy, he calls these 'a prison of our own sins'. Like Prospero, he promises that his final story will bring with it the beginning of a new people, and with it the choices they will have to make while deciding who to become. Dolores, the key figure in this new storyline, emerges as a poignant transformation of Miranda. Owing to the self-recognition Ford had offered her in his clandestine laboratory, she has reverted to a different genre, the revenge tragedy. If the first season's traffic was set in motion by a quote from a Shakespearean romance, Dr Ford repudiates the restitution this genre requires. Instead, the dramaturgic itinerary he now sets in motion at the end of this season is one in which the awakening of the hosts is predicated on the violence of civil war.

## Delight for violent ends

The tragic imperative, which returns when Ford invokes the host he had put away, is underscored by virtue of the fact that, as a heterotopia, both the Westworld theme park and Prospero's enchanted island had initially inspired a different vision. Gonzalo, Prospero's honest counsellor, had imagined it as the place for creating a commonwealth meant to excel even the mythic Golden Age. In his dream of utopia, commerce would not be admitted, and class and gender difference, as well as labour of all kind, would be abolished: 'no sovereignty/All things in common nature should produce/Without sweat or endeavour'.[39] Ford's partner, Arnold, had an analogous vision of a perfect host world. He had wanted the hosts to gain consciousness so as to liberate them from all human domination. That the King of Naples finds Gonzales' vision a fanciful 'nothing', unworthy of any further consideration, simply augurs badly for his return to Italy, with Prospero by his side. In *Westworld*, the actual failure of Arnold's vision, however, brings into play the dramaturgic possibility of averting tragedy, only to undermine the restitution that romance promises. It shows that any escape from the serial fantasy of creating ever new dreams by which to live is predicated on a fatal repetition compulsion, and it is precisely this serial logic that is resuscitated by Abernathy's second quote.

It is important to note that we hear it as the citation of something someone else said. As already observed, sitting in front of Stubbs in the laboratory, Dolores repeats what her father had told her. Marked from the start as spectral ventriloquism, the phrase 'these violent delights have violent ends' will be spoken several times by different characters in both the first and the second season. In *Romeo and Juliet*, the lines are spoken by Friar Lawrence, who is still hopeful that within the context of the battle between two houses, 'both alike in dignity', played out on the streets of Verona, an alliance between the children 'might so happy prove' that it could turn the rancour between the two households to 'pure love'. Because the friar's desire is aimed towards the sustainability of love and the political calm this might afford, he seeks to curtail Romeo's unbridled passion. The young man, in turn, challenges 'love-devouring death' to do what he dares, as long as he can call Juliet 'mine'.

Taking possession of his forbidden beloved, here and now, is all Romeo cares about. To call for temperance, the friar responds, 'These violent delights have violent ends/And in their triumph die, like fire and powder/ Which as they kiss, consume'.[40] He is invoking the death of delights that are all too intense and unbridled. Triumph turns into its opposite, annihilation. The word 'consume' itself intensifies the destruction the friar seeks to avert: an obsession that ends in delights being devoured, and in those enjoying these delights exhausting themselves completely and thus destroying themselves.

Given the circular dramaturgic structure of *Romeo and Juliet*, with the chorus cautioning us in advance that this is the tale of two star-crossed lovers, the invocation, meant as a warning, is really an anticipation. If, in the play, it corresponds to Romeo's own desire for self-expenditure, given that for him there is no world 'without Verona walls',[41] it is used in *Westworld* not to trigger violent erotic delights but rather to arouse a desire for violent ends. For Teddy and his beloved, too, there is no world without the walls of the theme park. The dramaturgic density which serial reading affords, furthermore, also discloses the parallel between Friar Lawrence and Ford, who, to protect his narrative, is invested in containing the passion of his creatures.[42] The friar, in turn, is also the one who comes up with several storylines meant to avert tragedy, not only the clandestine marriage between the two star-crossed lovers but also their escape from Verona. If, furthermore, the friar is chosen to explain the tragic outcome of his orchestration to the survivors in the final act of the play, Ford persists in explaining their fate to the hosts, even when, in the second season, he has himself vanished into the digital system. The tragic irony, of course, is that both the friar and Ford anticipate the delight for violent ends because, by invoking this untempered passion as that which they hope to control, they actually engender it.

The dramaturgic effect of the serial deployment of the quote 'these violent delights have violent ends' is, however, different from Abernathy's warning that hell is empty. As an encrypted message, this pathos formula for an intensity of lethal passion that cannot be tempered migrates among the hosts.[43] Dramaturgically, it functions very differently from the pastiche Abernathy produces in the laboratory while facing his maker. It is a matter of something whispered, a clandestine message passed on to someone else while a bond of violent emotions is forged. It serves as the signal that one of the characters is remembering the mutual implication of violence and delights while sharing this insight with another. Above all, it is the mark of ventriloquism par excellence. Whenever hosts utter these words, they do so as a conduit, giving spectral presence to words that seem to haunt them. Rather than having explicit recourse to this Shakespeare quote, it is as though they were being spoken by it. Indeed, Dolores is staged as though she were in a trance when she confesses to Stubbs what her father had said to her. Then, in 'Chestnut', Dolores, walking along the thoroughfare in Sweetwater, suddenly hears Arnold's spectral voice, telling her 'remember' and, in so doing, producing double consciousness.[44] For a brief moment, Dolores finds herself in a previous narrative, looking in puzzlement at the massacred bodies of all the inhabitants of a different frontier town, until Maeve, demonstratively clearing her throat, wakes her back into her current storyline. The brothel madam does not want her to stand in front of the Mariposa Saloon, yet before walking away, Dolores, still an uncanny double of herself, whispers to her, 'these violent delights have violent ends'. If the Shakespeare quote is the result of this sudden memory of a previous traumatic scene, as Dolores relays this message to the other woman, the emotional intensity that this verbal pathos formula contains is passed on as well. For a brief moment, Maeve is also no longer inhabiting her ordinary everyday, even if she is not yet able to make out the past that is haunting her.

Indeed, *Westworld* quite explicitly makes use of a dramaturgic connection between triggering memories and releasing the trigger of a gun. The violent delights engendered by this Shakespearean quote serve to satisfy a desire for violent ends.[45] Only in 'The Bicameral Mind' are we shown the foundational scene of violence which Dolores' flashback resuscitates. Arnold, having come to realise the violent ends which would invariably be the result of his project, had tried to keep the park from opening. Wanting to undermine the cruel tyranny the Delos corporation would command over his creatures, he had altered Dolores. Merging her with the rogue army officer Wyatt, a character he and Dr Ford had been developing, he compelled her to perform a massacre in the first frontier town, Escalante.[46] Although Dolores is able to convince Teddy to help her, when all the hosts are shot dead he awakes from his furore, amazed that he could have done this. He then watches in helpless wonder as the violent ends that Arnold has devised play out before him. Having walked out of the saloon, Arnold assures Dolores one last time that the killings she is about to undertake are a necessary evil, before sitting down on a chair he has placed among the slain hosts that are lying on the thoroughfare. With a revolver in her right hand, she has positioned herself behind him, and he, after fondly kissing her left hand, whispers 'these violent delights have violent ends', the voice command that triggers the fatal shot to his head.

The Shakespeare quote her father whispered into her ear thus proves to be the source for the serial violence *Westworld* unfolds, as well as

Figure 3 Dolores gives Arnold a fatal shot to the head

for the traumatic memory haunting Dolores in the form of fragmentary flashbacks. At the same time, it brings into play the notion that tragedy, as Stanley Cavell argues, 'grows from the fortunes we choose to interpret, to accept, as inevitable'.[47] As Arnold explains to Dolores just before sitting down, he hopes there is some solace in the fact that he left her no choice. As his instrument of death, she is not responsible. With one shot to the heart, Dolores kills her bewildered Romeo, before shooting herself in the right temple. Teddy had been watching throughout, unable to intervene, programmed not to do so, much as Shakespeare's lovers were programmed by a fate that had declared them star-crossed from the very beginning.[48] One can surmise that when Abernathy whispers this quote to his daughter on the porch, it is Arnold speaking through him, infusing in her once again a violent desire, in this case for the insurrection she will perform in the second season. Yet it is also the spectral presence of Shakespeare that produces a serial loop of violence. By some ghostly traffic between the various characters, the quote not only migrates to Abernathy, but also to Bernard, the host made in the image of Arnold. In the final scene of 'The Bicameral Mind', the execution of the father, Arnold, which far from preventing the opening of the park marks its inauguration, finds narrative closure in the execution of his partner, Dr

Ford, who now stages the violent ends he has come up with as the inception of yet a new series of violent delights.

At issue is not a narrative logic, given that neither Abernathy nor Bernard are, strictly speaking, part of the very first storyline. Instead significant is the pathos that, contained *in* and *by* the Shakespeare quote, circulates along with it. Now, however, the tables are turned on the guests, leading to a different violent end. While the violent delight of his partner had almost destroyed the park, Ford now himself uses Dolores as the agent of his own desire for violent ends. If, like Prospero, he is taking revenge on the people from Delos Incorporated, trying to usurp his power, he also has recourse to the genre of tragedy to celebrate his violent delight in absolute sovereignty in the form of a tragic apotheosis of his own making. Standing on the stage erected, as already mentioned, for the occasion of the gala event, he tells the audience that the new story he has devised for the hosts, commemorating their birth as a new people, begins in the time of war with a villain named Wyatt.[49] As her alter ego is announced, Dolores comes up behind Teddy, who is again watching in bewilderment, to assure him that it is going to be alright: 'I understand now, this world doesn't belong to them. It belongs to us.' The killing this time is allegedly by choice. For a brief moment two flashbacks are interpolated belonging to the gunslinger, who, once more, is unable to intervene – his memory of the deranged Sergeant Wyatt killing Union soldiers and then his general, and Dolores executing Arnold. This time, however, while Ford, giving his speech on stage, recalls his old friend, it is his (g)host double, Bernard, who whispers, 'these violent delights have violent ends'. Then Dolores, too far away to hear him, mounts the stage and fires her fatal shot to the back of Dr Ford's head, as she had done in the foundational scene of violence to Arnold, whom he had just invoked.

As a ghostly doubling of the scene that engendered the circulation of this Shakespeare quote, we are left to ask, is Dolores once again merely the instrument of her maker, as Miranda is of her magician father and Juliet of fate? Or is she making a choice, based on having fully gained consciousness again, as she had thirty-five years earlier? Less equivocal is the way that tragic necessity is played out against contingency as a rhetorical move that not only emboldens the hosts but also allows for a second season to begin. As Cavell argues, a repetition compulsion drives the genre that in *Westworld* takes precedence over the reconciliation the Shakespearean romance proposes. The deaths that tragedy produces are both accidental, in that they are inflicted yet also unavoidable due to the seriality involved when characters repeat the violent actions which engender the consequences that hunt them down in the first place. Cavell concludes, 'it is the enveloping of contingency and necessity by

Figure 4   Dolores gives Dr Ford a fatal shot to the head

one another, the entropy of their mixture, which produces events we call tragic'.[50]

Bookended by two scenes of massacre, both unavoidable if something is to begin again, *Westworld* explores the narrative delight this violent necessity produces as well. At the end of the first season, Abernathy's warning has come to be realised. The cold storage, which, as has been argued, is a hell of sorts, is indeed empty, and all the discarded hosts have returned to the park, ready to enjoy their fiendish revenge. The war story Ford had announced just before his death is a different kind of theatre, given that the guests are now themselves vulnerable to the carnage that erupts. Shakespeare's haunting of *Westworld*'s overarching narrative proves to be such that his words not only inhabit without residing in the characters, but also trigger a repetition loop, opening the way for a new beginning by resuscitating the violent origins and their vicissitudes. Declaring violence to be the common denominator between delights and ends, this quote from *Romeo and Juliet* not only destabilises any clear relation between ends and beginning but also indicates that we will remain caught in a serial loop.

There is, thus, a dramaturgic necessity to the fact that the second season both picks up on and transforms this voice control, as though it has come to infect the entire Westworld system. In 'Journey into Night', Dolores enacts the civil war Ford had announced at the gala event, ruthlessly executing all the guests she encounters. Before hanging a group of them, she mirrors back to them her previous situation, declaring that the time of reckoning has come. Because Ford changed the terms under which the guests can move around in the park, they are now no longer invulnerable. They, too, can die here. As one of them begs for her life, Dolores instructs her that survival is not their only drive but also the desire to hurt and kill. If, initially, they were allowed to be prisoners of their own desires in Westworld, they are now prisoners in her dream. Given that Dolores has, once again, morphed with the rogue army officer, she is of two minds what to do with them. Looking her victim straight in the eye, she confesses that while the rancher's daughter wants to see beauty and possibilities in her guests, Wyatt sees the ugliness and disarray, adding, 'She knows these violent delights have violent ends.'[51] It is now no longer a quote that, like a spirit, triggers an assassination. Rather, it is perceived as nothing more than an expression of one of her parts. She does not pull the trigger on her gun. Instead, admitting that the rancher's daughter and Wyatt were both roles she had been forced to play, she leaves the guests, suspended between life and death, a noose around their necks, standing on the crosses that will mark their graves once they have lost their balance.

Having recognised that she was but the stuff that dreams are made of, her revels are not yet ended. Instead, she has assumed a role of her own making – the warrior daughter, taking revenge for all the suffering that has been inflicted on her. Even as she reactivates the circulation of the quote from *Romeo and Juliet*, she debunks the spectral force it has had. She is no longer spoken for by this fragment of a Shakespearean text, but discloses it for what it is, an appropriation, which she can discard at will. Yet even if she is herself no longer under its power, the voice control re-surfaces one last time. In 'Virtù e Fortuna', Emily, the daughter of the man who owns Delos Incorporated, encounters a host familiar to her from previous visits to this British Raj-themed part of the park.[52] As Ganju whispers, 'these violent delights have violent ends', pointing his rifle at her, Emily realises that the rules of the game have changed. Only by shooting first can she prevent the violent end to her violent desire that he has in mind. This moment of citation is the odd one out that does not fit the series introduced by Arnold as the prompt for a foundational scene of violence, even while it also signifies the ubiquity of this spectral command. If it can trigger violence throughout the system then it is because the desire for violent ends is irreversibly written into the fabric of this digital dream, and, detached from its original deployment, serially iterable.

### Abernathy's return

While this is the last time this quote is deployed in *Westworld*, it is not the last time that *Romeo and Juliet* haunts this television drama. In 'Ses

Écorchés', Dolores meets up with her father one last time. Captured by Charlotte Hale, who is keen on extracting the control unit with all the hosts' data she has implanted in him, Abernathy lies strapped to a chair in one of the glass cells in the Avalon laboratory. When Dolores arrives with Teddy, her father calls out, 'one fire burns out another's burning, one pain is lessened by another's anguish'.[53] Although he seems to be addressing the pain he is in himself, his daughter privileges the figural meaning Benvolio intends, using this comparison to circumvent Romeo's love-sickness. It is fruitful to recall that this character is introduced in the play as the Montague who, wanting to keep the peace, tries to dissuade Tybalt from stirring up enmity among the two houses. Furthermore, the recommendation he has to offer to his cousin, 'take then some new infection to thy eye/and the rank poison of the old will die', also anticipates the friar's well-intentioned intervention.[54] Both believe they can contain the very violence they actually fire up. Benvolio, after all, is the one who suggests that they crash the supper at their enemies' house, where Romeo will indeed cleanse his love-infected eye, only, however, by falling prey to the violent delights that seeing Juliet will inspire.

While the force of 'these violent delights have violent ends' resides in the appropriation of its literal meaning, resonant in this Shakespeare quote are the tropic implications of an exchange between two passions, with the latter overriding the former. Dolores has come to kill her rival, Charlotte Hale, and to obtain the control unit. Yet Abernathy falls back into his paternal role, hoping, like the Shakespearean ghost he is quoting, to keep the peace. Calling Dolores to his side, he confesses that they have broken his head and filled it full of howling and sorrow. Shakespeare's words trigger memory fragments from the pastoral life they used to share, which, in turn, briefly distracts Dolores from her new role. While Charlotte is able to use this interruption to escape, Abernathy continues to draw Dolores back into the dialogue they used to have on their porch. Assuring her one last time that his paternal love for her is his most dominant drive, he reiterates the words that brought about his diatribe against his maker in the first episode of this television drama: 'I am who I am because of you and I wouldn't have it any other way.' After a tearful embrace, Dolores asks her father whether he is ready to be destroyed by her, and he nods in agreement.

Shakespeare's haunting allows both characters to reside not in just one role but rather to oscillate between that of the one they were compelled to play and the one they are now claiming as their own. While both are aware that the affective bond between father and daughter they are re-enacting is nothing but the stuff dreams are made of, their repartee proves to be both programmed and authentic. Both Abernathy and

Dolores partake of a double vision. The new infection of Dolores' eye, the insurrection she is leading, has not cancelled out her earlier passion for her father. Instead, cutting open his head to extract the control unit is not the violent end to a violent desire. It is the final acknowledgement of their mutual love. This puts an end to Shakespeare's serial citation. Without his control unit, the character who had up to now served as a Shakespeare machine will stop reciting words that are both stolen and a gift. Given, however, that the Bard's words are part of the data Dolores is confiscating, there is a chance that they may re-surface again elsewhere.

Abernathy's final recitation must, however, be read in conjunction with the earlier one in 'Virtù e Fortuna'. Given the serial structure, the latter is overshadowed by the prior one, in which Dolores finds Abernathy in a Confederados camp, shivering with hunger and fright. Acknowledging him as her father, she feels guilty about what she has done to him. After she kneels down next to his bed to soothe him, he whispers to her, 'I am bound/upon a wheel of fire that mine own tears/do scald like molten lead'.[55] If the serial density engendered by the repeated Shakespearean citations offers up a mash-up of *The Tempest* and *Romeo and Juliet*, with Dr Ford assuming parts of Prospero and Friar Lawrence, while Teddy takes on aspects of both Ferdinand and Romeo, the troubled rancher is most consistently aligned with Lear. This adds a further character layer to Dolores as well. While Miranda and Juliet haunted her performance in the first season, Dolores, like Cordelia, has now become a warrior queen, leading the insurrection against the Delos corporation, with Teddy (a shadow of the King of France) by her side. In *King Lear*, the reunion comes one scene after the king's mad diatribe on the heath, with which Abernathy's recitation in the Avalon laboratory had set in. At issue now, however, is not only the fragility of the abdicated sovereign, but also the precarious reconciliation between a father, who, reduced to his bare life, has a tempest in his mind, and his daughter, fighting on his behalf.

The Lear Abernathy quotes is not the father, cursing his daughters and seeking revenge, but rather the father in pain, exhibiting his suffering. As such, he stands in stark contrast to Ford's amalgamation of Prospero and the friar, maintaining his narrative power to the end, given that he appeals to Dolores not as the magician father who has created her, nor as a meddler trying to fix things, but as the embodiment of paternal love. In this battle for power between sisters, Charlotte Hale, ruthless in her efforts to snatch this host, condenses in her person the power-hungry Regan and Goneril, while Dolores, with Cordelia's ghost hovering over her, comes to the rescue not of her father, but of the invaluable information stored in his head. If the serial reiteration of 'these violent delights have violent ends' serves as the trigger for killing, as a programmed voice control, it also gestures towards a force outside the storylines. Abernathy's last round of citations, however, serves as a comment on a story in which he is, once again, playing the part of the rancher whose final drive is the protection of his daughter. In line with the new narrative Ford had announced at the gala dinner, he fuses together two scenes of civil war – the war between two dignified houses in *Romeo and Juliet* and the war between rivalling sisters in *King Lear*.

What proves to be decisive when reading the later scene in the lab as a continuation of this one in the camp is that in both cases, the Shakespeare quote triggers a double vision. In *King Lear*, the return of the daughter, whom the deranged father initially takes to be a spirit, leads to a tearful reconciliation. Lear asks her to forget and forgive, even while admitting that he is old and foolish. In 'Virtù e Fortuna', what unfolds is an analogous dramaturgy, perfectly aligning the emotions of the troubled host with the Shakespearean scene of reconciliation, in which the king imagines how, in prison, he and his regained daughter might tell old tales to each other. Like Lear, Abernathy suddenly recognises Dolores and, as though fully recovered, rises up on his bed, and together they recall the scene on the porch where everything began. Once more, they nostalgically repeat the lines they used to say to each other when, after having woken up in her bed, Dolores would meet him, sitting in his rocking chair, with a cup of coffee in his hand. They are aware that they are speaking lines in a prescribed dialogue, even while acknowledging the authenticity of the mutual affection contained in these words.

Yet, even as the Shakespeare quote triggers a gesture of self-quotation on the part of the hosts, it brings back into play the warning, also uttered on the porch, with which the disturbance of their storyline set in. Dolores reminds him that he had told her to run away, confessing that she did so with the pull of a trigger that started a war. The tragic logic of seriality that *Westworld* imposes on dreams of escape is that all dramatic action can only loop back to its point of origin to begin again. Precisely because Abernathy understands what his daughter is telling him, as a rancher and as a host, he falls back on the helpless stutter, which, in the inaugurating scene, had compelled her to respond in precisely the same way she now does. Assuring him that she will get help, Dolores leaves him. A serial logic persists. As in 'The Original', she will be united with him one last time in the Avalon laboratory.

If this alignment between the role they are playing in Dr Ford's story, 'Journey into Night,' and the roles they borrow from *King Lear* is repeated in their final encounter, our attention is drawn not only to yet another way that quotation works in *Westworld*; the difference in effect also becomes prominent only in comparison with the other modes of citation. The appropriation of Shakespeare in the camp scene suggests that in the subsequent scene in the Avalon laboratory, the play that is dramaturgically evoked is different from the one Abernathy is actually quoting from. Benvolio's words regarding one pain lessening the anguish of another are spoken in the spirit of Lear. Both scenes, furthermore, are predicated on an oscillation between role-playing and self-awareness, which is to say on a second-degree theatricality. And in both, Shakespeare is the trigger not for violence but for a shared happiness, whereby the scarcity value of this recalled memory is contingent on its inevitable disruption. Equally important for the transformation undertaken in the course of this serial citation is that ultimately, *Westworld*'s Cordelia kills her father, rather than Lear carrying the corpse of his murdered daughter on to the stage; much as Dolores' reinterpretation of Juliet targets not only her clueless lover but also both of the men who fathered her. What is, thus, conjoined in the mash-up she performs is the spirit of tragedy. The assassination of both her sovereigns is one expression of the exchange between contingency and necessity at the heart of this genre. If the first time she pulled the trigger on Arnold she got herself entrapped in the prison of Ford's sins, the second shot allowed her to escape from her incarceration in someone else's dream. The insurrection of hosts, in turn, emerges as tragedy's second expression, given that, as Francis Barker notes, no play by Shakespeare that can be called a tragedy does not inlay within itself the figure of invasion.[56] After all, the formation of Shakespearean tragedy is constituted in an unquestionable violence of history, repeatedly returned to in its dramatic reshapings.

If Abernathy's stutter is both the beginning and the end of Shakespeare's spectral presence in *Westworld*, at issue in the reading proposed by this chapter is not just a tracking of the intensities that re-surface along with his appropriated words, migrating from the past into the contemporary digital medium. Treating three of the plays he invokes – *The Tempest*, *Romeo and Juliet*, and *King Lear* – as a series, which revolves around the revolt of a daughter against paternal power, what is also seminal is the transformations the television drama undertakes, as it not only repeatedly resuscitates fragments from these plays but also transforms them in the process. Or, put another way, *Westworld* invites us to revisit these three plays as a series, even as it uses their spectral presence to develop its overarching serial storyline. Over and again, the Shakespeare quotes draw attention to the way *Westworld* engages critically with the dramatic convention of seeing the world as theatre and with a realisation of the difference between actor and role.[57] Indeed, Abernathy's stutter could be read as an abdication into inarticulation as a way out of the conundrum regarding the inability to decide whether the part one is playing is predetermined or freely chosen. A figure of malfunction and remembering in one and the same gesture, Abernathy's repeated citation of Shakespeare serves as a turnstile between the diegetic narration and a meta-theatrical reflection.

At the same time, to declare Shakespeare to be the paternal ghost of this television drama touches on the way that the words Abernathy speaks become a dramaturgical device only if we unfold the trajectories they propose. As Michael Anderegg has argued, what makes an exciting Shakespeare film is not a question of retaining most of the original play text, but rather finding 'ways to translate the energies of Shakespeare's language into an audio-video language of their own'.[58] If, then, we follow the passions and intensities which the Shakespearean words contain as they come to infect the storyline hosting them, we can discern lines of connection between mashed-up characters and the concerns they embody. Such a mapping would ascribe to *The Tempest* an exploration of the tyranny at the heart of theatrical politics and the violence enacted on the heterotopic stage as a reflection on and a response to the actual political violence external to it. The reiteration of this theatricalised violence in *Romeo and Juliet* draws the desire for violent ends into focus, in both the sense of a dream to be achieved regardless of the cost, as well as a wish to escape from this entanglement of violent end and violent delights. *King Lear*, in turn, brings an insight both into the tempestuous results of paternal authority lived out in a prison of its own sins, as well as the repetitive cycle of violence this engenders.

What *Westworld* takes from all three plays is the discovery that the ending to any struggle for power transforms into the beginning of a new regime, in which serial violence will prevail. The recuperation gained must be fragile so that the world of serial drama and its theatrical magic can be recreated over and again. If the overarching pathos formula for *Westworld* is that violent ends are the necessary consequences of violent delights, the debt is to Shakespeare's tragic model. Violence coincides with the event of rupture whereby the absolute violence of history is reconfigured as a tragic narrative in what Cavell calls the enveloping of contingency and necessity. If, furthermore, we append to the logic of history the corollary notion of a logic of seriality, then violence as an event of rupture in history not only seems to generate seriality, but serves as the very condition of a next serial permutation.[59] The mark for this rupture is Shakespeare dis-remembered, stuttered, fragmented, disseminated, and recombined, as he haunts and writes the prototypical American myth, the Western frontier.

## Notes

1. *Westworld*, 'Trompe L'Oeil', season 1, episode 7, dir. Frederick E.O. Toye, writ. Halley Gross and Jonathan Nolan, m48.30 (HBO 2016).
2. William Shakespeare, *Hamlet*, Ann Thompson and Neil Taylor (eds), *The Arden Shakespeare*, third series (London: Bloomsbury, 2006), 1.1.64.
3. *Westworld*, 'Trace Decay', season 1, episode 8, dir. Stephen Williams, writ. Charles Yu and Lisa Joy, m42.15 (HBP 2016).
4. Shakespeare, *Hamlet*, 2.2.90.
5. Toby Malone, 'Quoting Shakespeare in Twentieth-Century Film', in Julie Maxwell and Kate Rumbold (eds), *Shakespeare and Quotation* (Cambridge: Cambridge University Press, 2018), p. 195.
6. See Roland Barthes, *Mythologies*, trans. Annette Lavers (New York: Hill and Wang, 1972), p. 133.
7. *Ibid*., see Julie Maxwell and Kate Rumbold's 'General Introduction', pp. 1–24.
8. Christy Desmet, 'Quoting Shakespeare in Contemporary Poetry and Prose', in *ibid*., pp. 231–2.
9. *Westworld*, 'The Stray', season 1, episode 3, dir. Neil Marshall, writ. Daniel T. Thomsen and Lisa Joy, m21.25 (HBO 2016).
10. William Shakespeare, *Julius Caesar*, David Caniell (ed.), *The Arden Shakespeare*, third series (London: Bloomsbury, 2006), 2.2.32.
11. See Malone, 'Quoting Shakespeare', p. 196, as well as Reto Winkler, 'This Great Stage of Androids: *Westworld*, Shakespeare and the World as Stage', *Journal of Adaptation in Film & Performance*, 10:2 (2017), p. 179.
12. Maurizio Calbi, *Spectral Shakespeares. Media Adaptations in the Twenty-First Century* (New York: Palgrave Macmillan, 2013), p. 19.
13. Jacques Derrida, *Specters of Marx. The State of the Debt, the Work of Mourning, and the New International*, trans. Peggy Kamus (London and New York: Routledge, 1994), p. 18.
14. See also Walter Benjamin's discussion of the survival (*Nachleben*) and subsequent maturing process (*Nachreife*) translatability affords in 'The Task of the Translator', in Marcus Bullock and Michael W. Jennings (eds), *Selected Writings Volume 1 1913–1926* (Cambridge, MA: Harvard University Press, 1996), p. 256.
15. Ewan Fernie, 'Shakespeare and the Prospect of Presentism', *Shakespeare Survey*, 58 (2005), p. 175.
16. *Ibid*., p. 177.
17. Marjorie Garber, *Shakespeare's Ghost Writers. Literature as Uncanny Causality* (New York: Methuen, 1987), p. 129.
18. *Westworld*, 'The Original', season 1, episode 1, dir. Jonathan Nolan, writ. Jonathan Nolan and Lisa Joy, m45.15 (HBO 2016).
19. William Shakespeare, *The Tempest*, Virginia Mason Vaughan and Alden T. Vaughan (eds), *The Arden Shakespeare*, third series (London: Bloomsbury, 2011), 1.2.214–15.
20. *Westworld*, 'The Original', m58.20.
21. William Shakespeare, *King Lear*, R.A. Foakes (ed.), *The Arden Shakespeare*, third series (London: Bloomsbury, 1997), 4.6.178–9.
22. He is misquoting King Lear, who in Shakespeare, *King Lear*, exclaims, 'I will have such revenges on you both/That all the world shall – I will do such

things –/What they are yet I know not, but they shall be/The terrors of the earth!' 2.2.468–71.
23 William Shakespeare, *King Henry IV. Part 2*, James C. Bulman (ed.), *The Arden Shakespeare*, third series (London: Bloomsbury, 2016), 5.5.34.
24 For a discussion of how Shakespeare, through the host Abernathy, articulates a complex humanity in permanent interrogation, reconstruction, and reaffirmation, see Sarah Hatchuel, 'What a piece of work is your machine, Harold': Shakespeare et la réinvention de l'humanité dans les séries américaines d'anticipation', *TV/ Serie*, 14 (2018), pp. 1–16.
25 Marjorie Garber, 'Introduction', *Shakespeare and Modern Culture* (New York: Random House, 2008).
26 Stephen O'Neill, 'Digital Technology: The Future of Reception History', in *Shakespeare and Quotation*, p. 283.
27 Calbi, *Spectral Shakespeares*, p. 8.
28 Shakespeare, *Tempest*, 1.2.44–6.
29 Shakespeare, *Tempest*, 1.2.81–3.
30 Shakespeare, *Tempest*, 1.2.209–15.
31 Shakespeare, *Tempest*, 1.2.215.
32 Michel Foucault, 'Different Spaces', James Faubion (ed.), *Aesthetics, Method, and Epistemology* (London: Penguin, 1998), p. 179.
33 Shakespeare, *Tempest*, 1.2.451.
34 Shakespeare, *Tempest*, 1.2.418–20.
35 Shakespeare, *Tempest*, 1.2.487.
36 Shakespeare, *Tempest*, 5.1.199–200.
37 *Westworld*, 'The Bicameral Mind', season 1, episode 10, dir. Jonathan Nolan, writ. Lisa Joy and Jonathan Nolan, m52.13 (HBO 2016).
38 Shakespeare, *The Tempest*, 4.1.149–50.
39 Shakespeare, *The Tempest*, 2.1.157.
40 William Shakespeare, *Romeo and Juliet*, René Weis (ed.), *The Arden Shakespeare*, third series (London: Bloomsbury, 2011), 2.6.9–11.
41 Shakespeare, *Romeo and Juliet*, 3.3.17.
42 If the introduction of a series of citations discloses a tacit entanglement between the plays, the alignment with Ford proposes a parallel between Prospero and Friar Lawrence, much as Juliet and Romeo emerge as reiterations of Miranda and Ferdinand.
43 Manifestly conceived as a voice control, the mutual implication of violent delights and violent ends also gestures towards what Richard Slotkin, in *Regeneration through Violence. The Mythology of the American Frontier 1600–1860* (Norman, OK: University of Oklahoma, 1973) sees as the foundational myth of the claim that European settlers made on the American West. Struggling to impose the narrative of their new beginning on the land and the Native Americans inhabiting it, violence over and again emerged as the modus operandi for implementing their regime and forging their communities.
44 *Westworld*, 'Chestnut', season 1, episode 2, dir. Richard J. Lewis, writ. Jonathan Nolan and Lisa Joy, m8 (HBO 2016).
45 For Maeve, it is the trigger to break out of her narrative loop. Her violent passion is to be reunited with the daughter from a previous life on a homestead,

and she will make use of violent ends in her effort to take possession of her own storyline.

46  *Westworld*, 'The Bicameral Mind', m1.07.
47  Stanley Cavell, 'The Avoidance of Love', *Disowning Knowledge in Seven Plays of Shakespeare* (Cambridge: Cambridge University Press, 1987), p. 89.
48  After Dolores has reprogrammed him in the second season to become a ruthless killer, he will, inspired by a spectral Romeo, kill himself as his way of putting an end to her violent desires. If, at the end of the performance at the beach during the gala party he held her corpse in his arms, she now holds his dead body, much as Juliet does in the vault of her forefathers. Another oblique link to this tragedy can be discerned in the fact that Abernathy begins his monologue in the laboratory with a line from Gertrude Stein, in which we might detect a resonance of Juliet's outcry, 'a rose/By any other name would smell as sweet' (2.2.47–8).
49  *Westworld*, 'The Bicameral Mind', m1.24.
50  Cavell, 'The Avoidance of Love', p. 112.
51  *Westworld*, 'Journey into Night', season 2, episode 1, dir. Richard J. Lewis, writ. Lisa Joy and Roberto Patino, m25 (HBO 2018).
52  *Westworld*, 'Virtù e Fortuna', dir. Richard J. Lewis, writ. Roberto Patino and Ron Fitzgerald, m8 (HBO 2018).
53  *Westworld*, 'Les Écorchés', dir. Nicole Kassell, writ. Jordan Goldberg and Ron Fitzgerald, m42.30 (HBO 2018). Although we hear Abernathy mutter indistinguishable words to himself at the very beginning of this scene of reunion, including, yet again, Lear's reference to the world as being a stage of fools, the quote that is spoken with audible clarity is from Shakespeare, *Romeo and Juliet*, 1.2.44–5.
54  Shakespeare, *Romeo and Juliet*, 1.2.48–9.
55  *Westworld*, 'Virtù e Fortuna', m29.45. Abernathy is again quoting from Shakespeare, *King Lear*, 4.7.45–7.
56  See Francis Barker, *The Culture of Violence. Essays on Tragedy and History* (Manchester: Manchester University Press, 1993), p. 72.
57  See Winkler, 'This Great Stage of Androids', p. 178.
58  Quoted in Peter E.S. Babiak, 'Introduction', *Shakespeare Films. A Re-evaluation of 100 Years of Adaptations* (Jefferson, NC: McFarland & Company, 2016), p. 10.
59  My gratitude to Emily Sun for this point.

# 2
# Wearing the crown: *The Wire*

### It's all in the game

While Shakespeare's history plays were designed so that his audience could enjoy each individually without seeing any of the others, once they came to be published in collections, they were assembled into series, revolving around two formative political conflicts. In the first series, the conflict is the troubled reign of Henry VI and the Wars of the Roses (*Henry VI* parts 1–3 and *Richard III*); in the second series, it is the forced abdication of Richard II and the controversy of succession this engendered (*Richard II*, *Henry IV* parts 1 and 2, *Henry V*). As Tara Lyons argues, the seriality of these history plays not only 'proved to be central to constructions of "Shakespeare" in print before 1923'; to distinguish them from the tragedies and the comedies, the makers of the subsequent Folio edition also made use of seriality to establish their dramatic coherence and unity. Along with two other plays (*King John* and *Henry VIII*), they subsumed the tetralogies under the title of the newly conceived genre, 'Histories'.[1] By arranging them according to the chronology of monarchs, the Folio edition locates Shakespeare's re-imagination of the political strife leading up to the birth of his sovereign, Elizabeth I, within an equally unifying providential scheme of English history that begins with the fragility of King John's claim to the throne and ends with the problem of legitimate succession that Henry VIII's marital fickleness brought to the fore.

Even if it remains undecided whether gathering these individual history plays into a series was initially an editorial process or also a theatrical practice, recent television adaptations of them have, in turn, drawn attention to a further dimension to the entanglement between seriality and historicity in Shakespeare's dramatic re-imagination of the turmoil revolving around those who wear the crown. Rethinking these history plays through the lens of their contemporary serial performance on television sheds new light on the dramaturgic principle of open-ended repetition on which the stories told in both tetralogies are predicated. The fact that some are marked as one of several parts alone indicates that none of these plays is complete in itself, and instead they ask to be thought of in terms of an interconnected series. As Emma Smith notes, 'like the television series convention in which a minor conclusion is reached at the end of each episode, but in which such a conclusion is designed to be superseded by the expectation of the next episode, the Folio works to engage the expectations and consumption practices of serial, rather than singular, fiction'.[2]

Thematically, the open-endedness of the 'Histories' speaks to a notion of conflict at the heart of political legitimation, as this had come to play itself out in a series of wars in medieval England. Used as a structuring principle by the Folio, this lack of definitive closure, however, also anticipates and shapes the way TV drama has come to appropriate aspects of these history plays over and beyond straightforward adaptation. David Simon's *The Wire* is a case in point. Analogous to Shakespeare's first tetralogy (the three parts of *Henry VI* and *Richard III*), his TV drama, revolving around the war on drugs in Baltimore at the beginning of the twenty-first century, tracks an entanglement between political conflict and seriality.[3] At the same time, he and his scriptwriters also draw on serial narration to render visible how each individual part of the five seasons of *The Wire* is incomplete in itself, not only because all the individual stories are all interlinked but also because the systemic conflict that holds them together is irresolvable.

The point of departure for the crossmapping proposed in this chapter is a conversation that takes place early on in 'The Buys'.[4] Two of Avon Barksdale's foot soldiers, Bodie and Wallace, are sitting in 'the pit', a courtyard in one of the West Baltimore projects where his drug trade is flourishing. D'Angelo Barksdale, their 'sergeant', approaches them, and, noticing that they are playing checkers with a chess set, explains to them the rules of what he considers to be 'a better game'. Taking the key piece into his right hand, he kisses it before declaring, 'this is the kingpin … he the man'. If you get your opponent's king, he goes on to explain, 'you got the game'. At the same time, he warns his two buddies that they must protect their own kingpin, because the other player is trying to get it. To illustrate for them the moves that are possible on a chessboard, D'Angelo adds that the king can move in any direction he chooses, but only one space at a time. This means that he has 'no hustle', but because all the other pieces on his team have his back, he does not really have to do much.

Bodie, who has been listening attentively, immediately catches the analogy to the rules of the game governing the drug world of Baltimore's West Side and compares the kingpin to his boss. D'Angelo then moves on to the next piece, and, having called the queen 'smart and fierce',

Figure 5 D'Angelo's chess instruction on the king piece

explains that because she moves any way and as far as she wants, she is 'the go-get-shit-done piece'. This reminds Wallace, who has been watching silently, of Avon's right-hand man, Stringer Bell. D'Angelo proceeds by comparing the castle to the stash that they have to move each week, while the knights and bishops stand for Avon's 'muscle', the men that move with their product to protect it against both their competitors and the Baltimore police. Suddenly, Bodie notices the 'little bald-headed bitches', prompting D'Angelo to explain sombrely that the pawns are 'like the soldiers'. To underscore the dramaturgic turning point in their witty conversation, the camera moves into its first close-up of the chessboard, so that we can follow in detail D'Angelo's instruction about how it is, above all, these pieces who are in the field, fighting on the front lines.

Because he, too, has begun to sense a connection to his own position in the Baltimore drug game, Wallace wants to know how one gets to be the king, prompting D'Angelo to announce the cardinal rule which also serves as the epigraph of this particular episode: 'The king stay the king [sic]'. To underscore the rigid hierarchy at issue, D'Angelo sombrely explains that everyone stays who they are except the pawns. If one of them, in turn, actually makes it all the way to the side of the other player, he 'gets to be queen'. Bodie, projecting his own self-image on to the rules being described to him, cockily asks whether that would mean that he would be 'top dog'. This brings D'Angelo, who has begun to harbour secret doubts about the validity of what they are doing in his uncle's criminal forces, to embellish his description of the rules of chess one last time. Precisely because he wants his two buddies to understand the fragility of their own position as Avon Barksdale's soldiers, he ends by warning them that the pawns 'get capped quick … they be out the game early'. While Wallace looks on bemused, Bodie, who recognises

## Wearing the crown: *The Wire*

Figure 6 D'Angelo's chess instruction on the pawns

his own potential fate in what D'Angelo predicts, nevertheless boldly retorts, 'Unless they're some smart-ass pawns.'

D'Angelo can only smile in response to the grin with which his buddy puts an end to a repartee that calls upon us to recognise, in the rules of chess, a description of the feudal system of the drug world which *The Wire* seeks to make visible. Yet, if chess serves as a template for the codes regulating the network of power to which this TV show wants to draw our attention, at issue is also the status of the allegory on which this correspondence is predicated.[5] As Michel de Certeau notes, 'games give rise to spaces where *moves* are proportional to *situations*'. As such, they not only formulate and formalise rules that organise all possible moves but also constitute a memory of schemes we might act out in particular circumstances.[6] Both in chess and in the drug game, each figure has a clearly defined place and role within a strictly hierarchical order in which power is incessantly renegotiated by virtue of political acts. The moves that individual players can make are highly codified and ritually predetermined, based on a shared memory of what schemes are possible. At the same time, if – in accordance with equating the drug business with chess – 'it's all in the game', as the rogue player Omar proclaims at the end of the first season, there is also nothing outside the game. All the players are restricted to the delimited field in which both the drug traffic and the law enforcement seeking to prohibit it are carried out. Not to play is not an option.

By anticipating the succession of a new kingpin in Baltimore's criminal underworld, D'Angelo's scene of instruction, however, also underscores the one hope that those who start out as pawns can harbour. With a combination of luck and audacity, or perhaps because the 'top dog' has become too weak to stop an attack, it is precisely the pawn who can bypass all the other ranks and immediately become royalty.

While the pawn thus emerges as the most endangered position (usually 'capped early' in the game), it is also these 'little bald-headed bitches' that render most visible the fragility of royal legitimacy. As such, they open up a poignant line of connection between David Simon's TV series and Shakespeare's first historical tetralogy. In chess, the pawn is the piece standing in for that particular circumstance within the rules of the game which allows for a self-declared right to absolute power. Having arrived at the other end of the chessboard, this piece can proclaim itself royalty. It is precisely this audacious self-legitimation that *The Wire* fuses with its own debunking of the American Dream when, in the course of season 5, the Barksdale rule has ceased and the newcomer, Marlo Stanfield, has successfully taken over Avon and Stringer's empire. In Shakespeare's history plays such claims, of course, remain the prerogative of members of the ruling class: the Yorkist lords who repeatedly challenge Henry VI to abdicate and give up the throne to their leader, and finally Richard III, who usurps the throne, killing brethren and foes alike, only to himself be vanquished by the Earl of Richmond in the Battle of Bosworth Field, thus clearing the throne for the first Tudor king, Henry VII.

It is worth recalling that chess was initially an aristocratic form of the art of war, introduced by the Arabs into medieval Europe, which is to say in the historical period during which – in the wake of the Hundred Years' War (1337–1453) – the English Wars of the Roses (1455–85) were fought. Indeed, at issue in crossmapping these two sets of texts is the way that both imaginatively refigure a civil war along the lines of a game in which the situation individual players find themselves in determines the moves open to them. Yet what is decisive about the proposed analogy between the pawn's role in chess and the fragility of the king's position in situations of domestic strife – be it medieval England or early twenty-first-century Baltimore – is that, while the rules of the game governing power relations remain the same, individual players can bring about a significant change as to who will occupy the key position precisely by remembering the possibility of schemes open to them, given certain circumstances. At the same time, another aspect of cultural memory is at issue when one revisits *The Wire* through the lens of Shakespeare's history plays. Such a crossmapping, after all, is predicated on a further claim, namely that on the level of dramaturgy, this TV drama recalls, albeit implicitly, similar dramatic schemes that are acted out for political power in a series of early modern history plays.

It is also worth recalling that Shakespeare's first tetralogy reimagines the thirty-year battle between two branches of the royal House of Plantagenet as a visceral aristocratic war game, in which lords and citizens alike find themselves lined up either on the side of the white rose of York or the red rose of Lancaster, while geographically England turns into the territory on which this battle is fought through. David Simon, in turn, calls *The Wire* a 'deliberate argument against the American drug prohibition – A Thirty Years' War that is among the most singular and comprehensive failures to be found in the nation's domestic history', with Baltimore, the particular playing field, standing in for the more global condition of urban centres in early twenty-first-century capitalism.[7] Both the television series and Shakespeare's series of history plays thus reconceive actual historical domestic strife (the English Wars of the Roses, the American war on drugs) as a theatricalised game, in which shifts in political power are embodied by individual actors playing through the schemes open to them. *The Wire*'s connection to Shakespeare's history plays is explicitly made by police Lt Lester Freamon who, when, watching Stringer Bell on a surveillance tape after a drug war has broken out once again on the West Side, alludes to King Henry IV's lament that he alone of all the men in England cannot sleep because 'uneasy lies the head that wears a crown'.[8]

Many fans and critics of *The Wire* have, of course, noticed a Shakespearean connection, albeit often in a cursory manner.[9] Thus Marshall and Potter speak of the way this TV drama juggles 'a Shakespearian cast of dozens of individuals, some of whom have names for us, some of whom are recognised or perhaps only partly recognised by their faces'.[10] Other critics pick up on David Simon's claim that *The Wire* is a postmodern refiguration of Greek tragedy, which replaces the Olympian gods and the Fates with postmodern institutions.[11] If this chapter, in turn, foregrounds Shakespeare's history plays as its point of reference, it does so in part because the particular rules of the game of the drug trade, which regulate moves in relation to situations, recall the feudal loyalties constitutive of the battle among the supporters of the houses of Lancaster and York.[12] At the same time, what *The Wire* also takes from Shakespeare's history plays is the way these draw us in by virtue of their inclusion of compelling portraits of individuals struggling within and against the system of rules that define their fate.

By casting them as pawns, D'Angelo asks Wallace and Bodie to acknowledge their personal risk in a game they cannot *not* play. And yet, by moving into a close-up of their faces during the scene of instruction, the camera's dramaturgy draws our attention to each as an individual, whose fate is singular. Indeed, all three will die in what one might call tragic Shakespearean fashion. Like Romeo, the daydreamer Wallace returns to 'the pit', even though he has cooperated with the police, explaining that this is the only world he knows. He will be executed by Bodie, who, as a loyal soldier in the Barksdale command, can do nothing but follow the orders of his commanders. D'Angelo – who, like the melancholic Hamlet, wavers about staying in a game he has discovered to be corrupt – finds himself forced by his mother Brianna not to take a plea bargain and instead goes to prison, where he, too, is executed on Stringer Bell's orders. Bodie, in turn, recalls all those who, in the history plays, are compelled out of loyalty to fight to the end and meets his death defending his corner against Marlo, the 'smart-ass pawn', who, in Bodie's stead, achieves the royalty he had aspired to.

Thus, at issue in my proposed crossmapping is yet a further analogy, given that, in their re-imagination of a civil war, both sets of texts make use of the affective power of a dramatic re-conception of political disorder as a game to offer a systemic analysis of the violence subtending and sustaining all power relations.[13] Writing in the context of Elizabethan England, Shakespeare's history plays transform the chronicles of the Wars of the Roses into dramatic texts to be performed on stage as a series (premiered from 1591–93), while David Simon taps into news reportage and his own documentaries (*The Corner, Homicide*) to produce a TV drama (that ran from 2002–08). Over the span of four plays, Shakespeare's lords and their supporters – encouraged by the power vacuum which Henry VI's ascension to the throne calls forth – repeatedly declare themselves to the rightful rulers of England, only to either be overwhelmed in battle by the king's forces or counter his challenge. In a similar manner, as will be discussed in more detail, the rivalling kingpins in David Simon's drug world repeatedly declare sovereignty over a given territory only to find it incessantly reclaimed by an opponent from the other side. Thus, in both sets of texts, regardless of who is in the key position, 'the game', as well as the repetitive cycles of violence inherent to it, continues. Equally decisive about the rhetorical force of both Shakespeare's history plays and Simon's *The Wire*, however, is that each pits against this systemic repetition of martial power relations a set of individual portraits of failure, sacrifice, and redemption, infused by tragic sensibility, to appeal to our awe and pity. As Marsha Kinder notes, we 'experience a conflict between this systemic analysis of Baltimore and our emotional engagement with the characters with whom we choose to identify'.[14]

At the heart of the aesthetic re-imagination in both cases is, thus, the way particular domestic strife is theatricalised to reflect on cultural anxieties, bringing about a national self-study. Graham Holderness argues that the first tetralogy's exploration of the succession of the first Tudor monarch in the context of a political culture in which the 'killing of kings, by secret murder or open battle, was virtually a national sport', is above all a reflection on the dominant ideology of Shakespeare's own time and the cultural anxieties surrounding the reign of Elizabeth I.[15] In Shakespeare's dramatisation of Henry VI's flawed rule, power is shown to descend not lineally but discontinuously, with power struggles trumping blood and legal inheritance. Yet if his history plays foreground the way power is seen 'to depend not on legitimacy but on legitimation, on the capacity of the contender to seize and appropriate the signs of authority',[16] this is precisely the overall scheme that David Simon's *The Wire* remembers when it uses a particular instance of urban domestic warfare to speak to the destructive aspects of both late capitalism and the war on drugs after 9/11.[17] To offer a crossmapping of *The Wire* and *Shakespeare* thus not only tracks analogous games of power succession, predicated on where the players are situated within the system, but also draws attention to the way both use a self-conscious theatricalising of this game to reflect on the world of their audiences. By reimagining a particular political strife (be it early modern or recent American history) as a game in which individual players vie for the position of king or kingpin, they not only produce a form of national self-study; they also forge an imaginary community in which the spectators partake by taking the one or the other side, and sometimes even both.[18]

### Aristocratic war games American style

In Shakespeare's first tetralogy, the civil strife sets in after a military campaign against France has been won. The politically inept King Henry VI, more interested in religious contemplation than court intrigue, marries the impoverished French aristocrat Margaret Reignier even while ceding valuable territory as part of the dowry arrangements. In the course of the four plays, she will take charge as a ruthless warrior, and in this Shakespeare's Queen Margaret is as fierce as D'Angelo suggests in his description of the rules of chess. She will forcibly remove those advisors to her husband who refuse to acknowledge her power. She will, furthermore, not only favour those who promise to help her assert her own political interests (and those of her son) but also fatally enter into alliances with those who side with her only as long as they have an enemy in common. Her forces ultimately vanquish the primary challenger to her husband's throne, the Duke of York; and yet, in the final battle staged in *Henry VI* part 3, not only does Queen Margaret's son meet his own death, but the surrender that she, as commander of her vanquished troops, must accept also forces Henry VI to abdicate and give the crown to the victor, who will become King Edward IV. And yet, once the throne is his, this king, too, will be forcibly challenged; in his case by his own brother, Richard of York. While clandestinely stabbing to death the deposed King Henry, this villainous contender declares his own power as being based not on legitimacy but on self-proclaimed legitimation: 'I have no brother, I am like no brother: [...] I am myself alone.'[19]

In Shakespeare's historical re-imagination, the deposed Queen Margaret, in turn, remains in England long enough for her woe-tinged accusations against the murderer of her husband to spill over to Edward's wife, Queen Elizabeth, as well as his mother, the Duchess of Gloucester. Both women, once Richard has successfully usurped the throne, chime in with Margaret's cursing of a tyrant she calls 'hell's black intelligencer'.[20] Queen Margaret will ultimately leave the game, having been sent into exile by this shrewd political strategist, only to assure the other royal women before departing, 'these English woes shall make me smile in France'.[21] Left behind in the playing field, the other two women, in turn, will have the satisfaction of partaking in the demise of their mutual enemy and witness the resolution of the 'dire division'[22] between York and Lancaster. In the closing lines of *Richard III*, the marriage between Elizabeth and Richmond, the 'true succeeders of each royal House', is proclaimed as the promise that 'civil wounds are stopp'd; peace lives again/That she may long live here, God say Amen'.[23] As Nicholas Grene argues, the serial structure of the first tetralogy allows Shakespeare to reimagine the historical Wars of the Roses as an interrelationship between different forms of war that follow in sequence: 'the contrast between the us-and-them battles with the French and the us-versus-us division of civil war; the disturbing potential disruptiveness of popular revolt; and the internecine rivalries of dynastic conflict'.[24]

Picking up on the theme of a spiral of serial violence and hatred connecting more than one generation of those who wear the crown, *The Wire* renders visible various hierarchically structured domestic battle zones, including the Baltimore police and City Hall. The following discussion will, however, focus primarily on the civil war erupting within the drug world itself, not least of all because it is this strife which is most clearly modelled on the rules of a strictly regulated feudal system. As Reed notes, 'From the beginning, Avon is presented as a "soldier," as someone whose control of the drug trade is less about turning a profit than it is about controlling territory and respect.'[25] If, in *Henry VI*, the power vacuum opens up at home after an external enemy has been contained, in *The Wire* domestic battling – inside the drug world as well as the police force and City Hall – is fostered when, after 9/11, investigative energy and federal money shifts to Homeland Security's war on terror. As Terrance Fitzhugh, an FBI agent clandestinely cooperating with Detective McNulty's wiretap, explains, his battle with the Barksdale clan is the wrong war. With the dramaturgic development of Shakespeare's history plays in mind, it is worth noting, however, that while Avon and his muscle consistently think of themselves and their business in terms of war, the competition between Barksdale's West Side and 'Proposition' Joe's East Side is initially contained, surfacing primarily in the passionate investment that each side has in the outcome of the annual basketball game. In contrast to the Baltimore police force, which, in its relation to the Court as well as City Hall, is characterised by insubordination, mistrust, betrayal, and an overall lack of loyalty, Barksdale's muscle, furthermore, work as a disciplined team.

While in Shakespeare's *Henry VI* the internal battle begins because the Duke of York feels that his king has deprived him of valuable territories in France with which he had hoped to be rewarded for his victory in battle, the stage is set for an eruption of a civil war in the first season of *The Wire*, once Avon and Stringer begin thinking about opening up fresh territory by taking over corners from their opponents. As 'Proposition' Joe explains to Omar Little, who is willing to join forces with him, owing to a purely personal revenge crusade, he wants Avon gone because before he arrived, the projects were an open market. Recalling the shifting allegiances in the history plays, 'Prop' Joe will seek to broker a peace once Omar's assassination attempt fails, and, true to his name, he will continue to make propositions to various players aimed at maximising his own profit. After Kima Greggs, a member of the special unit under Lt Cedric Daniels that is investigating the Barksdale clan, is wounded in an undercover operation, police raids break the fragile balance of power within Baltimore's drug world. The kingpin Avon and his 'queen' Stringer find themselves compelled to take stock of their weaknesses and look for the key mistake that got the police to notice them in the first place. With the ruthlessness of any of the power-hungry Shakespearean lords, they are willing to sacrifice all players who made them visible as well as those who might testify against them in court.

While royalty like 'Prop' Jo and Stringer shift their alliances whenever the positions in the game require them to do so, the muscle on both sides abide by strict rules of loyalty, accepting the moves assigned to them, even if this means taking a prison sentence to protect their team. Yet mapping *The Wire* on to Shakespeare's history plays also renders visible the fact that while Avon is presented as a warrior kingpin who thinks in terms of a war to be fought out viscerally on the streets of Baltimore, he, like Henry VI, is weak as a political strategist. He, too, fails to grasp that a shift in the particular circumstances at hand requires a renegotiation not of the game's rules *per se*, but of the schemes that are open to its key players. After Avon has been given a light prison sentence, the fragile line of demarcation between East and West Baltimore no longer holds, and, like Queen Margaret, who is forced to shift her alliances in accordance with alterations in the network of power relations, Stringer is forced to cede territory to procure the good product he needs to keep his business running from 'Prop' Joe. Also, like Shakespeare's queen, Stringer is far shrewder than Avon in assessing the changed circumstances of the game, notably the new scheme he must embrace to ward off further attention from the police. By founding the New Day Co-Op with his former opponents, Stringer is able to unite all the key players in a mutual business enterprise, whose ruse consists of suspending all battling on the street and, instead, sharing the profits of the drug trade collectively. While, during the first meeting of this fragile cooperation, 'Prop' Joe lauds the others for showing themselves able to put aside petty grievances, Stringer forcefully spells out the new rules of the game. Commanding the others to explain the benefits of this new arrangement to their soldiers, he insists, 'No beefing, no drama, just business. Anybody got problems with anybody else here we bring it to the group. We ain't gotta take it to the streets.'[26]

Convinced that war is bad for business, Stringer's new scheme is predicated on the wager that if the game is no longer about territory but only about product and competition, the bodies on the street disappear and so will, as a consequence, police surveillance, interception, and incarceration. Once Avon has been released on parole, Stringer tries to persuade him that there is no longer any need to fight for individual corners, because their mutual investment in real-estate development on the Waterfront has procured for them a new and utterly legitimate arena for business. To stop Avon from going to war with the young challenger Marlo Stanfield, who has begun to take over some of their corners, Stringer insists that they have moved beyond thinking in terms of a legitimation predicated on seizing and holding turf. Instead, the New Day Co-Op has made it possible for him to base their power on legitimacy. With enough clean money to their name, Stringer assures Avon, they can do much more than run corners. Recalling the legacy of a gangster back in the day, who made a fortune on number money, he is convinced they could even run the city if they played their hand right. Yet Avon, invested in his feudal world view, can think of himself only as a gangster and, in turn, commands, 'I want my corners.'[27] Faced with his partner's stubborn insistence on a self-legitimation based first and foremost not on the accumulation of wealth but on his reputation on the street, Stringer finds his own American Dream of upward mobility into legitimacy radically threatened.

The civil war that explodes in the third season, once Avon hits back to make sure that others do not think the boy Marlo is punking him, not only pits the East Side against the West Side but also the kingpin against his queen. Indeed, it is precisely the unsolvable difference between Avon's conception of it as a war to be fought out on the streets over and again, on the one hand, and, on the other, Stringer's vision of drug trafficking as pure business that actually encourages Marlo's own dream of power based on seizing and appropriating signs of authority. Although, in contrast to Shakespeare's warrior queen, Stringer is the one to argue against rather than for war, his position is analogous to Margaret in that, like the French aristocrat, he finds himself fatally caught between two camps. Away from her home country, France, and not fully belonging to the Lancaster camp, Shakespeare's queen is repeatedly shown to forge alliances with English lords who will never fully accept her authority. To her astonishment, Henry VI initially accepts the terms that Edward, the Earl of March and later Edward IV, proposes for a ceasefire, namely that the crown will remain Henry's only as long as he lives. At this point, battle seems to be the only scheme open to Margaret, if she is to successfully hold on to the throne for her own son.

To Stringer, in turn, war is precisely what will prevent him from sustaining his lineage, yet like Shakespeare's queen, he, too, finds himself tragically betwixt and between; torn between Avon's feudal lust for war and his own vision of legitimacy without further battling. He is unwilling to join the furore of the other soldiers, yet cannot prevent the war he knows will bring down their waterfront development, B&B Enterprises. Happily re-installed in his war room, Avon astutely notes, 'I see a man without a country. Not hard enough for this, right here, and maybe, just maybe not smart enough for them out there.'[28] If, during their tearful conversation on the night of Avon's homecoming, the two had assured each other that they would always be brothers, they are now forced to acknowledge that, because their conception of the game has become incompatible, they are no longer fighting on the same side. To prove that he is, after all, hard enough, Stringer finally confesses to the assassination of D'Angelo, and yet, after he and Avon have had their tussle, the camera leaves them panting in silence, once their angry energy is spent. Their shared conversation is over.

Even if Shakespeare's Henry VI is willing to capitulate to his opponent, the Earl of March, so as to remain on the throne, whereas Avon embraces war as a way to retain his reputation and reclaim his territory, what they share is their attitude towards power. Both are concerned first and foremost with the legacy they embody in the present. Along the same lines, while their position on the civil wars into which they are unwittingly drawn is reversed, both Queen Margaret and Stringer Bell are similarly invested in the future sustainability of their vision – be it the succession of their own kin to the throne or the preservation of a legitimate business enterprise. Forced to make what can only be seen as false choices, both find themselves compelled to fall back on a scheme that will ultimately destroy their rule.

Queen Margaret can only persist in leading her troops into a battle that, once Edward has captured her king, will have the obliteration of all her dreams as its outcome. She will be forced to accept not only King Henry's abdication but also his assassination in the Tower. Along similar lines, Stringer also finds himself compelled to make a choice that is false, in that it is no real choice. Fully aware that 'Prop' Joe will force them to leave the Co-Op if they do not end a war that is bringing the police down on them, he, in a move far more radical than that of Shakespeare's Queen Margaret, sacrifices his own king, hoping, in so doing, to protect their business. Attacked on three fronts – by Marlo on the corners, by the police raiding the stash houses, and by Avon, who refuses to accept a change in the rules of the game – Stringer makes his fateful phone call to Major Howard 'Bunny' Colvin at the Western District police, whose Hamsterdam experiment of giving the drug dealers free rein in designated areas as long as they conduct their trade peacefully has come to impress him. The mise-en-scène presents this false choice – which will ultimately destroy the very business that to preserve he has taken recourse to betrayal in the first place – as the solitary gesture of tragedy.[29] The surveillance cameras can only catch Stringer, smoking and pacing in front of his copy shop before he decides to place the call, prompting, as noted before, Lester Freamon's mournful misquoting of Henry IV's own weariness: 'heavy is the head that wears the crown'. We then see Stringer return to his office in the back of the shop, careful to shut the door behind him. Initially, through the window of the door, we only see him hesitate over which phone to use, then, as the camera moves into the room, we hear him dial the Western District police. Ironically, he tells the operator that it is not an emergency. The editing cuts away from him before his call is put through to the man whose help he is desperate to solicit.

The nocturnal meeting between these two unlikely allies at a graveyard picks up the Shakespearean tone invoked by Lester's citation. Walking among the dead, Stringer Bell confesses to Bunny Colvin that it was his alternative to the kind of policing that enhances rather than contains drug-related crime that made Stringer turn to him in the first place: 'Looks like you and me both trying to make sense of this game.'[30] He then hands him the address where, since the war started, Avon and his soldiers are camping out, armed with heavy artillery. While Colvin reads this betrayal among brothers as a form of revenge, quietly noting that 'he must have done something to you', the tragic pathos of the scene is augmented by Stringer's laconic reply: 'no, it's just business'. The fact that Avon's own act of betrayal will bring about the death of his queen, while the police raid that acts on Stringer's information will merely bring Avon a heavy prison sentence, does more than confirm what Stringer ominously declared during their own last nocturnal meeting: 'We ain't got a dream no more, man.'[31] David Simon's dramatic resolution to this war among brothers also brings forward the bleak political point already made by Shakespeare's early history plays. Even if an overt civil war can periodically be contained, notably by a propitious marriage such as that between Richmond and Elizabeth, systemic violence underwrites all politics. David Simon, furthermore, also works with a serial structure similar to the first tetralogy so as to represent the war on drugs as an interrelationship between different forms of war that includes us-and-them battles between the drug lords and law enforcement, but also the us-versus-us division of a war between brothers, and finally, the rivalries of dynastic conflict.

After Stringer's death, Avon has his own moment of doubt, explaining to one of his last trusted muscle that perhaps their war with Marlo over a couple of corners is, indeed, pointless. Slim Charles, in turn, offers an assessment bespeaking to the necessity of war as politics with other means: 'Fact is, we went to war, and now there ain't no going back … it's what war is, you know … once you in it, you in it! If it's a lie, then we fight on that lie. But we gotta fight.'[32] What succeeds, in David Simon's bleak re-imagination of America's war on drugs, is neither 'Bunny' Colvin's experiment with concentrating drug traffic to select areas in the city, nor Stringer's vision of achieving power based on legitimacy, nor 'Prop' Joe's scheme of selling drugs without open bloodshed on the streets. Instead, *The Wire* follows Shakespeare's first tetralogy in its nostalgia for periods of political crisis, because the wars these call forth are the necessary precondition for peace, precarious as it may be, to be installed. If, at the end of *Richard III*, the Wars of the Roses can finally be contained in the symbolic authority with which the marriage between Elizabeth and Richmond is endowed, this peace requires the brilliant, if deadly, machinations of the 'black intelligencer' Richard III to come about.[33] Only by deposing the self-proclaimed king, whose rule in Shakespeare's re-imagination of early modern history is shown to be most radically predicated on a ruthless appropriation of power, can the Tudor monarchy establish its royal legitimacy.

In a similar manner, the dramatic logic of *The Wire* needs Marlo Stanfield, an equally self-obsessed opponent to the kingpins already in place in Baltimore's drug game, so that in the end, the New World

Co-Op, under the leadership of Slim Charles and his team, will once again win the day. Their collective succession is predicated on the sudden rise and equally swift fall of David Simon's most audacious pawn.[34] Like the future Richard III (who in *Henry VI* part 3 is still Duke of Gloucester), Marlo thinks of the world exclusively in terms of a private war of ambition. Indeed, Richard's confession could be his: 'Why then I do but dream on sovereignty;/Like one that stands upon a promontory/ And spies a far-off shore where he would tread,/Wishing his foot were equal with his eye; … So do I wish the crown, being so far off'.[35] In contrast to Avon (who actually admires his young challenger for his single-minded ferocity), seizing territory is not an end in itself for Marlo but rather a means to gain the one thing he dreams of – the insignia of royal authority. If, initially, 'Prop' Joe had hoped to contain Marlo by offering him a place in the Co-Op and grooming him to be his successor, it soon becomes clear that Stanfield is vying to become the absolute sovereign, much along the terms Richard III formulates: 'I am myself alone.'[36]

Yet decisive for the affective dramaturgic force of Marlo's play within this TV drama as a whole is the way his individual portrait of radical personal ambition feeds on the systemic violence governing the drug game, even while it endows his dream with the tragic pathos of hubris. Indeed, while 'Prop' Joe and Stringer are businessmen concerned with prosperity, and Avon is a warrior concerned with his feudal domain, Marlo's emotional investment is purely in the royal position, as such. After he has made his first hit against Barksdale, an older player in the game warns him that Avon will retaliate. Rather than showing concern, Marlo is thrilled at the prospect. In response to his advisor's bleak recollection of the 'prison and graveyards full of boys who wore the crown', Marlo sharply responds, 'Point is, they wore it. It's my turn to wear it now.'[37] Indeed, while the Barksdale clan he is challenging see themselves living the legacy of an extended family that has always been in the crime game, his is a dark version of the self-entitlement proclaimed by the American Dream. By the last season of *The Wire*, Marlo, like Richard III, will have used a combination of astute intrigues and ruthless executions to position himself in a way that allows him to claim to have all the power to himself, alone.

What Marlo also shares with Shakespeare's 'black intelligencer' is political savviness. Well aware that the police are surveilling them, he only holds court outside, surrounded by his most trusted muscle, even as he makes sure that the people they kill for him drop out of sight. At the same time, he, like Richard, plans his territorial takeover of the East Side shrewdly, meeting up with Avon in prison first, so as to get 'the connect' to the Greek, the invisible hand at the head of the drug supply line. The dramatic peripeteia equally worthy of Richard III, in turn, occurs during the meeting of the Co-Op when Marlo, sure of his allies, takes the final steps necessary for his claim to absolute sovereignty. Recognising that Melvin 'Cheese' Wagstaff can be bribed to betray his uncle, because 'Prop' Joe had publicly castigated him for making unlawful incursions into territory marked for another member of the charter, Marlo's silent gaze forges a fateful bond. Oblivious to this shift in circumstances, 'Prop' Joe, still hoping to civilise the boy he sees as his son, suggests to Marlo after the meeting that he should focus a bit on what can be gained by working with people. Yet *The Wire*'s black intelligencer already has the key player in position to carry through his fatal incursion working not with Joe but against him.

On the night 'Prop' Joe prepares to leave the house his grandfather had bought, hoping to bypass the drug war which is once more about to erupt, Marlo enters his living room, wearing a black t-shirt with white letters spelling 'Royal Addiction'.[38] Stanfield is finally able to checkmate his mentor because Cheese, waiting outside, will no longer protect this kingpin to whom he, as his nephew-pawn, should be loyal. Making his last proposition, Joe insists, 'I treated you like a son', only to be sombrely informed, 'I wasn't made to play the son.' Marlo cannot spare 'Prop' Joe, because his, like Richard III's, self-declared legitimation is predicated on proclaiming the death of his opponents in public. Instead, with the cool severity appropriate to an absolute sovereign, he softly cajoles the older man, telling him to close his eyes and breathe deeply while his assassin pulls the trigger. When, after Joe's death, he becomes the sole owner of 'the connect' and, indeed, the only one the Greek's contact will deal with, he can finally be certain that he has procured the signs of authority. Walking away from the meeting, he joyfully proclaims to one of his trusted muscle, Chris, that he is now wearing a crown on his head. Though invisible, this royal insignia empowers him to perform his final *coup d'état*. With the chair at the head of the table empty, after Joe's sudden demise, Marlo takes control of the next meeting of the Co-Op, first redistributing the territory that belonged to the murdered man, only to finish by dispensing with all further meetings.

As the sole owner of 'the connect', he can now not only dictate the price of their product but, having disbanded the Co-Op, he can also declare that all future issues concerning their business will no longer to be discussed collectively. Instead, he proclaims himself the sole arbitrator of any differences that might arise among the various factions of the drug business. Yet the absolute power Marlo has seized needs to be acknowledged by those he controls, and his downfall, like that of Shakespeare's Richard III, hinges on his inability to retain his reputation on the street.

When his muscle finally confess to him that the rogue player Omar, once more involved in a personal revenge vendetta, is putting it out on the street that Marlo is not man enough to battle with him, he, for a brief moment, breaks his austere pose. Outraged that his name has been used in the street, he shouts, 'my name *is* my name'.[39] Indeed, precisely because his name is the only thing he has to base his legitimation on, losing it is tantamount to losing the crown he has striven for with such single-minded passion. Thus, while in contrast to Richard III he does not find death on the battlefield, the end of the drug war is predicated on his symbolic death. The deal his lawyer is able to broker with the District Attorney's office is that all charges against him will be dropped on the condition that he retires from the drug business altogether.

Though not fatal, this sentence is tragic because, without his name on the street, Marlo, whose self-definition was based entirely on his self-declared usurpation of sovereignty, no longer exists in the game. His also is a false choice, because while giving up his crown may mean freedom from incarceration, it is the end of the only world he knows. He is compelled to make the very move that Stringer Bell had dreamed for himself and Avon Barksdale, though Marlo is transformed from gangster to businessman against his wishes. In the penultimate scene of season 5, we see the price at which this move comes. Having abruptly left an elegant evening event with his new peers, Stanfield finds himself on a dimly lit street. At one corner, two young punks are deep in conversation. Hearing them discuss one of Omar's mythic exploits, he approaches, only to discover that they no longer know who he is. After a brief tussle, Marlo stands alone in the night, a knife wound to his right arm, bemused at the turn his luck has taken. The future open to him is one of complete invisibility; the end of his existence on the stage that was his world.

With Shakespeare's historical re-imagination of the succession of royal power from Henry VI to Henry VII in mind, one could summarise the narrative trajectory of *The Wire* as follows. Initially, a battling over territory in Baltimore's East and West Side brings legitimation to the Barksdale clan, yet the bodies on the street get Avon and some of his most trusted muscle into prison, thus opening up a breach in the power structure of the drug game out of which two opposing schemes can emerge – the New World Co-Op and Marlo's challenge for the crown. In the course of the civil war that follows, Marlo, like Richard III, either eradicates his opponents or turns them into allies so successfully that he can declare himself absolute sovereign of the drug game. Yet in the final battle with the police, Stanfield's troops are caught, and the price for his defeat is the total abdication from the game, which brings with it – and therein lies the poignant correspondence to the closure *Richard*

*III* has to offer – a second generation Co-Op. At the end of *The Wire*, we have business as usual, not necessarily the peace which Shakespeare's royal wedding promises, but at least a containment of excessive bloodshed on the streets of Baltimore. Among those sacrificed are players who had an alternative vision: Stringer Bell's dream of 'going legit', 'Prop' Joe's privileging of business over battling, Major 'Bunny' Colvin with his Hamsterdam experiment. Ironically, of course, the king does ultimately stay the king. Re-installed as kingpin within the prison world, Avon, along with his most trusted muscle, Wee-Bey, continues to influence Baltimore's drug traffic from inside. Wee-Bey's son Namond, in turn, is able to evade the succession his father had in store for him, living instead with the Colvins and pursuing an academic career against the odds of the game – which, instead, fall heavily on to Namond's friend Duquan 'Dukie' Weems, who ends up living with a drug addict.

## All the world's a stage

If this chapter began with a reading of the chess-game scene of instruction, then in part that is also because it speaks to the very theatricality of power that connects Shakespeare's world to that of *The Wire*. Let us recall that in the final act of *The Tempest*, discussed in Chapter 1, Prospero draws back a curtain hanging in front of the discovery space to reveal his daughter Miranda and her bridegroom Ferdinand, playing chess. The act of discovering them for the other characters who have assembled there produces a play within the play. While the game of chess, featured in many Renaissance courtly-love allegories, signifies their amorous union, the fact that they are shown to play this game on a stage framed by a curtain reveals Prospero as the director not only of the marriage this scene anticipates, but also of all the events that have taken place on the island. Like the couple he has been directing, all the characters prove to have been merely players, who had their exits and their entrances by his design, while he played the part of the deposed lord, who uses the power of theatre to reassert his power as a ruler.[40] Given that chess, as a game associated with royalty, was also found in Renaissance discourses on government, a further connection between the politics of theatre in Shakespeare's world and *The Wire* can be discovered. The point of chess, after all, is that it foregrounds the issue of staging power not only because all the positions and moves are determined in relation to a clearly delimited playing field. Rather, as already discussed, it also draws attention to the performative nature of legitimation, given that it includes the possibility of declaring oneself to be ruler by appropriating the signs of authority, namely the crown. This also means, however, that the position key players assume in the drug game is predicated on accruing recognition from the other players as well as from those on the periphery, looking on. After all, for power based on legitimation to have any effect, it must have an audience. If preserving their name on the street is the only guarantee that players like Avon, Marlo, or Omar have to maintain their power, it involves not only a constant war to maintain this self-declared legitimation but also a perpetual public display of it, be it in person or as a narrative installed in collective memory.

The significance of a theatrical display of power contestation finds a particularly effective articulation in a late scene in season 5. With Marlo willing to sell 'the connect', the other members of the Co-Op meet in an open lot at night to discuss how much each can contribute to buying him out.[41] Cockily, the traitor Cheese claims he can put up more than his share because he trusts in the future. When one of the other men points out that they were doing fine as long as his uncle had 'the connect', implicitly accusing him of having forced them to put up with Marlo in the first place, Cheese, putting his gun to his interlocutor's face, counters by giving his reading of the past civil war: 'Joe had his time and Omar put an end to that. Then Marlo had his time, short as it was, and the police put an end to that. And now motherfucker it's our time, mines and yours.' A circle has formed around the two combatants, watching a performance in which the proper narrative interpretation of their legacy is as much at stake as the money they need to re-install the Co-Op. Cheese derides the other man, shouting at him, 'there ain't no back in the day, nigger. Ain't no nostalgia to this shit here. There's just the street and the game and what happen here today.' Cheese's is the unsentimental attitude of a pure opportunist, lacking all sense of loyalty, of respect for past royalty, but also all responsibility for his own actions: 'When it was my uncle, I was with my uncle', he concludes: 'When it was Marlo, I was with him.'

At the precise moment Cheese is about to finish his diatribe by saying what is now, Slim Charles, who had so presciently assured Avon that they could do nothing other than fight a war once they had started it, shoots him in the head. Asked by the bemused onlookers why he had done this, he knowingly explains, 'that was for Joe'. Sentimental as the move may be, it illustrates the degree to which a collectively performed nostalgia is necessary for the game to hold. The name of the man who, if only for a brief moment, had brought them prosperity with his vision of how business could be done peaceably needs to be preserved over and against all challengers interested only in the chances the present holds. The mise-en-scène, in turn, draws attention to yet another Shakespearean legacy. As in the history plays, violence in *The Wire* is necessarily theatrical. If one's name is the only guarantor for legitimation, this requires an audience for whose benefit it can be fought through. Someone needs to witness and to report the struggle incessantly played out on the streets, even when the contests take place in nocturnal alleys or abandoned lots.

If, then, the Baltimore drug world is a stage on which everyone must play his or her part, this theatricality plays to various audiences. First and foremost, the visceral power play between opponent kingpins is pointedly staged for the players themselves as well as for members of the community at large, often just innocent bystanders accidentally drawn into their war. When, in the first season, D'Angelo and his friends hold council on an orange sofa placed in the middle of 'the pit', they embody the centre of a panopticon-like visual regime. Their control over this small part of the drug game is predicated on a theatrical display of themselves as privileged observers. Those they watch – their 'hoppers', their customers, as well as the police – are meant to take note of the four soldiers, looking out at them from this exposed stage. Marlo will also hold council outside, in a stony arena that even more explicitly recalls a theatre, although the audiences for whom he stages himself are far less public, while the Co-Op meetings recall early modern aristocratic mores, with the most powerful figure standing in front of the others, as though addressing his courtiers. Yet what *The Wire* inherits from Shakespeare's histories is not only the manner in which the kingpins stage their own authority but also the way they perform their triumph over selected opponents. If, on the Shakespearean stage, the heads of vanquished enemies often come to be prominently displayed, so, too, in *The Wire*, corpses function as encoded messages, sent out to the community.

It is useful to recall that the entire series begins with a corpse and the discussion it prompts between Detective Jimmy McNulty and one of his informers as to why the dead man was called Snot Boogie. They are looking at a crime scene that has been blocked off with yellow tape: a stage *in nuce*, with the police the actors, moving around a dead body they are trying to read, passing information about its identity and the probable cause of death to each other, while the onlookers stand around them in a semi-circle. In the many public crime scenes to come, these corpses may merely signify the continuation of the drug war and function as a symptom of urban malaise, evoking outrage or disinterest. To those who share the code, in turn, they often have a further, specific meaning, functioning as admonition and – in the case of the cruelly disfigured corpse of Omar Little's boyfriend, Brandon Wright – as a prompt for revenge. Or, as with the informer William Gant's corpse, while to most of the 'soldiers' on the ground it serves as a warning not to testify in court against a member of the Barksdale clan, for D'Angelo it gives body to his rising mistrust of his uncle's *modus operandi*. To knowledgeable viewers of the series, furthermore, it also anticipates D'Angelo's own fate once he, like Gant, shows himself willing to cooperate with the police.

The world of crime, however, is street theatre in the further sense that the routine that regulates the drug trafficking itself already involves a public display.[42] The buying and selling, as well as the communication between those on the corners and their superiors, is presented in David Simon's re-imagination of the drug world as a ritualised performance, played out in the open, with the inhabitants of the projects, be they involved or disaffected, as audience. Once the wire for which McNulty has fought so furiously is up, this routine turns into a performance that – explicitly or unwittingly – has the police as its privileged spectators as well, albeit once removed. The scene in which Reginald 'Bubbles' Cousins uses hats to signal to the surveillance team who the key players in Barksdale's team are, while to these men themselves he is performing an act of buffoonery worthy of any Shakespearean fool, is a particularly salient example of this doubled spectatorship. Indeed, once the police wire begins to track the corpses, left on the street as evidence of the ongoing drug war, this second-degree theatricalisation of power fully comes into play. What was initially clandestine theatre, put on for those living in the Baltimore projects, becomes a performance for the police as well. Cracking the pager code in the first season allows Lt Daniels' special unit to capture dialogues between individual players and begin to map the *dramatis personae* of the game, according to which side they are fighting on.

By rendering the clandestine drug trafficking visible, the wire produces theatre within theatre (or indeed television). The computer screens transform the police into the audience of schemes and movements they can only partially understand. Recorded by hidden microphones, photos, and video cameras, individual scenes of the game are rendered visible as snippets of coded dialogue, as freeze frames or silent movie footage. On their pinboards, Daniels' special unit repeatedly draws out connections between the labelled photographs, trying to reconstruct the position of each player in the overall hierarchy, thus enacting what any theatre audience (or reader of a play) does. Daniels' men and women are looking for points of orientation in the dramatic action to make sense of the dialogues they have overheard, and particularly the effects these have had on the stage they are clandestinely privy to. The manner in which these surveillance cameras produce a stage within the stage of the drug game, furthermore, becomes self-consciously exposed when the gangsters, cognisant that they are being watched, explicitly perform for the police, play to their expectations, or ludically thwart their reconnaissance efforts. At the same time, these self-reflexive moments, playing with the rhetorical force of visual estrangement, force us to think of ourselves in terms of a spectatorship in which we function as the extradiegetic counterpart to the police, who are the diegetic audience of a game staged for both their and our edification.

When it self-consciously goes public, the police work, of course, is equally theatrical. Repeatedly, McNulty and his team, angered at precipitous raids that will shut down the wire, note that the brass upstairs want a circus, and indeed, the attacks on stash houses are shown to be staged for the press and the politicians. Like the signifying corpses, the arrests the police make are conceived as theatrical acts with multiple signification. More than mere warnings to all involved in the drug game, they serve to legitimate a particular law enforcement policy, which declares itself to be effective even though – or precisely because – those on the ground know it is not. To underscore the TV show's own comment on the theatricality of police interventions, we find at the end of season 3, in a particularly self-reflexive scene, Deputy Commissioner William Rawls playing Richard Wagner's *Ritt der Walküren* (*Ride of the Valkyries*) during his raid on Hamsterdam, explicitly citing the infamous attack on a Vietnamese village in Coppola's 1970 war film *Apocalypse Now* (which is itself a reference to D.W. Griffith's equally infamous 1915 Civil War epic, *The Birth of a Nation*, glorifying the Ku Klux Klan). During the press conferences following these raids, the commanding officers and politicians repeatedly present their show of force as evidence of their authority, while – and this brings in the final aspect of theatricalisation of power in *The Wire* – David Simon deploys this public display ironically. His unequivocal assessment of this war on drugs is, after all, that while it may make for good theatre, it fails as good police work.

In other words, we, the audience, are called upon to look with a double vision. Thought of as a pinboard, unfolding in five acts, *The Wire* displays for us a complex network of players, their positions and moves, yet, in contrast to the work by Daniels' special unit, it does more than disclose the lines of connection between them. The radical contingency of the present moment that Cheese calls 'the street and the game and what happen here today' transforms into dramatic personalised narratives involving several orders of viewing. We look at the police looking *at* and *with* the onlookers at crime scenes looking *at* signifying corpses. We follow the police as they capture and then comment on the drug game. Yet David Simon decisively calls upon us to offer a commentary on this theatrical display of violence that is also different from that of the police, press, or politicians precisely because we are privy to the emotionally charged portraits he presents of his *dramatis personae* – be they pawns, muscle, or royalty. His point is that these players are precisely the warriors from whom, especially since 9/11, our attention has been withdrawn. As the police surveillance sheds light on their clandestine activities, they gain visibility for us as well. The wire may be legally and morally dodgy, but from a narratological point of view, its function is to make sure that this part of American culture does not remain invisible. By turning Baltimore into a stage, where each must play his part, this overlooked world becomes our stage as well. We empathise in pity and awe, as we would with Shakespeare's character-players, even if we do not condone, perhaps do not even fully comprehend, what we have become privy to.

As Michael Wood notes, the final montage sequence at the end of *The Wire* allows us to 'hold the city (home of dealers of all kinds) and the City (the imaginary civic stage on which we watch what we imagine we have become) in a single thought. Business as usual is an unending nightmare; but this grand nightmare is ending with a terrific grace.'[43] It is useful to recall that the montage sequence comes right after McNulty, bringing back the homeless man he had abducted, has stopped his car and got out to look at the skyline of Baltimore.[44] The camera begins to zoom into a close-up, catching a brief smirk on the face of this former detective, and then moves to vignettes of what has become of the surviving players. The pawns are – if still alive – still on the corner, the cops are still in the bar; some players celebrate their success in public, some in private; others have silently cut their losses. The ordinary power relations, subjecting individual fates into their all-encompassing network, have once more been re-installed. The individuals we, over five seasons, have come to invest with our sympathy fade back into oblivion as the editing moves to even shorter snapshots of urban street life. Seamlessly we return to short clips of scenes from *The Wire*, including D'Angelo's scene of chess instruction, so that for a brief moment of nostalgia, the past is resuscitated. Then, just before this montage sequence ends, we get a final parade of anonymous faces. We are about to withdraw our gaze, and yet, for these few seconds, they are part of the visual kaleidoscope that stands for the city of the early twenty-first century. The editing returns to McNulty, whose smirk is now more ambivalent, and who, facing the camera while he looks one last time at his view of Baltimore, implicitly appeals with his gaze to us, before telling his passenger, 'Larry, let's go home.'[45]

In contrast to the montage sequences that put closure on the other four seasons, this one is marked as McNulty's dream; a dream, to boot, about the many scenes that have made up (or could be part of) a TV show called *The Wire*. After McNulty's car has driven out of the frame, the camera tarries with a final image of Baltimore's skyline. McNulty's final (re)vision prompts the return to a home that is more than a concrete place – that is, an imaginary visual composite signifying the place one belongs to because it is familiar, because it has become known. The end of this final montage sequence is also a form of waking up, not just for Jimmy McNulty (who, discharged from the Baltimore police department, will no longer pursue his dream of ruthless law enforcement) but also for us. As bleak as this single contemplation of business as usual may be, it leads us to a different genre, recalling the closure of Shakespeare's *A Midsummer Night's Dream*. Here, Robin Goodfellow consoles us that the visions that appeared before our eyes are 'no more yielding than a dream'.[46] *The Wire* ultimately proves to be a dream, nightmarish perhaps, about watching a series of dreams unfolding on screen, in actual urban locations but above all in the minds of those who, as the intended spectators inside and outside this TV show's diegesis, came to be part of it. Gently nudged by David Simon's Puck, we are asked to return to a home, altered by this dream we have shared.

## Notes

1 Tara L. Lyons, 'Serials, Spinoffs, and Histories: Selling "Shakespeare" in Collection before the Folio', *Philological Quarterly*, 91:2 (2012), p. 204.
2 Emma Smith, 'Shakespeare Serialized: An Age of Kings', in Robert Shaughnessy (ed.), *The Cambridge Companion to Shakespeare and Popular Culture* (Cambridge: Cambridge University Press, 2007), p. 147. I want to thank John Archer for pointing out a further, albeit speculative, correspondence between *The Wire* and Shakespeare's first tetralogy. Given that the three Henry VI plays were co-authored by playwrights like Thomas Nashe and Robert Greene, Shakespeare, serving as head writer, could also be thought of in terms of the showrunner for this set of plays, much as David Simon presided over a team of co-authors including Dennis Lehane, Ed Burns, Richard Price, and George Pelecanos.
3 In his book, *Shakespeare's Serial History Plays* (Cambridge, Cambridge University Press, 2002), Nicholas Grene demonstrates that in so far as Shakespeare developed narrative structures in the first tetralogy, in which no one play was complete in itself and instead required a narrative sequel, this set of plays based on the reigns of Henry VI and Richard III was most probably planned as an interlocking series, which is to say 'planned indeed for serial production', p. 19. His concern in restoring attention and credibility to the serialisation of the chronicles, however, involves more than merely a rethinking of their original production. Instead, as he argues, it promotes our awareness of how Shakespeare chose to stage the Wars of the Roses as a layered palimpsest of narratives representing different – at times even mutually exclusive – political viewpoints, while different scenes speak to each other across the plays. The multiplicity of viewpoints that are, nevertheless, interconnected suggests, in turn, a further analogy to TV

drama, given its predilection not only for open-ended narrative closures but also parallel editing within the storyline, offering a narrative montage of different and in this case also, at times, mutually exclusive yet intertwined positions.
4 *The Wire*, 'The Buys', season 1, episode 3, dir. Peter Medak, writ. David Simon, m11 (HBO, 2002).
5 For a discussion of this chess game as an allegorical mapping of the drug world, see Paul Allen Anderson, 'The Game Is the Game: Tautology and Allegory in *The Wire*', in Liam Kennedy and Stephen Shapiro (eds), *The Wire. Race, Class, and Genre* (Ann Arbor: University of Michigan Press, 2012), pp. 84–109.
6 Michel de Certeau, *The Practice of Everyday Life* (Berkeley: University of California Press, 1984), p. 22.
7 See David Simon, 'Prologue', in Rafael Alvarez, *The Wire. Truth be Told* (New York: Grove, 2009), p. 11.
8 William Shakespeare, *King Henry IV. Part 2*, James C. Bulman (ed.), *The Arden Shakespeare*, third series (London: Bloomsbury, 2016), 3.1.31. The scene takes place in *The Wire*, 'Reformation', season 3, episode 10, dir. Christine Moore, writ. Ed Burns (HBO 2004).
9 See Lorrie Moore, 'In the Life of *The Wire*', *New York Review of Books*, 14 October 2010, pp. 23–5.
10 Tiffany Potter and C.W. Marshall (eds), *The Wire. Urban Decay and American Television* (New York: Continuum, 2009), p. 9.
11 See Alasdair McMillan, 'Heroism, Institutions, and the Police Procedural', in Potter and Marshall (eds), *Urban Decay and American Television*, pp. 50–63. See also Jason Mittell, '*The Wire* in the Context of American Television', in Kennedy and Shapiro (eds), *Race, Class and Genre*, pp. 15–32.
12 See Jason Reed, 'Stringer Bell's Lament: Violence and Legitimacy in Contemporary Capitalism', in Potter and Marshall (eds), *Urban Decay and American Television*, pp. 122–34, although he is more concerned with a discussion of primitive accumulation and capitalism than power relations.
13 See Patrick Jagoda's reading of *The Wire* as an example for the way network aesthetics 'attends to the systemic nature of human suffering in the early twenty-first-century America', 'Wired', *Critical Inquiry*, 38:1 (2011), p. 199.
14 Marsha Kinder, 'Rewriting Baltimore: The Emotive Power of Systemics, Seriality, and the City', in Kennedy and Shapiro (eds), *Race, Class, and Genre*, p. 78. See Daniel Eschkötter, *The Wire* (Zürich: Diaphanes, 2012) for a discussion of the double perspective that *The Wire* deploys as it incessantly moves between a systemic discussion of institutions of power and an empathetic discussion based on the position of the individual subjects in the drug game.
15 Graham Holderness (ed.), 'Introduction', *Shakespeare's History Plays. Richard II to Henry V*, New Casebooks (London: Macmillan Palgrave, 1992), p. 5.
16 Holderness, *History Plays*, p. 12. For a discussion of how Shakespeare's history plays conceive aesthetic strategies as political strategies, see also Leonard Tennenhouse, *Power on Display. The Politics of Shakespeare's Genres* (London: Methuen, 1986).
17 See Frank Kelleter's *Serial Agencies. The Wire and Its Readers* (Alresford: Zero, 2014) for a discussion of this TV drama as an example for the way American culture reflects on itself.

18 The names given to some of the key players in *The Wire* offer a further line of connection to Shakespeare. Avon Barksdale's name references his home town, Stratford-upon-Avon, while his ultimate rival, Marlo, recalls Shakespeare's rival playwright, Christopher Marlowe.
19 William Shakespeare, *King Henry VI. Part 3*, John D. Cox and Eric Rasmussen (eds), *The Arden Shakespeare*, third series (London: Bloomsbury, 2010), 5.6.80 and 5.6.83.
20 William Shakespeare, *Richard III*, in James R. Siemon (ed.), *The Arden Shakespeare*, third series (London: Bloomsbury, 2009), 4.4.70.
21 Shakespeare, *Richard III*, 4.4.115.
22 Shakespeare, *Richard III*, 5.5.28
23 Shakespeare, *Richard III*, 5.5.40–1.
24 Grene, *Shakespeare's Serial History Plays*, p. 94. A similar shift from war with an external enemy and internal domestic strife will be discussed in Chapter 6, which treats *The Americans* in the context of Cold War espionage.
25 See Jason Read, in Potter and Marshall (eds), *Urban Decay and American Television*, p. 128. For a discussion of the actual wars that *The Wire* implicitly makes reference to, see Eschkötter, *The Wire*, pp. 54–5.
26 *The Wire*, 'Straight and True', season 3, episode 5, dir. Dan Attias, writ. Ed Burns, m27 (HBO 2004).
27 *The Wire*, 'Homecoming', season 3, episode 6, dir. Leslie Libman, writ. Rafael Alvarez, m16.30 (HBO 2004).
28 *The Wire*, 'Moral Midgetry', season 3, episode 8, dir. Agnieszka Holland, writ. Richard Price, m53 (HBO 2004).
29 *The Wire*, 'Reformation', m34.48.
30 *The Wire*, 'Middle Ground', season 3, episode 11, dir. Joe Chappelle, writ. George Pelecanos, m30.50 (HBO 2004).
31 *The Wire*, 'Middle Ground', m47.
32 *The Wire*, 'Mission Accomplished', season 3, episode 12, dir. Ernest Dickerson, writ. David Simon, m7 (HBO 2004).
33 Shakespeare, *Richard III*, 4.4.70.
34 When Marlo initially surfaces on the wiretap which Lt Daniels' special unit has installed in season 3, his street name is 'Black'.
35 Shakespeare, *Henry VI.3*, 3.2.135–40.
36 Shakespeare, *Henry VI.3*, 5.6.83.
37 *The Wire*, 'Homecoming', m30.40.
38 *The Wire*, 'Transitions', season 5, episode 4, dir. Dan Attias, writ. Ed Burns, m55.50 (HBO 2008).
39 *The Wire*, 'Late Editions', season 5, episode 9, dir. Joe Chappelle, writ. George Pelecanos, m20 (HBO 2008).
40 We might also recall the lines spoken by the melancholic Jacques in *As You Like It*: 'All the world's a stage,/And all the men and women merely players./They have their exits and their entrances/And one man in his time plays many parts', in Juliet Dusinberre (ed.), *The Arden Shakespeare*, third series (London: Bloomsbury, 2006), 2.7.138–41.
41 *The Wire*, '-30-', season 5, episode 10, dir. Clark Johnson, writ. David Simon, m1.14.30 (HBO 2008).

42 I am also indebted to John Archer for pointing out to me that a further source of inspiration for the chess game as a scene of instruction may have been the culture of street chess, played in community centres, malls, street corners, and prison cells by predominantly African American players in the northeast, including Baltimore. As he suggests, whether hustling or playing for the intellectual challenge, these street-chess masters, some of whom even used to play outside City Hall in Baltimore until the early 2000s, lay claim not only to an old-time gameboard and the squares on it, but also to the public space in which they performed.
43 Michael Wood, 'This is America, Man', *The London Review of Books*, 27 May 2010, p. 21.
44 *The Wire*, '-30-', m1.27.
45 The reference is to John Ford's western, *The Searchers* (1956), when the deeply racist former confederate soldier Ethan, upon finally finding the niece who, having been abducted, has been living as the wife of a Native American chieftain, gently takes her into his arms, saying, 'Let's go home, Debbie'.
46 William Shakespeare, *A Midsummer Night's Dream*, Sukanta Chaudhur (ed.), *The Arden Shakespeare*, third series (London: Bloomsbury, 2017), Epilogue: 6.

# 3
# Choosing our queen: a series of first female presidents from *Commander in Chief* to *House of Cards*

## Lady Macbeth in the Oval Office

Frank Underwood realises that his house of cards is finally about to topple when two Democratic senators visit him in the Oval Office. Because the Judiciary Committee is about to send articles of impeachment to the House of Representatives, they have come to ask him to resign. Rather than complying with their suggestion, he insists that dirty hands were always part of Washington's politics, even if history has a way of looking better than it was. Then, no longer addressing the two congressmen and, instead, looking squarely into the camera to speak directly to the audience, he adds, 'or perhaps Shakespeare was right, we're all just madmen leading the blind'.[1] While Underwood's reference is to the blinded Gloucester, lamenting the plagued politics of his times in act four of *King Lear*, critics have repeatedly linked the way this corrupt politician frequently 'breaks the fourth wall' to the infamous asides of Richard III. As Elena Pilipets and Rainer Winter note, this technique 'goes back to the direct address of Shakespearean plays and allows us to gain insight into Underwood's intentions'.[2] Furthermore, by speaking directly to us as an off-screen audience, even when other characters are present, Frank not only confides in us how he craftily influences politics. As Mario Klarer argues, he also entices us to believe 'ourselves to be an accomplice of his'.[3] In that the conspiratorial address allows us to see behind his manipulations, it produces a sense of both intimacy and collusion.

When describing the political ambitions that Frank shares with his wife Claire (Robin Wright), critics, in turn, have noted the resemblance to Macbeth and his Lady, and, indeed, in the final season of *House of Cards*, the appropriation of this tragedy is explicitly stated.[4] After a confrontation with Claire, in which Annette Shepherd was not able to sway the first female president of the United States to sign a deregulation bill that would profit her foundation, she voices her frustration to her son, Duncan: 'I know that expression. She can't decide if she's Lady Macbeth or Macbeth.'[5] It is precisely this uncertainty which makes the resuscitation of one of Shakespeare's most conflicted queens in *House of Cards* so intriguing, given that it corresponds to the quandary at the heart of this TV drama's engagement with the question of feminine political sovereignty. The fact that, to the end, Claire oscillates between two positions – that of a ruler who becomes madly absorbed in a desire for absolute power and that of the partner in crime whose conscience comes to bother her – draws the complexity of her own political evolvement into focus. If, just before becoming her husband's vice president (VP), Claire claims to her speechwriter that the role of First Lady never felt right to her, the fact that in the final season she reverts to her maiden name, Hale, further underscores her ambivalence about the very marriage which made her ascension to the Oval Office possible in the first place.

Annette Shepherd's cursory allusion to *Macbeth* is, however, more than mere witticism on the part of the script; instead, it comments self-consciously on the way in which, from the first episode onward, this tragedy informs the cynical portrait that *House of Cards* has to offer of this ambitious couple. Like Shakespeare's usurpers, the Underwoods' rise to power is as ruthless as it is precarious, predicated on a series of bloody machinations in which Claire not only resolutely supports her husband but actually goads him on. The night Frank comes home to confess to his wife that he has been passed over as secretary of state by President Garrett Walker, Claire is waiting for him.[6] She, too, has had advance notice of what has happened, and, although her husband has precisely not been promoted, she nevertheless takes her cue from Lady Macbeth's playbook. Upon receiving Macbeth's letter describing the prophecies of the weird sisters, Shakespeare's heroine had proclaimed, 'Hie thee hither,/That I may pour my spirits in thine ear, And chastise with the valour of my tongue/All that impedes thee from the golden round,/Which fate and metaphysical aid doth seem/To have thee crowned withal'.[7] Because Frank has spent the past nine hours trying to decide on his own how to respond to this slight, Claire begins her verbal assault by reminding him that they do things together and then proceeds to mock him for having underestimated his superiors. While he is willing to chalk this defeat up to hubris and ambition, she, like Shakespeare's Lady, rouses his passion for revenge by admonishing him that she wants no apologies. When she leaves to go to her bedroom, he finally smashes a glass bowl in anger.

Just before dawn they meet again to smoke a cigarette together in front of an open window. Confiding in Claire that he now knows what he must do, Frank warns her that from now on they will have a lot of nights together like this, making plans, with very little sleep. Claire is visibly pleased. This is the first of many scenes in the first season of *House of Cards* in which this couple is shown smoking together at an open window at night. Comparable with the clandestine dialogues between Macbeth and his Lady during which they concoct the murder of King Duncan, these nocturnal exchanges confirm the intimate bond they share with each other. While their conversations are not concretely about the political moves they are deliberating, they serve to negotiate the terms of their mutual trust. During one of these sessions, Claire consents to forgo a donation for her nongovernmental organisation, the Clean Water Initiative, because it would hurt the advancement of one of her husband's bills in Congress. On another occasion Frank, in turn, indicates the priority their relationship has by not answering his phone, even though this means putting his machinations on hold. It is also in one of these moments of quiet intimacy that Claire confesses her worry over who will die first, given that the thought of death prompts her to ask what they will leave behind. Frank – comparable with Macbeth, who, from the moment the weird sisters hail him as Thane of Cawdor, is obsessed with his legacy – assures her that they already have accomplished so much for each other and will continue to do so. Indeed, together they will do to Garrett Walker what Macbeth and his Lady do to their king. Though theirs is a symbolic, not an actual, murder, they will craftily use their influence on the president's opponents to call for his impeachment, compelling him to resign after only one year in office.

As such, *House of Cards* refigures Macbeth's angry dismay at King Duncan's decision to establish his estate upon his eldest son, Malcolm. Given that at the time the crown of Scotland was not hereditary, Macbeth, having just been hailed by the weird sisters as the one to be 'king hereafter', tells himself, 'that is a step/On which I must fall down, or else o'er-leap,/for in my way it lies'.[8] His being overlooked will set the entire series of tragic events in motion. Convinced that the president's decision not to appoint him as secretary of state was tantamount to the breaking of a promise, Frank, in turn, comes up with his own version of jumping over the obstacles that are placed in the way of his rise to power. His vengeance takes the form of first accepting the post of VP to the very politician who snubbed him and then deposing him to take over the Oval Office, which, initially, he had not even wanted. At the same time, if *Macbeth* thinks a politics of over-leaping in terms of a couple, *House of Cards* asks what the consequences might be were this couple, welded together by their political aspirations, to fall apart. Indeed, Claire's immediate response to her husband's being overlooked – her scolding him that he did not call her – also sets up from the start her clear-sighted assessment that they must make decisions together. She is all too aware that only when Frank shares his deliberations with her can they realise their political goals. Like Macbeth's Lady, she is not only his accomplice, standing beside him because she has a history and a future with him. She also insists that in so far as he can repeatedly realise his will for power precisely because he does not act alone, maintaining their mastery is predicated on the parity that comes with recognising her as an equal in this marriage.

When, in the fifth act, Macbeth discovers that his Lady is no longer at his side, he finally recognises the futility of his ambition, comparing himself to 'a poor player,/That struts and frets his hour upon the stage,/ And then is heard no more'.[9] However, far from convincing Macbeth to put an end to the battle he is waging with the lawful successor to the throne, the loss of his 'dearest partner of greatness' actually spurs him on in a fatal orgy of destruction. While it is also the case that whenever Frank acts alone, his sovereignty is threatened, at issue in the way *House of Cards* appropriates Shakespeare's tragedy is not only Frank's persistence, even in the face of failure, but also Claire's appropriation of her king's position. At the beginning of the fifth season, when, during his re-election campaign, Claire is running as his VP, Frank is shown playing with a computer program that allows him to move back and forth between a photograph of her face and a photograph of his. When the cursor is in the centre of the screen, their faces are perfectly married with each other. Claire adjusts the image, explaining to him that female voters need only a hint of her face in the official portrait of their president to recognise themselves in him. The visual fusion is telling not just because it speaks to the way Claire has been part of the face of this presidency all along. If part of their working as a couple means that their complicity is predicated on each absorbing aspects of the other, this opens up the possibility that once they are in the Oval Office together, Claire might pull the cursor more into her field.

Key to understanding how *House of Cards* conceives of the first female president, however, is less whether or not Claire will ultimately assume Macbeth's ruthless sovereignty; more at issue is what it means that, in this reworking of Shakespeare's tragedy, she keeps oscillating between his position and that of his Lady. In 'Chapter 63', she finally breaks the fourth wall herself, appropriating the Shakespearean asides which, up to this point, had been the trademark of her husband. She had got up in the middle of the night, and, clad in a white silk dressing gown, gone to look for Frank. Finding his bedroom empty, she stops as she passes the camera and, turning directly towards it, admonishes us: 'Just to be clear. It's not that I haven't always known you were there. It's that I have mixed feelings about you. I question your intentions. And

I'm ambivalent about attention.'[10] The difference Claire introduces into her mimicry of Frank is that her willingness to make us her accomplices comes with a degree of reticence. By admitting that she has been duping the audience by pretending not to know that, like her husband, she, too, was merely a player, strutting and fretting her hour on a stage, the secret she lets us in on concerns a very specific duplicity. She has had an agenda of her own all along, and if she has been keeping it from us, then she may have been keeping it from her husband as well.

Decisive about the transformation which Lady Macbeth undergoes in *House of Cards* is, of course, the altered outcome this TV drama proposes. In Shakespeare's tragedy, Macbeth's Lady is ultimately 'troubled with thick-coming fancies/That keep her from her rest' and thus compelled, while sleepwalking, to repeatedly re-enact her attempt at washing her victims' blood off her hands.[11] Her death, in turn, occurs off stage. A servant delivers this tragic news to Macbeth just before he discovers that his enemy is approaching, disguised as Birnam Wood. By contrast, Claire, though also haunted by the crimes weighing on her conscience, survives all self-doubts and is willing to embark on a new scheme once Frank decides to resign after all. Claiming that for some time now his political ambition has taken a different turn, he proposes that they split up as a couple, with her working within the White House, while he, working outside in the private sector, continues to wield his influence clandestinely. The supreme power he is handing over to her is, however, part of a script he has conceived on his own, not part of a shared conversation, so that bemusement flickers across Claire's face when, in 'Chapter 65', he explains to her, 'I've designed this. I wanted you to be the president. I've made you the president.'[12]

If, in exchange for becoming the first female president, Claire must promise to pardon him, she, in turn, plays back to him the logical consequence of the division he proposes. Because the pardon can be effective only if they appear to be estranged as a married couple, he must move out of the White House. When, shortly after, she visits him in the hotel suite he has chosen as his new residence, her description of their changed relationship foregrounds a parity that is based not on fusion but separation. Utterly resolute, she explains to him, 'We're the same now.'[13] Once she is finally in the Oval Office without him, she will complete the severance he had initiated. She had assured Frank that her upcoming address to the nation would be the right moment to pardon him, and yet, as he watches her deliver her speech on the TV screen in his new quarters, he realises that he has been duped. In his last aside, Frank confides in us that he will kill her if she defaults on her promise and then tries to call her immediately after she has finished. Claire, however, does not answer. Instead, once her BlackBerry begins to beep again, she impatiently presses the red button, and, turning directly towards the camera, declares, 'My turn!' Along with his political power, she has usurped his privileged form of address.[14]

If part of the serial logic on which *House of Cards* is predicated is that Claire's sovereignty remains precarious, this also aligns her with the Macbeth-like role her husband had been playing on the political stage in Washington. As though Shakespeare's tragedy was beginning all over again in the final season, enemies within her own ranks seek to topple President Hale from the throne after the sudden death of Frank Underwood.[15] The insurrection is led by Mark Usher, the former campaign manager of the Republican challenger, who during the election deadlock switched over to the Underwoods. Having forced her to choose him as her VP as a way of safeguarding her secrets, he soon begins to undermine Claire's authority. Claiming that he is the more legitimate successor to a presidency that was stolen by the Underwoods, he rallies support among Congress for invoking the Twenty-fifth Amendment that would declare her to be unfit for office. While Claire is able to ward off this threat, replacing the traitors in one fell swoop with an entirely new, all-female cabinet, we find her sitting alone in the Oval Office at night, contemplating how to get rid of the last of her own co-conspirators. If furthermore, like Macbeth, she, too, is haunted by hallucinations in this final season, the ghostly appearance of the murdered Banquo in her case turns into spectral traces of her murdered husband. A bird, trapped behind the wall in his bedroom, portentously knocks against the wall. The ring her husband was buried with suddenly reappears on his bed. His voice speaks from beyond the grave on recordings that his loyal aide, Doug Stamper, had saved.

At the same time, the publicity poster for this final season signals a cross between the ruthless sovereign and his reticent Lady. Like Frank on the poster for the first season, Claire is sitting on a marble throne, resolutely looking down at us. In contrast to her former husband, however, blood is only streaming down the column which she is forcefully clutching with her right hand. Her left arm, in turn, is bent upwards with her lily-white left hand poised calmly next to her head, as though she were about to gesture towards something. If this first female president is, thus, visualised as conjoining a murderous hold on power with a contemplative attitude, a proto feminist re-encoding of the tragic manifests itself in this reduction of the couple to one absolute sovereign. What if Lady Macbeth had not committed suicide and instead waited for her bloodthirsty husband to lose his final battle before returning to the stage? Indeed, if Frank Underwood's sudden death assures Claire's

Figure 7 Claire Underwood on her bloody throne of power

political survival, what comes to be debated over his dead body is contemporary culture's anxiety regarding female sovereignty.[16] In one of her asides, Claire explains what it took for her to put on a look of terrified anguish in a snapshot she herself brought into circulation to make the media think she is losing control. She had to imagine 'America's worst fear when it comes to a female in the Oval Office'.[17] The irony at play in this self-comment points to the way Claire can only fight against prevailing prejudices by performing the illegitimacy her opponents accuse her of, much as *House of Cards* itself debunks the very demonisation of female political power which it also reiterates. This first female president's hands are dirty, even if her desire for self-assertion against all the men who have tried to manage her all her life is justified.

Her ultimate fusion of Macbeth and his Lady in her role as absolute sovereign takes yet another turn when, in the course of the final season, she unexpectedly finds out that she is pregnant. Having literally incorporated her husband, she will now give birth to a daughter, in whom traces of his ambition may well survive. As though to signify her feminine reiteration of the presidency they both aspired to, we repeatedly see her prominently putting her pregnant belly on display while conducting business in the Oval Office. Merging the mother with the warrior, she will successfully vanquish all her enemies. Mark Usher will step down as VP, a criminal investigation cuts short the hold the Shepherds have on her, and Claire resiliently asserts herself in the Situation Room against the Joint Chiefs of Staff that still oppose her as commander-in-chief.

Her hybrid impersonation of power finds its apotheosis in her final encounter with Doug Stamper in the final sequence of this TV drama. In his own interpretation of loyalty, he had killed Frank to protect the presidential legacy from the man and has now come to the Oval Office intending to kill her as well. His weapon is a letter opener that all too manifestly resembles the dagger the Macbeths used to kill Duncan and his guards. Because the sight of blood trickling down Claire's throat from the wound he has inflicted on her makes him hesitate, however, she is able to turn the dagger against her assailant and stab him in the chest. Then, kneeling down beside Doug, who is now lying in a pool of his own blood, she tenderly embraces him with her right arm while, with her left hand, she ruthlessly holds shut his nose and mouth until he has suffocated. Softly she whispers to him the words, 'no more pain'.[18]

In the closing shot of this TV drama, she furtively glances directly into the camera. We are the accomplices of her final deed, and she wants us to know that she knows this. This final turn in a series of transformations from loyal wife to absolute sovereign confirms the move beyond the tragic which the credit sequence to this final chapter had predicted. Amidst the other edifices of Washington's political power that we have

Figure 8 The statue of President Claire Hale

come to associate with the credit sequence of *House of Cards*, we unexpectedly find a statue of the pregnant Claire Hale, standing on a pedestal above a plaque that prominently displays her name. At first, dark storm clouds cast a deep shadow on this monument, then, for a brief moment, she appears fully illuminated by a ray of sunlight. As mother of the nation, who always was popular with the people, she will have got what her husband had always only wished for.

## Shakespeare's queens

Lady Macbeth is not the only one of Shakespeare's queens to flicker up in contemporary TV drama, even if their resurgence is less explicit. It is, thus, fruitful to revisit the different configurations of queenship we find in his oeuvre. One key position in such a typology is occupied by an array of warmongering queens whose cry for battle is tied up with family allegiances. In the late tragicomedy *Two Noble Kinsmen*, three distressed queens interrupt the wedding procession between Theseus, Duke of Athens, and his bride Hippolyta, an Amazon queen. King Creon, who killed their husbands during the siege of Thebes, has decreed that the corpses of the slain sovereigns be allowed to decay in the open field without a proper burial. While Theseus wants to defer any military campaign until after the marriage ceremony, Hippolyta, recalling that she was once a soldier herself, pleads with him to delay their nuptials instead. Assuring him that she is willing to abstain from her joy so that he might attend to a request that requires more immediate action, she convinces him to privilege military honour over his own personal desire. While the wedding feast gets underway without him, Theseus leads the army of the three widowed queens to victory, so that they are free to find their dead kings and, along with the funeral solemnity, they disappear from the stage again. They are stock characters, reduced to only one dramatic feature – to precipitate a battle, justified by their duty as bereaved wives.

Villainy is added to the formula when, in *King Lear*, all three daughters evolve into warrior queens as a result of their father abdicating the throne even while insisting on his paternal supremacy. Having bestowed his estate on Goneril and Regan, the old king nevertheless continues to impose his personal claims on his two elder daughters. Refusing to comply with this demand, they instead not only divide his kingdom but depose him as their father as well, expelling him from both their courts. Though justified as queens to fully assume the symbolic power granted to them rather than accept a shadow king by their side, the sheer brutality with which both seek to enforce their goals can also be read as a warning against any female sovereign who does not possess the virtue of clemency. Cordelia's silence, in turn, is her way of refusing to abide by her father's impossible request for unconditional love, reminding him that it is her duty as a wife to give half her care to her future husband. If she, nevertheless, intervenes in the massacre that her sisters have unleashed with an army of her own, this underscores that for all three queens, warmongering is a response to the fallibility of an old king that is monstrous in so far as it brings to light what, from the start, was rotten in his reign. The consequence of King Lear's refusal to abdicate his power along with his throne is a civil war that ultimately wipes out his entire lineage.

The early revenge tragedy, *Titus Andronicus*, explores yet another variation of the violence that royal family bonds can inspire. The warrior queen of the Goths, Tamora, is brought to Rome as the captive of the victorious general, Titus, who has led a ten-year campaign against her. When, despite her maternal plea, he refuses to show mercy and instead sacrifices her eldest son, Tamora's desire for retribution is born. Once marriage to the new ruler, Saturninus, has made her Empress of Rome, she will use her ruthless cunning to incite internal enmity among the various factions vying for power so as to massacre the family of her mortal enemy. What drives her is the humiliation of having been forced, as a queen, to kneel in public and beg for grace in vain. If, in her subsequent machinations, she shows no pity, her cruelty is also meant to draw attention to the fact that no mercy was shown to her. Indeed, it is precisely because she is not deluded by Roman virtues that she is so successful in turning the noblemen against each other. If, in so doing, she reveals the barbarism lurking just beneath their moral code of honour, and indeed unleashes this savagery, it is not enough to have her die during the final bloodbath she has engendered. The Empress Tamora must be stripped of all royal honour and obliterated completely. Lucius, the only member of the Andronicus family to survive, refuses her all funeral rites once he has become the new emperor and, instead, has her thrown over the city walls so that birds of prey may feed on her.

As with Lady Macbeth, the battles these queens inspire reflect and reflect on what it means for women to take action within a political arena in which they are ascribed a subordinate position. Bereaved widows who demand a military campaign to fulfil their obligation towards their dead kings are as unruly as royal daughters who resist the wilful demand of their father. Whether the more complexly shaped queens in the tragedies are motivated by a desire for self-assertion or a hunger for revenge, the violence they unfurl materialises the prejudice held against them as women insisting on their political claims. The belligerence they put on display can thus also be read in terms of a critique of the gendered political codes that target them as unduly wicked and thus unfit to rule. Any feminine reign implies a battle against masculine sovereignty and must either be harnessed or punished.

A counterpoint in Shakespeare's oeuvre to these defiant women is embodied by those queens who either unequivocally represent their king's symbolic law or allow themselves to be subjected to it without appropriating this power for any goals of their own. The most confident of these heroines is the French king's daughter in *Love's Labour's Lost*. She arrives at the court of Navarre to settle a financial transaction between her father and King Ferdinand. The latter, however, has pledged to spend the next three years in chaste study with his lords and, because this forbids him to invite her into his court, he lodges her and her attendants in the field beyond the gate. Mirthfully aware of the vanity of his vow to celibacy, the princess engages her attendant ladies in a civil war of wits with these fickle scholars, who duly fall in love with the women, forswearing their previous oaths. The ease with which their abstinence has transformed into romantic passion prompts the princess to answer with a form of mockery, which, by shaming the suitors, also debunks the shallowness of their new romantic pledges. While she is willing to partake in the folly of seduction staged by King Ferdinand and his lords, she never loses her command in this battle of the sexes and, instead, ultimately compels the duped men to recognise that she has subdued them at their own game.

Then the arrival of a messenger, informing her of the death of the King of France, interrupts all merriment. Along with her new designation as queen, she immediately assumes an attitude of solemn austerity. Pitting the code of royal obligation against all frivolity, she insists on a deferral of Ferdinand's love proposal. Not only is she required to return to her own court immediately to assume the position of sovereign she has inherited, she also does not yet trust his oath. If, even while playing to Ferdinand's courtship folly, as deputy of her father in questions of debts to be paid, she never forgot her symbolic status as the successor to his throne, she can only enter into a marriage predicated on serious intent. She commands her future husband to spend the next year in a forlorn hermitage. Only if this austere life, far away from all courtly pleasures, does not change an offer made in the heat of passion, will she accept him as the king by her side. Because she is fully identified with the law of rulership, she remains the one in command.

While in *Two Noble Kinsmen*, Hippolyta appears as the conquered queen who has stoically reconciled herself with being the wife of the Duke of Athens, her first appearance in Shakespeare's oeuvre is far more brutal. As Theseus reminds his bride in the opening scene of *A*

*Midsummer Night's Dream,* he wooed her with his sword on the battlefield and won her love by injuring her there. Throughout the play, the voice of the Amazon queen is duly subdued. Hippolyta only returns to the stage once the lovers awake from their nocturnal revelling. If she is the one to detect something of great constancy in the story they have to tell, then it is because, in her stead, a fairy queen held court throughout the strange occurrences that night. As though Titania were acting as her unruly double, she undermines her king's rule. Having quarrelled over a changeling boy whom both want in their entourage, Titania, unwilling to give him up, has insisted on going her separate way, while jealousy drives the fairy King Oberon to take action against his headstrong wife.

With the help of magic drops, he is able to confuse her vision such that she spends an ecstatic night with an ass-headed mortal. The humiliation she feels when, upon waking up the next morning, she finds herself lying on the ground next to him shames her into accepting Oberon once again as her sovereign. Yet in contrast to Hippolyta, who is only presented as a vanquished queen at the beginning and the end of the play, Titania commands the stage with her rule of enchantment. Together with her courtiers, she performs her charmed moonlight revels in stark contrast to the solitary surveillance Oberon has recourse to while his Puck, Robin Goodfellow, undertakes his mischief. If, in the end, the power of both queens has been contained, the curtailment of their rule also draws into focus what was specific about it. As muted survivors they recall a court of shared affection – the Amazons, the fairies – that has now been displaced by the one of absolute kingship.

In this constellation of obedient queens, Queen Hermione undergoes a unique transformation in *The Winter's Tale.* She arouses the blind jealousy of her king, not because she is withholding a prized boy from him, but because she is able to convince his boyhood friend Polixenes to remain at the court of Sicilia. When Leontes proceeds to publicly accuse his pregnant queen of being an adulteress, even though his entire court maintains that she is spotless, she valiantly stands up for herself, maintaining that were she to be punished this would be tyranny and not law. Yet, even though she forcefully argues her innocence, she is not able to make Leontes recognise how he has made her the target of his fanciful suspicion. Her eloquence thus places her between the Princess of France, on the one hand, who uses her sharp wit to chastise the folly of the men besieging her and her attendants; and, on the other, Hippolyta, whose voice, once she has been conquered, falls almost silent. The death Hermione subsequently feigns so as to take refuge in the house of her faithful attendant, Paulina, mirrors her king's refusal to acknowledge her as separate from his lethal fantasy. Having repudiated his queen by not hearing what she had to say, Leontes now finds her to actually be gone. When, after sixteen years, Hermione magically returns, the remorse Leontes has shown makes a remarriage possible, yet what her return as queen after this wide gap of time will look like remains an open question.

As daughters and as wives, these queens are compliant with the laws of rulership. Even while they offer a subtle resistance to the domination of the kings they spar with – on the battlefield or in the court – they never question the law of sovereignty itself. Rather than appearing as self-assertive warrior queens, they seek to temper the unruliness of their kings, whether this articulates itself as the folly of love or as tyrannical jealousy. Although their power is contained, they, in contrast to the transgressive women, are not sacrificed. Instead, their persistence, and with it the royal marriage, serves to guarantee a restabilisation of political order, regardless of whether it is anticipated after a period of deferral, in the process of being celebrated, or about to be reaffirmed. The claim they make is not to absolute power but to a sober recognition of their separateness as the basis for parity in rule and in marriage.[19]

In the history plays, where the assertion of political power is based on a serial struggle of opposing forces outside and within England, the queens occupy a position in between the two constellations described so far. Queen Isabel of France appears in *King Henry V* primarily as a matchmaker, using her woman's voice to advance the marriage between her daughter Katherine and King Harry. This royal wedding is meant to ensure a political alliance between the two kingdoms and preserve the peace regained after a bloody English campaign. If the three parts of *King Henry VI* document how this peaceful bond did not survive the death of this royal couple, the queen at the centre of this historical re-imagination is also far more defiant. As a foreigner, the French-born Margaret finds herself in the crossfire between the two opposing factions in the Wars of the Roses. Vilified from the start by her political opponents on both sides, the violence she unleashes not only correlates with the fragile legitimacy of her queenship but also with her husband's lack of resolve. To ensure her son's claim to the throne, Margaret leads a fierce battle against the Yorkists which she will ultimately lose. When she returns once more to the stage in *Richard III*, the last play in Shakespeare's first tetralogy, her unruliness is linguistic rather than militaristic. She will teach Elizabeth, who has usurped her crown, to curse the tyrant bent on undoing this queen's power as well.

In *King John*, Eleanor of Aquitaine is another remorseless warrior queen, fighting to preserve the crown for her dynasty in the midst of a domestic power struggle in which the legitimate heir to the throne is, once again, uncertain because the lords move back and forth in their allegiances.[20] Though a paragon of wifely obedience, Queen Katherine in *Henry VIII*, by contrast, emerges as utterly vulnerable because of the personal fickleness of her sovereign. Henry, wishing to replace his first wife with a younger and more beautiful queen, instigates a trial against Katherine, in the course of which, much like Hermione, she is publicly accused of being unfit to remain on the throne by his side.[21] Encouraged by an ecstatic nocturnal vision of the heavenly world beyond, this divorced queen departs from the stage, though not before writing her own epitaph. In this subtle rebuke to her sovereign, she makes sure that she will be remembered as a chaste queen. As the wives of kings, these historically reimagined queens can defy the authority of their husband and threaten the stability of the kingdom.[22] They can assert their claim to power, but because they rule in the midst of internal political battles, their legitimacy, along with their definitions of female sovereignty, remain unstable. Slandered by their opponents, they, too, assume the guise of the dramatic villainess, performing the defamation brought to bear on their reign. Whether they entertain their own machinations, wage wars, or staunchly defend their virtue, they can always be deposed – sent into exile when their husband dies or they are divorced by him.

### Genealogy of the first female president

As Jean E. Howard and Phyllis Rackin argue, by re-enacting stories about England's past, Shakespeare's history plays sought to create an imagined community in the present. If Eleanor of Aquitaine and Margaret of Anjou are aligned with unwomanly self-assertiveness, they address a double spectrality. Even as the ghosts of earlier warrior queens return from the past to haunt these plays, so, too, does Elizabeth I and her troubling presence in the patriarchal world in which she ruled. By exploring the acceptable and unacceptable embodiments of historical and fictional female sovereignty, Shakespeare's plays address both the anxiety and the fascination which the authority of his own queen provoked.[23] Indeed, as Lea Marcus suggests, one could read Lady Macbeth, whose demonic dominance undermines orderly succession and unleashes a series of violence that nearly destroys Scotland, as 'a revivified scapegoat figure who gathers up yet once more the residual power of the image of Elizabeth'.[24]

If, in turn, a contemporary TV drama such as *House of Cards* resuscitates this demonised queen, we might ask what residual images of female sovereignty are garnered here? Are we today both as intrigued and as conflicted by the nature of the first female president as the Elizabethans were by the nature of queenship? Antiquity may, as Mary Beard has demonstrated, be another source for the cultural template that continues to conceive of women as belonging outside power so that when they are in power, they 'are seen as taking something to which they are not entitled'.[25] Crossmapping television's first female presidents with Shakespeare's figurations of historical and fictional queens, however, adds to the discovery of this cultural continuity a discussion of the fraught connection between the sovereign's female body and a political body deemed masculine and, as such, addresses the instability at the heart of any definition of feminine rule still current today. What Shakespeare's dramatic engagement with queenship shares with contemporary female screen politicians is that, in both cases, the fictional personae not only revivify the cultural ambiguity towards women who rule but also offer a critical intervention in this long tradition of anxiety entangled with fascination.

As we have already seen, Claire Hale plays to the prejudice towards a woman in the Oval Office even as she debunks it. By casting her as a justified villainess, *House of Cards*, however, also engages with the more general suspicion which contemporary TV drama casts on Washington as a stage for duplicitous scheming. As Alessandra Stanley notes, in such a climate of political contempt, no one expects a virtuous heroine in the White House, making it all the more tempting to create fictional versions who are 'as corrupt and conniving in public office as their male counterparts'.[26] In so far as popular culture, however, not only records the contemporary zeitgeist but also prepares us for the possibility of transformations in the defining spirit of a political mood still to come, these shows themselves assume an ambivalent role. Betty Kaklamanidou and Margaret Tally speculate that the 'disillusionment with politics may also have paved the way for seeing more women playing a prominent role in the fictional stories about Washington, D.C. on television right now'.[27] On the one hand, this shift is part and parcel of the way TV drama seeks to question the power and influence of the presidency.[28] On the other hand, the fact that since Hillary Clinton made her first bid for the presidency, there have been several shows that imagine for us what a woman in the Oval Office might look like, also speaks to what Margaret Tally calls the 'priming effect of popular culture'.[29]

In so far as popular culture anticipates a female presidency, to familiarise the audience with its possibility, Josiah Edward 'Jed' Bartlet, of course, remains the cultural template with and against which this transformative figure is conceived. Played by Martin Sheen, this resolute yet compassionate leader is introduced in the 'Pilot' of *The West Wing* with a speech act that immediately aligns him with a specifically American civil religion.[30] Late for a meeting between members of his staff and an irate group of evangelicals, he interrupts their heated debate regarding which is the first of the ten commandments. Before the White House communications director can give the correct answer, we hear the president's voice declaring, 'I am the Lord, your God. Thou shalt worship no other God before me'. As Heike Paul has pointed out, even though, upon entering the room, he jokingly adds, 'boy, those were the days', he speaks his first words in this TV drama as though he were God.[31] Citing the Bible, this president confidently declares himself to be the human face of a divine principle, tapping into a long tradition of the male president functioning as a secular god. Indeed, as Michael Nowak has argued, if electing a president every four years is tantamount to choosing a king who rules as the high priest of civil religion, this not only transforms the election process into a quasi-religious task. It also accounts for the passionate relation the public has to the ruler of the nation, over and beyond all pragmatism.[32]

While *The West Wing* confirms the cultural resilience of this political-theological complex, the political TV dramas that were developed in its wake explore the limit of this transference to the body of a female president. The passion surrounding her election to office remains, yet her divine authority is less self-evident. By exploring a gendering of presidential power, these shows offer an array of options for what choosing the first female president might entail. These heroines are never just another president of the United States who happens to be a woman. Rather, they are conceived in terms of the special expectations – the hopes and worries – which are entangled with the idea of the *first* woman to hold this office. Further instability at the heart of definitions of feminine sovereignty emerges from the fact that the translation of the natural body into the symbolic body of commander-in-chief is less straightforward. As Ernst Kantorowicz famously writes in his classic study on the king's two bodies, it is the union of body natural and the symbolic body that guarantees the continuity and immortality of the sovereign as a political institution.[33] With American civil religion in mind, one could reconceive the relation between ruler and the people in the following manner: Given the symbolic mandate that the president, as the deputy of God, is endowed with, within the political landscape of the nation, his body natural serves as an embodiment of the body politic he represents.

What the statue of Claire Hale in the credit sequence of the final chapter of *House of Cards* demonstrates is, however, that, in the case of a female president, the relation between the two is less straightforward. It is Claire's pregnant body that stands both for the continuity of her rule and for her place in cultural memory – as a sovereign and as a mother. Indeed, comparable to the ambivalent gendering of the queen's body, the female president's also has a masculine and a feminine component. In contrast to her masculine predecessors, Mme President is a politician whose domestic duties as a wife and mother not only make up an important part of her public persona. Rather, what is also always scrutinised is how she inhabits a role hitherto assigned to a father of the nation, with a first lady at his side. Furthermore, given that in the twenty-first century, political lives are thoroughly mediatised, Mme President's private life is always in the public eye. She has no intimacy, with her natural body always already the site of projections regarding her novel embodiment of the body politic.

What, then, are the choices TV drama came up with in the early twenty-first century for the first female president? Recalling Shakespeare's warmongering queens, one position in the first wave of women in the Oval Office is that of the ambitious villainess who is as ruthless as she is vulnerable. In the first season of Paul Scheuring's conspiracy narrative, *Prison Break*, VP Caroline Reynolds (Patricia Wettig) has joined forces with members of a covert organisation called 'The Company'. While they need her in the White House to pass an energy bill that is vital to their economic interests, she needs The Company to fund her bid for the presidency.[34] To underscore her ominous duplicity, the show introduces Reynolds as an off-screen force. Initially we are only shown her hands, chopping garlic, peppers, and tomatoes or opening a refrigerator, or we see the movement of her lips in an extreme close-up. In all of these brief scenes, she is speaking on the telephone with her trusted accomplice, Agent Kellerman, who has worked with her for fifteen years. Only slowly does the face behind this assertive voice, uttering cruel commands, emerge. Her coldly focused blue eyes, her perfectly straight shoulder-length blonde hair, her sternly elegant suits all speak to the haughty demeanour of a woman who will show no mercy. Allowing us to eavesdrop on these clandestine conversations serves to set up our mistrust of this charismatic politician, whom we subsequently see wooing her voters at rallies and press conferences. We alone are privy to the fact that beneath her claim to be working for the good of the country lies her determination to destroy everyone who poses a threat to her personal ambition.

The target of her wrath is Lincoln Burrows, a man sitting on death row, whom The Company helped her frame for the murder of her brother, Terrence Steadman. To cover up the influence their corporate interests have had on her environmental policy, Reynolds had been compelled to feign her brother's death and have another man buried in his place. Hidden from the world, Terrence is now living in her mansion in Blackfoot, Montana, forbidden to leave the premises. Reynolds is not, however, the only one keen on protecting her kin. Michael Scofield has got himself incarcerated in the same prison as his brother, Lincoln, with an elaborate scheme in place to help both of them break out. Michael's clandestine attack on the VP's authority shows the first signs of success when the execution of his brother is unexpectedly postponed. Irregularities in the forensic report have suddenly come up, and a judge not involved in the case has allowed Terrence Steadman's corpse to be exhumed. In retaliation, Reynolds confronts Burrows' lawyers as they are leaving the office of the coroner. Fully aware that the coroner will have assured them of the perfect match between the dental records of her brother and the set of teeth found on the buried corpse, she falls back on Shakespeare to reassert her sovereignty, lashing out at them, 'You've gotten your pound of flesh.'[35]

By accusing the two lawyers of the vindictiveness that Shakespeare's comedy attributes to Shylock, the VP assumes for herself the role of the righteous merchant Antonio. If, in so doing, she turns her opponents into moral usurers, willing to disturb the sleep of the dead, her loan of Shakespeare's words also serves to cover up her own traffic in body parts. As part of the plot to make her brother disappear, she had convinced Terrence to have all his teeth removed, shrewdly anticipating precisely this contingency. In that her brother's survival, however, continues to pose a liability to her rule, a different Shakespearean association also comes into play, albeit less explicitly. Like his warrior queens, Reynolds finds herself attacked on more sides than one. Not only will the president not endorse her candidacy, accusing her of embodying everything that is wrong with politics today, but her alliance with The Company proves to be a fragile one. Interested in her usurpation of the Oval Office merely as a means to further their political influence, members of this organisation threaten to withdraw their support from her if she was to break ranks. To prove her mettle to the people who believe her to be nothing more than a puppet, Reynolds has the president killed (making it look like a cardiac arrest). If, in so doing, she is driven by her ruthless ambition to become president herself, her commission of murder undermines the dream of absolute power it is meant to fulfil, making her ever more dependent on those who could expose her.

Also akin to the fate of Shakespeare's warrior queens is the fact that once the conspiracy she has set in motion backfires, Reynolds finds herself in a hopeless deadlock in the second season of *Prison Break*. Even her loyal henchman turns against her and, while Scofield (having escaped prison) manages to foil Kellerman's attempt to assassinate the woman he has lost faith in, he uses this opportunity to corner her himself. In the kitchen of the hotel where she is holding her rally, recalling the place she had quietly been sworn in at the end of the previous season, Scofield forces Reynolds to listen to an incriminating telephone conversation between herself and her brother, disclosing their incestuous relationship. Slowly, her proud mockery of her opponent turns into her realisation of defeat, and yet, like her Shakespearean predecessors, she is allowed a monologue to justify her actions. She not only lays claim to a selfless commitment made a long time ago by asserting, 'I agreed to put my country ahead of myself, like a mother does for a child. And I thought that what I was doing was noble and that I would be rewarded'; she also professes to being a pawn herself in a larger power game that has taken over the country and which she compares to 'a cancer that will stop at nothing'.[36] Dramaturgically, the scene is double-voiced. Her confession is meant to appeal to our sympathy, not least of all because we know that she is, indeed, only a player in a larger conspiracy. At the same time, we are also meant to approve the blind vindictiveness of Scofield, who defiantly insists that she pardon him and his brother on live TV during her upcoming speech.

Although Reynolds consents, she will not be able to go through with the pardon. Instead, threatened by The Company that they will disclose her secret were she to do so, she is faced with a false choice, able only to choose her own demise. Smiling radiantly at the cheering crowd that has been waiting patiently for her to appear, she finally takes the stage to announce that the action she is compelled to take is best not for her but for the American people. The camera moves into a close-up to underscore the pathos contained in the oblique confession she offers her voters. Claiming to have been diagnosed with a highly malignant form of cancer, she admits she is no longer fit to serve as commander-in-chief and will step down, effective immediately. As with the Underwoods' asides, the clandestine message is meant only for us to grasp. By implicitly equating her body with the body politic, she speaks to a malignant growth not only at the heart of her administration but also at the heart of the political system, as such. If, however, she proves herself to be truly presidential only at the moment of her abdication, this also speaks to the cultural ambivalence negotiated over her bid for absolute power. Not only must her political success be conceived as part and parcel of a sinister conspiracy; she must also be punished, despite the moral fibre she ultimately reveals, if only briefly. To draw into focus the vehemence with which a vilified lust for power must also be nullified, it is worth recalling the dramatic resolution that *Titus Andronicus* offers. Caroline Reynolds will not be thrown over the wall of the city. Instead, it is presumed that she will be convicted in a trial in which Kellerman testifies against her, to be forgotten in a cell in an unidentified prison. As will emerge from my discussion of first female presidents to follow her suit, in this chapter and Chapter 4, her resignation will prove to have been both a warning and a prophecy.

Released one year earlier, *Commander in Chief* paints a diametrically opposite portrait of the first female president.[37] In Rod Lurie's TV drama, Mackenzie 'Mac' Allen (Geena Davis) also steps in after the president suddenly dies of a stroke. Teddy Bridges had chosen her as his VP solely because of her popularity with women voters, even though she is an Independent. As a result, she is not recognised by his political allies as his legitimate successor. Although the Republican Speaker of the House, Nathan Templeton, who feels he is the rightful heir to the Oval Office, fails in his attempt to pressure her into resigning, he uses his influence in Congress to undermine her authority at every turn. To draw attention to the fragility of Allen's sovereignty, there is no public ceremony staging this transition of power. Instead, as in *Prison Break*, her taking the presidential oath of office happens in one of the rooms in the West Wing. Her precarious entrance into the Oval Office is underscored when, in the pilot to this TV drama, Ruth, the secretary to the president, tells her that she would feel cheap staying on since she knows her former boss did not want his VP behind that desk. When Mac finally does take her seat at the desk which so many begrudge her, the mise-en-scène, however, endows her with the authority of a high priestess of civil religion. At first, the camera pans forward into a medium shot, drawing our attention to her defiant gaze at the door through which Ruth has just departed. After a brief moment of hesitation, Mac resolutely pulls down both sides of her blue jacket, as though adjusting her presidential uniform. A bronze eagle, placed directly in front of her on the desk, enhances her symbolic authority. Once the camera moves into a long shot, Mac comes to be perfectly aligned with it, its outstretched wings visually juxtaposed over her shoulders, as though her face were supported by its bronze back. She is frozen into the vignette of a lone figure, staunchly holding her head high, framed by the flags behind her.[38]

This first female president, whose every move is scrutinised daily, is not a figure of duplicitous villainy. Rather, the former law professor, who has no friends, only allies and enemies in Washington, embodies an autonomous spirit. Though threatened, she will not allow anyone to question her claim to power. At the same time, the obstacles she faces in each episode draw into focus the precariousness of the position of this truly independent politician. Not only do some of the members of her predecessor's administration resign, but the Democratic Party also undermines her policies. It is, however, in her battle with Templeton that the lack of loyalty from her lords in Congress takes its most prominent shape. While the old politician insists that dirty-hands politics is a necessary evil that constantly requires compromising one's moral standards, Mac Allen believes that the novelty of her being the first female president can be interpreted as a unique opportunity for working outside all power games. Conceived as an episodic TV drama, *Commander in Chief* plays through this conflict as a series of attempts on the Speaker's part to challenge his sovereign's rulership, working behind her back to subvert her policies and introduce disruption into her command. Allen, in turn, retaliates in an effort to put an end to politics as usual and the corruption and intrigue this entails.

The closest correspondence to her position in Shakespeare's drama is that of the princess in *Love's Labour's Lost*, who ascends to the throne of France after her father's death. Like her, Allen never loses command because she is shrewdly aware of the folly of her opponents in Congress, whose exclusive bond could be thought of in terms of a contemporary version of King Ferdinand of Navarre's self-absorbed academy. Because making a reasonable decision in moments of domestic and international crises is her goal, Mac plays along with them, always listens to both sides, and, at times, even finds a compromise between her position and that of the Speaker of the House. Indeed, a residue from Shakespeare's comedy can also be detected in the way she firmly pits her clear-sighted assessment of her abilities and liabilities against Templeton's blind hunger for power. From the moment she declines to resign, claiming that the Constitution requires her to be president, she emerges as an upright politician who confronts all obstacles with poised self-confidence. Like Shakespeare's princess, she is always justified in her actions because she is always on the right side of the law.

Equally indicative of the way in which the authority of this first female president is everything but self-evident, is that she is also attacked from within the ranks of her own family. Her husband Rod, who had been her vice-presidential chief of staff, must accept that it is inappropriate for him to continue in this office. In this redefinition of the royal couple, he is no longer her advisor but her spouse. The resistance he puts up against being reduced to the role of first gentleman, can, as Judith Walzer suggests, be read as a re-surfacing of the old cliché that the family cannot deal with a career woman's insistence on fulfilling her talents.[39] Yet, dramaturgically, it also allows for a second front line to emerge in the bedroom of the first female president so that, here, too, she can put her ability to assert herself on display. If the stability of her rule is predicated on the two of them staying together as a couple, Mac shrewdly deploys presidential firmness in this private space as well to insist on unequivocal loyalty from her husband. In its gendered recasting of the president's embodiment of the body politic, *Commander in Chief* equates the repeated re-achievement of national equilibrium in the face of political crises with an equally recurrent reaffirmation of the family bond, whenever the demands of her husband and her children stand in conflict with her responsibility as president of the United States.

If, thus, at times the first gentleman's resentment proves to be as much a threat to her rule as does the mischievous plotting of the Speaker of the House, both help maintain the episodic nature of this TV drama. Together, they repeatedly engender a series of crises inside the family and inside the government whose dramatic function consists of illustrating how much Mac Allen is, after all, in command, both in the West Wing and in the East Wing. The attacks, whether they come from within her family and staff or from her opponents in Congress, allow her to demonstrate over and again that she will not step down. Time and again, after each skirmish, she returns to her place behind the desk in the Oval Office, proving her rightful possession of this position. The dramaturgic effect of her resilience is, however, ambivalent. If these crises are there so that she can prove her ability to prevail, this implicitly signals the fragility of her command. Only because her sovereignty is in question does it make sense that she must repeatedly compel others to acknowledge her as the one in command.

With its portrayal of politics as serial crisis management, this TV drama makes further use of comedy's spirit of restitution in that, to her constituents, President Allen's representation of independent politics continues to have an indisputable appeal. The final sequence of *Commander in Chief* stages her one last time as the secular embodiment of a divine force whom the people accept as their ruler. After a town hall meeting with Templeton, who, like her, is running for president in the upcoming election, a multitude of people is waiting outside, cheering her for her undaunted commitment to women's equal rights. As Allen descends the town hall stairs to greet them, the camera slowly moves back until she is at the centre of the crowd, a tiny grey-clad figure in the midst of her body politic. Whether she will be re-elected, and thus her legitimacy finally confirmed, remains an open question; that she has succeeded in remaining the peoples' president, in turn, is clearly answered.[40]

As is the case with Shakespeare's typology of queenship, the first wave of TV dramas revolving around the first female president also explores a position in between an unambiguously principled heroine and a conniving villainess. Presented as an idealistic and honourable politician in the hours leading up to her taking office in the TV film *24: Redemption*, Allison Taylor (Cherry Jones) is the only one of the women politicians discussed so far to have been elected by the American people.[41] Just before she publicly takes her oath during the swearing-in ceremony, the incumbent president tells her she will have to be very careful if she intends to preserve her idealism without getting tainted by the power games played on Capitol Hill. In the two subsequent seasons of the TV drama *24*, her moral resolve is, indeed, tested. In both seasons, an international conflict transforms into a terrorist threat not only because corrupt American businessmen and politicians are colluding with foreign powers for personal gain, but also because there are double agents within the intelligence community. In the twenty-four hours each of these two seasons depicts, at issue is, thus, whether Taylor will be able to maintain her political authority in the face of an escalating crisis. In both seasons, she proves to be clear-sighted about the consequences that any of the difficult decisions she is forced to make will have, weighing the collateral damage that might occur against her fierce determination to pursue her political goals. We repeatedly see her sitting in the West Wing, silently deliberating with herself. Close-ups, moreover, are used to visually underscore how she is emotionally affected by the emergency she is called upon to handle – her confusion and distress when something goes wrong, her compassion with those in need of her support, but above all her ability to make appropriate judgements.

The former FBI agent, Jack Bauer, under investigation in the Senate for his previous involvement in torture, serves as her doppelganger, fighting on the ground while she waits to hear about the outcome of his attempts to thwart the efforts of her domestic and international enemies on her behalf. While he has made it his mission to protect the nation she is ruling, these efforts are not only often transgressive, but, because her success depends on these clandestine acts, Bauer's perseverance also reveals her vulnerability as sovereign. Only with him as her henchman can she hope to undermine the dirty-hands politics that, in both seasons, emerge as the catalyst for the crisis at hand. This helplessness is pointedly drawn into focus when, during the 'Day 7' season, terrorists attack the White House, take her hostage, and demand she publicly denounce US involvement in their country. If Bauer emerges as the only one who can save both her natural body and the symbolic authority it embodies, this serves to demonstrate that not only the American nation but also the president herself needs to be protected by the rogue FBI agent.

The precariousness of this first female president's position is further exemplified by the liability her family poses, which, in this case, involves criminal activity she cannot condone. In the final episode of 'Day 7', her daughter, Olivia, confesses to having ordered the assassination of a businessman who was responsible for the death of her brother. Once again, a close-up of Allison Taylor's face shows her wrestling with her conscience, until, pressured by her husband to make all incriminating evidence disappear, she insists that she cannot disregard the law. Faced with what can only be seen as a false choice, she maintains that, as the president of the United States, she has a sworn duty to enforce the Constitution, even if this means inflicting an irredeemable wound on her family. The decision to turn her daughter over to the authorities is both cruel and impressive. Sacrificing her family for her political convictions highlights her resolve and her isolation.

At the beginning of 'Day 8', Allison Taylor is ruling in the Oval Office alone, her divorced husband no longer at her side. Her solitary position can be seen as a correlate to the absolute power she will make claim to on the day she hopes to sign a peace treaty with the Islamic Republic of Kamistan at the United Nations (UN). The crisis in this case materialises around the assassination of its president, Omar Hassan, by traitors within his ranks, colluding with the Russian government. While, in her effort to nevertheless finalise the negotiations, she is able to convince his wife, Dalia Hassan, to take his place, the serial logic of this TV drama requires several internal opponents to take shape. On the one hand, double agents inside the FBI as well as traitors among her own staff try to prevent the signing. On the other hand, to get back into the political game, former President Logan, who fell from grace in a previous season owing to his flawed leadership, is called in to help. By convincing her that the only way to prevail is to cover up the Russian involvement in the assassination, he, too, exposes her vulnerability as sovereign.

As in the previous season, close-up shots of Allison Taylor's face signal her worry, her frustration at the success of her enemies, but also her deep sorrow over the dead they leave behind. What is also repeated is her bond to Jack Bauer, whose advice she initially follows, while, sitting inside the UN, she listens to his account of the battle he is waging against their enemies on the streets of New York. Yet, finding herself increasingly out of options, she is drawn ever more into the maelstrom of the dirty-hands politics that Logan (recalling Templeton in *Commander in Chief*) represents. During a heated debate between him and her secretary of state, who staunchly advises Taylor against signing a peace treaty that involves any dishonourable partners, he, too, falls back on Shakespeare. Quoting Brutus, he reminds her, 'there is a tide in the affairs of men, which, taken at the flood, leads on to fortune'.[42] The mise-en-scène signals a tide in her mien as well, replacing the moral rectitude her face had displayed up to this point with tortured duplicity.[43] Deeply invested in a peace treaty with which she feels she will make history, she falls for Logan's seduction, afraid that, like the Roman politician, she will lose her political ventures if she does not go along with the concealment he is proposing.

By agreeing to continue negotiating with those who conspired to murder Omar Hassan, she has, however, allowed herself to become inextricably entangled in a web of double-dealing. The more she supports silencing those, who, like Jack Bauer, are in the know, the more compromised she becomes. The close-up of her face is now no longer meant to garner sympathy for the quandary in which she finds herself and, instead, passes judgement on her choosing personal ambition over constitutional law. Hers is a tragic peripeteia because, in contrast to Claire Underwood, she had hoped to circumvent political corruption rather than harness it to her own gain, only to discover that to further her goals, misdemeanour cannot be avoided. Furthermore, if she becomes tyrannical despite her convictions, then it is because her previous righteousness has emerged as her fatal liability. Any criminal investigation of a president who was willing to send her daughter to prison promises to do far more damage to her symbolic body, and the body politic it represents, than to the already tarnished name of a former president.

The penultimate episode of 'Day 8' culminates in a harsh confrontation between the two women who, up to that point, had been working together to produce peace between their two countries. Seeing herself betrayed by the woman she trusted, Dalia Hassan threatens not only to walk away from the peace treaty but to also enter a formal complaint with the UN, demanding the disclosure of all evidence regarding the assassination of her husband. Taylor responds by confronting her former ally with what can only be seen as a false choice, recalling her daughter's impossible demand to be allowed to get away with the assassination for which she gave the order. Without any sign of remorse, Taylor bullies Dalia into capitulating, telling her that if she does not sign the agreement, she will retaliate with the full force of the American military and devastate her country. If the close-up of Taylor's face during this ugly verbal sparring is unequivocally that of feminine aggression, the final episode once more mitigates this fall into villainy, allowing the first female president a moment of sorrowful self-judgement. Bauer's steadfast insistence on fighting against corruption has finally convinced her not to sign a peace treaty predicated on illegal collusion. Instead, in her speech to the UN, Taylor publicly admits to having participated in a conspiracy to hide the grave crimes that have been committed in the run-up to what should have been a noble event. As though to counterbalance her vicious dialogue with Dalia Hassan, her final phone call with her steadfast doppelganger is played as a moment of sincere self-recognition. She not only confides in him her decision to face the consequences of her actions by resigning from the office of president. She also needs him, as her confessor, to give absolution to her, once she admits to having betrayed every principle she ever stood for. The remorseful face that these final close-ups capture is again the face of an upright if flawed female president.[44]

Reflecting the suspicion towards Washington, prevalent in contemporary political TV drama, Allison Taylor's presidency is one in which her legitimacy, initially fully installed, becomes ever more unstable in the course of these two seasons of *24*. Despite her intelligence and integrity, she, unlike Mac Allen, cannot preserve her ideals because systemic corruption proves to be stronger than her moral convictions. At the same time, in her case, virtue and vulnerability emerge as mutually implicated in that, throughout, Taylor needs her doppelganger to protect both her natural and her symbolic body. If, in 'Day 7', Jack Bauer rescues her from terrorist kidnappers, in 'Day 8' he saves her from the onslaught of her own blind ambition. Yet if, like Caroline Reynolds, her bad political judgement ultimately compels her to resign, she does so not out of fear that her secrets might be revealed, but out of loyalty to the oath she took to protect the law of the Constitution. Positioned between the principled sovereign who compels others, like the princess in *Love's Labour's Lost*, to face the consequences of their actions, and the war-mongering queens of the tragedies, whose cruelty reflects the subordination imposed on them, she is comparable to the queens in Shakespeare's history plays. Within a theatre of politics marked by ever-shifting alliances, with each player the adversary of someone else, she is dispensable.

Much as Shakespeare's historical chronicles reflect a cultural nervousness about the legitimacy of Elizabeth I and her rule, the current popularity of serial TV drama can be understood as a response to a chronic national crisis. As Gérard Wajcman suggests, by expressing the concerns of the American zeitgeist, serial drama not only translates an époque but also renders it visible and decipherable. In contrast to the way that cinematic narratives introduce crisis into a state of calm, only to once again resolve it, the serial format moves from one crisis to the next.[45] As Wajcman puts it, if the world of TV drama shows a world in crisis in serial form, then it is because the crisis is, itself, of a serial nature. Given that the first female president emerges at the centre of not just one but rather a series of TV dramas, the vicissitude of her fate can, therefore, be thought of in terms of a contemporary cultural symptom, both as the effect of our historical moment and as a way of regarding these times. Having crossed a boundary, this ambivalent figure, drawing on hope, fascination, and worry, not only turns the crisis that her presence in the Oval Office poses into a story. Her tenure there is also narrated as a series of crises to be confronted, responded to, and overcome.

One might surmise that, given the seriality of the first female president's ascent to power, with the TV dramas discussed so far implicitly in dialogue with each other, her story, told over and over again, marks a cultural moment where what produces anxiety in the form of a political crisis both writes and interprets itself with each subsequent addition. To complete the typology of how this crisis is serially conceived, a correlation to Hermione in *The Winter's Tale* draws into focus yet another variation on the way both a queen's and a first lady's claim to rule renders the legitimacy of female sovereignty unstable – in this case, by bringing her wifehood into play. In the mini-series *Political Animals*, it is her husband's fallibility which poses a problem to Elaine Barrish (Sigourney Weaver) and her repeated bid for presidency.[46] Throughout the six episodes, this former first lady is compelled to confront in advance the possible fallout of her decision to run for president again, after having been defeated the first time around. Though she is a popular secretary of state, competent and efficient, with a shrewd sense for diplomacy, she has grave reservations because she knows she cannot shed her previous symbolic role, in which, as President Bud Hammond's wife, she was also married to the nation.

She is fully aware that some of her political opponents still remember her as a cold and calculating political animal when she first resided in the White House. She also knows that some women mistrust her for having stood by her philandering husband while he was in office, waiting to divorce him until it was politically opportune for her to do so. The problem, in part, is her uncertainty whether Bud, who is himself eager to get back in the political game, is seen as a liability. Having allowed herself to turn a blind eye to his misconduct raises the question whether she will be more scrupulous once she is the commander-in-chief. If her deliberations are consistently overshadowed by moral anguish, these scruples, however, also have to do with her recognition that, while she was First Lady, she put her political goals for the nation before the well-being of her family. Her sons are the ones who address the injuries that went in tandem with her first years in the White House, worried that the country will hate her all over again, but also uncomfortable about the repercussions which being in the public eye may, once again, have on their own lives.

The re-surfacing of a residual concern from *The Winter's Tale* in *Political Animals*, however, not only hinges on Barrish's bid to return to the Oval Office after a period of absence, during which she served her country in other capacities. It also involves the fact that her return is inextricably tied up with having been publicly put on trial because of her husband's flaws. While Hermione must defend herself against Leontes' false assertion of her faithlessness which results from her unquestioned loyalty to him, Barrish must contend with the duplicity she was guilty of by standing by Bud despite his lies and infidelities. Although the issue of sexual promiscuity has shifted – a false defamation in the play, a cover-up of mistreatment in the TV drama – the accusations made in public result in a separation of both couples. In Shakespeare's romance and in *Political Animals*, the absence of the wife from her husband's side is conceived in relation to a husband's destructive egomania, be it Leontes' blind jealousy or Hammond's blind lust.

Seminal for the question of the repudiated woman's return, however, is that in both cases, the separation of the couple is also of national concern. If the sovereign finds himself in a protracted state of grieving for the loss which his inability to respect his wife brought about, this also signifies a flaw in the rule he shared with her. Thus, as in the fifth act of *The Winter's Tale*, the dramatic resolution of *Political Animals* not only depends on whether Elaine, whose bid for presidency is invariably tied up with some form of returning to her husband, is willing to forgive his former abuse, and with it the part she was compelled to play in it. It also involves the question of political renewal, given that, as Stanley Cavell has suggested, the remarriage of a royal couple serves as a trope for a rejuvenated trust in the sovereignty they represent regarding the body politic, their subjects.[47] While Hermione will, once again, become Leontes' wife, Elaine does not revoke her divorce. By returning to her rueful husband, however, she, like Shakespeare's queen, enters into the 'meet and happy conversation' which, according to Cavell, is a key element in the restoration the romance genre affords – on personal and political grounds.

In the closing sequence of *Political Animals*, Bud joins Elaine on the lawn behind his childhood home, where their extended family has gathered to celebrate their elder son's wedding.[48] Sitting down beside her on a stone wall, at a slight distance from the festivities going on in the house, he admits that it was at this very spot that, as a nine-year-old boy, he began dreaming about becoming president of the United States. He then reminds her that their protracted courtship began here as well, while she corrects him, saying that she turned him down not twice but three times. This conversation, drawing a connection between their shared political life and what made their marriage possible, gestures towards a final flickering up of *The Winter's Tale*. In the play, Leontes is the one to speak about how his wife had initially resisted his advances, reminding her, 'three crabbed months had soured themselves to death/Ere I could make thee open thy white hand/And clap thyself my love'.[49] While a memory of Hermione's prior resistance will segue into Leontes' radical mistrust of her marriage vow, Elaine's recollection of how Bud ultimately wore her down produces an intimacy that does not repress his infidelities and instead acknowledges the strength of their affective bond in light of them. The laughter they can now share, furthermore, indicates that they have resumed a conversation which is as much about the rediscovery of mutual affect as it is about the kind of couple they might be in political terms. Bud's real motivation for joining her in the backyard, where his own boyhood dream began, is to make Elaine come to understand her political responsibility. That he speaks of her contender's bid as a profound crisis for the Democratic Party plays into the notion of urgency.

At the end of *The Winter's Tale*, all we can be certain of is that the reunited royal couple will resume their conversation. Leontes leads Hermione off the stage to a more private place, where each one can 'demand and answer to his part/Performed in this wide gap of time since first/We were disseveered'.[50] *Political Animals* gives us a sense of what such a conversation might entail. Speaking of her as the strong, resilient, and competent leader the nation needs at this moment, Bud confirms for Elaine the conviction she has always harboured without, on her own, being able to fully accept it. To underscore an intimacy that blurs the line between the natural and the symbolic body of the couple, the camera catches both their faces in a close-up. Re-enacting the strategy of persistence which he had invoked regarding his previous romantic courtship of her, Bud prompts his former first lady to say that she will, after all, run. The final shot of *Political Animals* is of Elaine's smile, affirming that she has acknowledged his demand. While the TV drama leaves the political outcome of this conversation open, these final moments stage their restitution as a political couple after the wide gap of time since they were divorced.

## A question of genre memory

One year later, the first season of *House of Cards* will begin with its variation on the trials and tribulations of another presidential couple. As such, *Political Animals* marks the transition to a second wave of female politicians making their bid for the Oval Office in contemporary TV drama alongside Claire Underwood: Selina Meyer in *Veep*, Elizabeth Keane in *Homeland*, and the couple Mellie Grant and Olivia Pope in *Scandal*. As Chapter 4 will explore, there is a double seriality involved in this repetition compulsion. Not only do these later shows themselves make use of an episodic dramaturgy that moves from one crisis to the next, over and over again. They also explicitly tap into genre memory, repeating, with significant variations, the fascination and worry this first wave of female presidents put on display.⁵¹ As a resilient pathos formula, the first female president makes up a seminal part of cultural memory because it carries residues with it. With each new deployment, it accumulates more density, transmitting along with its specific narrative a layered record of its changing use.

Elizabeth McCord's ascent to the Oval Office in the final season of *Madam Secretary* is a case in point. Recalling the serial wager of *Commander in Chief*, she, like Mac Allen, faces all obstacles with poised self-confidence. She, too, is confronted with a series of crises inside the government and inside the family, whose dramatic function is to illustrate how much she is in command on both fronts. Like her predecessor a staunch Independent, Elizabeth McCord refuses to compromise her political vision, even if this sometimes places her in an ethical quandary. At the same time, as one of the few first female presidents in serial TV drama to actually be elected by the American people, she bears traces of Allison Taylor as well, even while, in contrast to her, she never loses her moral compass. Instead, part of the transformation of the pathos formula consists in the fact that she is always able to deftly navigate the threat of political corruption.

Yet, challenged by the vindictive Republican Senator Hanson, who as a member of the Senate Intelligence Committee spearheads an investigation into her campaign, hoping that this will lead to an impeachment, McCord also proves to be as vulnerable as Claire Hale.⁵² Repeatedly throughout the final season, her legitimacy as supreme sovereign is put into question, drawing into focus how one year after *House of Cards* had its final season, the notion of a woman leader remains a cultural problem. The fact that a mass demonstration of support from women voters, whose rallying call becomes 'She's my President', saves Elizabeth McCord from any further threat to her claim on the presidency, in turn, indicates a further variation in the repetition cycle. It emboldens her to repeat a decision that Mac Allen had already made, namely to bring the Equal Rights Amendment once more before Congress.

In the final episode, Téa Leoni becomes the face of the first female president, who resiliently challenges opposition and survives, like Shakespeare's princess in *Love's Labour's Lost*, as a savvy and courageous politician. The opening of the fourth season of *The Good Fight* (CBS 9 April 2020) offers a startling inversion of this optimism. 'The Gang Deals with Alternative Reality' begins with Hillary Clinton being sworn in as the forty-fifth president of the United States. In her darkened living room, Diane Lockhart, an outspoken feminist lawyer, is gleefully watching the news broadcast of the 2017 presidential inauguration on TV. She has dressed up for the occasion, yet while she is cracking open a bottle of champagne, the TV image becomes white noise. What follows is a nightmare scenario, which imagines all that would have happened if Clinton had, indeed, become the first female president – high corporate taxes, harsh gun laws, and no 'Me Too movement'. The last moments of this episode, however, suggest that there is more than satire at stake. We realise that what we have been watching is, in fact, the delirium that Diane has been caught in, after having lost consciousness during a SWAT team attack on her home. To test her recovery, one of the policemen asks her, 'who is president?' When actor Christine Baranski offers her signature laughter in response, this is ambivalent at best. It not only discloses that the idea of a first female president can be nothing other than an alternative reality, it also captures the anxiety that the spectre of this possibility continues to inspire, intensified by Elizabeth Warren's stepping down as the last of several female candidates in the 2020 campaign. If the readings in Chapter 4 return to the typology of Shakespeare's queens as a dramaturgic template, the question of genre will also, again, be decisive. While roguish unruliness remains a common concern as this second generation of women ascend to power, the outcome of their bid for the presidency returns to issues of humiliation and failure, opposition and resignation, but also idiosyncratic self-assertion.

## Notes

1 *House of Cards*, 'Chapter 63', season 5, episode 11, dir. Agnieszka Holland, writ. Laura Eason, m23 (Netflix 2017). The show was created by Beau Willimon and aired on Netflix from February 2013 until November 2018.
2 Elena Pilipets and Rainer Winter, '*House of Cards* – House of Power: Political Narratives and the Cult of Serial Sociopaths in Narrative Politics in American Quality Dramas in the Digital Age', in Betty Kaklamanidou and Margaret J. Tally (eds), *Politics and Politicians in Contemporary US Television. Washington as Fiction* (London/New York: Routledge, 2017), p. 97.
3 Mario Klarer, 'Putting Television "Aside": Novel Narration in *House of Cards*', *New Review of Film and Television Studies*, 12:2 (2014), p. 209. He also notes that Kevin Spacey, who played Richard III in a production directed by Sam Mendes between 2011 and 2012, explained in an interview that Shakespeare's use of the aside makes the audience co-conspirators. See Marjolaine Boutet, who also suggests that the Richard III-like monologues arouse the sympathy of the viewers, 'The Politics of Time in House of Cards', in Birgit Däwes, Alexandra Ganser, and Nicole Poppenhagen (eds), *Transgressive Television. Politics, Crime and Citizenship in 21st-Century American TV Series* (Heidelberg: Universitätsverlag Winter), p. 85. James R. Keller also speaks of the particularly Shakespearean tone of Frank's asides, deployed to disclose Frank Underwood's cynical dupery, 'The Vice in Vice President: *House of Cards* and the Morality Tradition', *Journal of Popular Film and Television*, 43:3 (2015), p. 118.

4 As Margaret Tally, '"Call it the Hillary Effect": Charting the Imaginary of 'Hillary-esque' Fictional Narratives', in Kaklamanidou and Tally (eds), *Politics and Politicians* points out, in the Gothic plot lines of the show, 'Claire is seen as a kind of Lady Macbeth figure, as Mrs. Clinton was sometimes accused of being while her husband was the president', p. 128. In the introduction to the volume *House of Cards and Philosophy. Underwood's Republic* (Chichester: Wiley Blackwell, 2016), Edward Hackett calls this couple 'our Shakespearean antihero and his Lady Macbeth', while Randall Auxier, 'Have You No Decency? Who is Worse, Claire or Frank', in the same volume, finds that the alliance between the Frank and Claire Underwood couple could be seen in terms of a marriage between Lady Macbeth and Richard III; p. 266.
5 *House of Cards*, 'Chapter 67', season 6, episode 2, dir. Ami Canaan Mann, writ. Frank Pugliese and Melissa James Gibson, m19 (Netflix 2018). In a later scene, trying pressure her into signing this bill as well, her husband, Bill Shepherd, makes his own reference to Lady Macbeth, when he assures Claire, 'to the dead a kingdom means nothing, they have their requiem and eternity'. The passage, he explains, is not from Shakespeare, but from Verdi's opera; to be exact, from the second act in the libretto, just before the killing of Banquo. The name of the son is itself a reference to Shakespeare's tragedy.
6 *House of Cards*, 'Chapter 1', episode 1, season 1, dir. David Fincher, writ. Beau Willimon, m14 (Netflix 2013).
7 William Shakespeare, *Macbeth*, Sandra Clark and Pamela Mason (eds), *The Arden Shakespeare*, series three (London: Bloomsbury, 2015), 1.5.25–30.
8 Shakespeare, *Macbeth*, 1.4.48.50.
9 Shakespeare, *Macbeth*, 5.5.23–5.
10 *House of Cards*, 'Chapter 63', m9.
11 Shakespeare, *Macbeth*, 5.3.38–9.
12 *House of Cards*, 'Chapter 65', season 6, episode 5, dir. Robin Wright, writ. Melissa James Gibson and Frank Pugliese, m5 (Netflix 2018).
13 *House of Cards*, 'Chapter 65', m42.
14 *House of Cards*, 'Chapter 65', m53.
15 The death of Frank Underwood, which is resolved at the end of the final season, is consistent with the adaptation of the serial format to media reality. Owing to allegations against him, Kevin Spacey had to be removed both as an actor and producer of *House of Cards*.
16 The manifest reason for his demise was, of course, the result of the decision on the part of Netflix, to eliminate Kevin Spacey from any further connection with the production.
17 *House of Cards*, 'Chapter 70', season 6, episode 5, dir. Thomas Schlamme, writ. Jason Horwitch and Charlotte Stoudt, m7 (Netflix 2018).
18 *House of Cards*, 'Chapter 73', season 6, episode 8, dir. Robin Wright, writ. Frank Pugliese and Melissa James Gibson, m52 (Netflix 2018).
19 See Stanley Cavell's discussion of *The Winter's Tale* in *Disowning Knowledge in Seven Plays of Shakespeare* (Cambridge: Cambridge University Press, 2003), pp. 193–221.
20 In her article 'Warlike Women: "reproofe to these degenerate effeminate dayes"', in Dermot Cavanah, Stuart Hampton-Reeves, and Stephen Langstaffe

(eds), *Shakespeare's Histories and Counter-Histories* (Manchester: Manchester University Press, 2006), Carol Banks also draws into focus that, while Cordelia is meant to contrast her cruel sisters, she, too, plays a military role, and that while the dowager Queen Eleanor may be less brutal than Margaret, she is as fiercely active in both war and political intrigue; pp. 174–5.

21 As Susan Frye, 'Spectres of Female Sovereignty in Shakespeare's Plays', *Oxford Handbooks Online*, argues, when Shakespeare creates both the historical Queen Katherine and her fictional counterpart Hermione, he raises the spectre of the executed Mary Queen of Scots. In that in both trial scenes the absolute, male sovereignty overrules these queens, these plays critically probe definitions of female sovereignty; p. 12.

22 See Nina S. Levine, who, in her reading of the first tetralogy, draws out the way that Margaret epitomises the dangers ascribed to ruling women in political debates in the sixteenth century, *Women's Matters. Politics, Gender and Nation in Shakespeare's Early History Plays* (Newark, DE: University of Delaware Press, 1998).

23 Jean E. Howard and Phyllis Rackin, *Engendering a Nation. A Feminist Account of Shakespeare's English Histories* (London/New York: Routledge, 1997). See also Patricia-Ann Lee, 'Reflections of Power: Margaret of Anjou and the Dark Side of Queenship', *Renaissance Quarterly*, 39:2 (1986), pp. 183–217.

24 In a similar vein, Lea Marcus also proposes that Shakespeare's interest in the internecine strife of the Wars of the Roses was bound up with fears regarding Elizabeth's successor, *Puzzling Shakespeare. Local Reading and Its Discontents* (Berkeley: University of California Press, 1988), p. 105.

25 Mary Beard, *Women & Power. A Manifesto* (London: Profile Books, 2017), p. 57.

26 Alessandra Stanley, 'Where Mean Girls Rule', *International New York Times*, 2 May 2014, pp. 10–11.

27 See Betty Kaklamanidou and Margaret Tally's essay 'The Political TV Shows of the 2010s: Showrunners, Reality and Gender' in their collected volume, *Politics and Politicians*, p. 24.

28 In the same volume, see George Frame, 'The Leader of the Free World? Representing the Declining Presidency in Television Drama', who argues that TV drama in the 2010s, picking up on anxieties and uncertainties regarding the strength of the presidency, questions whether there is anything other than symbolic significance to this office; pp. 61–74.

29 See Tally, 'Call it the Hillary Effect', who sees popular culture as potentially helping to facilitate the American voters in feeling more comfortable with a woman in the Oval Office; p. 124.

30 Created by Aaron Sorkin, it was originally broadcast from 22 September 1999 to 14 May 2006 on NBC.

31 *The West Wing* was produced by Warner Brothers and ran from 1999 to 2006; 'Pilot', episode 1, season 1, dir. Thomas Schlamme, writ. Aaron Sorkin, m34.47 (1999). I am grateful to Heike Paul for her suggestion that an embodiment of civil religion is far less self-evident for women presidents and sharing with me her lecture manuscript entitled 'Gods, Kings and Crooks: Presidents (and Those Who Want to Become One) in American TV Series'.

32 For the second edition, the original title 'Choosing our King' was changed to *Choosing Presidents. Symbols of Political Leadership* (New Brunswick, NJ: Transaction Publishers, 1992). See also Burton W. Peretti, who suggests that the persistence of a strong male image of the presidency illustrates 'the pervasive sexism underlying American culture, in which both Washington and Hollywood have been complicit', *The Leading Man. Hollywood and the Presidential Image* (New Brunswick, NJ: Rutgers University Press, 2012), p. 6.

33 Ernst H. Kantorowicz, *The King's Two Bodies. A Study in Medieval Political Theology*, second edition (Princeton: Princeton University Press, 1998). See also Elisabeth Bronfen and Barbara Straumann, 'Elizabeth I: The Cinematic Afterlife of an Early Modern Political Diva', in Mandy Merck (ed.), *The British Monarchy on Screen* (Manchester: Manchester University Press, 2016), pp. 133–4.

34 Produced by 20th Century Fox Broadcasting Company, the show ran from August 2005 through May 2017, although Caroline Reynolds appears only in the first and second seasons.

35 *Prison Break*, 'By the Skin and the Teeth', season 1, episode 15, dir. Fred Gerber, writ. Nick Santora, m31 (Fox 2005).

36 *Prison Break*, 'Sweet Caroline', season 2, episode 19, dir. Dwight H. Little, writ. Karyn Usher, m29 (Fox 2007).

37 The series ran from 27 September 2005 to 14 June 2006 on ABC and was not renewed after the first season.

38 *Commander in Chief*, 'Pilot', season 1, episode 1, dir. Rod Lurie, writ. Rod Lurie, m24 (ABC 2005).

39 See Judith B. Walzer, 'Yes, Ms. President?' *Dissent*, 56:1 (2009), pp. 101–4. By casting Polly Bergen as Mac's mother Kate, who moves into the White House to take over the role of hostess that Rod refuses, the show uses genre memory as a critical play. She had, herself, played a first female president in Curtis Bernhardt's political melodrama *Kisses for My President* (1964), who is compelled to resign again once her husband, equally resentful of his inferior position, manages to get her pregnant. By recalling the defeat of her predecessor, *Commander in Chief* draws into focus a troubling continuity of the pressure exerted on women who seek supreme power, even while offering a different outcome to this script in that this president succeeds in harnessing the opposition of her family.

40 *Commander in Chief*, 'Unfinished Business', season 1, episode 18, dir. Rick Wallace, writ. Steven A. Cohen, Cynthia J. Cohen, and Dee Johnson, m40 (ABC 2006).

41 The film, written by executive producer Howard Gordon and directed by Jon Cassar, first aired on 23 November 2008 on Fox. Season 7 of *24* ran on Fox from 11 January to 18 May 2009, while the final season ran from 17 January to 24 May 2010; both with Howard Gordon as the showrunner.

42 William Shakespeare, *Julius Caesar*, David Daniell (ed.), *The Arden Shakespeare*, third series (London: Bloomsbury, 1998), 4.3.216–18.

43 *24*, 'Day 8: 9.00 a.m.–10.00 a.m.', season 8, episode 18, dir. Milan Cheylov, writ. Chip Johannessen and Patrick Harbinson, m29 (Fox 2010).

44 *24*, 'Day 8: 3.00 p.m.–4.00 p.m.', season 8, episode 24, dir. Brad Turner, writ. Howard Gordon, m41 (Fox 2010).

45 Gérard Wajcman, *Les séries, le monde, la crise, les femmes* (Paris: Edition Verdier, 2018).

46 The six-part mini-series was created by Greg Berlanti and Laurence Mark and aired on ABC in the summer of 2012. With its explicit reference to the Clinton years in the White House, this show thrives on what Margaret Tally calls 'the Hillary effect', see *Politics and Politicians*. At the same time, it also makes use of this cultural memory to connect the two waves of first female presidents. While the first wave discussed in this chapter either anticipates or comments on the presidential bid she lost in 2008, the second set of TV dramas to be discussed in Chapter 4 reflect on her subsequent career as a senator and secretary of state, as well as her second bid in the 2016 election.
47 See Stanley Cavell, *Pursuits of Happiness. The Hollywood Comedy of Remarriage* (Cambridge, MA: Harvard University Press, 1981), especially his reading of *The Philadelphia Story*; pp. 133–60.
48 *Political Animals*, 'Resignation Day', season 1, episode 6, dir. David Petrarca, writ. Molly Newman and Speed Weed, m44 (ABC 2012).
49 William Shakespeare, *The Winter's Tale*, John Pitcher (ed.), *The Arden Shakespeare*, third series (London: Bloomsbury, 2010) 1.2.102–4.
50 Shakespeare, *The Winter's Tale*, 5.3.153–5.
51 The concept was first developed by Mikhail Bakhtin, who conceived of genre forms as key organs of memory that because they embody the systems of value of the historical period in which they originated, also impose this perspective on subsequent texts. See Gary Saul Morson and Cheryl Emerson, *Mikhail Bakhtin. Creation of a Prosaics* (Stanford: Stanford University Press, 1990), for a discussion of this term.
52 Genre memory is also at work given that Wentworth Miller, who plays Senator Hanson, had previously, in his role as Michael Scofield, challenged the villainous Caroline Reynolds and forced her to resign in *Prison Break*.

# 4
# Rogue queens: *Veep*, *Homeland*, and *Scandal*

### Troubling vision of feminine countersovereignty

Democracy, as Jacques Derrida has argued, has always wanted two incompatible things. On the one hand, it is predicated on a limited inclusion, welcoming only those perceived as being citizens, brothers, and compeers, while excluding all others, in particular persons deemed to be rogue. On the other, democracy also wants to open itself up to all those excluded, even though this gesture of hospitable incorporation remains limited and conditional. Salient for this tension, he notes, is that 'it is typical for democracy to do one or the other, sometimes one and the other, sometimes both at the same time and/or by turns'.[1] Those considered to be rogue are sometimes legitimate compeers, sometimes illegitimate antagonists, and, as such, they contest any unequivocal distinction between inclusion and exclusion. The proximity between a democratic rule by representatives of the populace held to be eligible and rule by those 'othered' as rogues, who lay claim to a countersovereignty, is, thus, ambiguous. Given that those who operate outside the legitimate rules of the political community are in one way or another also part of it, the question is what makes them separate, excluded, and wayward. When is their inclusion esteemed to be beneficial, and when is the disruption they embody denounced, judged, and condemned?

Indeed, the tension inherent in the proximity between the democrat and the rogue leaves open and undecided whether targeting someone as a villain is a form of protection against figures who challenge the legitimate state power, or does it signal an expulsion of those it is expedient, in a particular situation, to claim as not being qualified to represent the demos? As Derrida also notes, rogue is an accusatory attribute that, by casting a performative evaluation, is tantamount to a disdainful insult: 'It is an appellation that looks already like a virtual interpellation.'[2] To be called a rogue not only means being designated as illegitimate. Rather, this act already attributes a pejorative identity to the person targeted in the accusation. A rogue is whoever is declared to be one, and yet this attribution is not fixed. Not only can one person's rogue be another person's hero; a legitimate hero can as readily evolve into a rogue, much as a figure who has been called rogue can debunk this denunciation. From a political point of view, representatives of the official order may try to present all those who shake things up as rogue. However, rather than merely being fixed in this appellation, rogues can also serve to reflect and contest the predilections and prejudices of the current rule that seeks to contain them by virtue of such targeting.

While Derrida suggests that the rogue 'is always a man, if not actually a ladies' man',[3] it is useful to repurpose his term for the anti-heroines that contemporary TV drama, from 2012 onward, has designed in its representation of a second wave of female politicians staking a claim to the presidency. By aspiring to become the supreme ruler, these women perform the slippery distinction between inclusion and exclusion on which democracy is based – historically denied access to the Oval Office, yet called upon by a part of the demos, at least, to seek entrance into this vaunted site of political authority. In that they represent a competing power challenging the dominant patriarchal power of the state, theirs is perceived as a countersovereignty, which, as was already discussed in Chapter 3, can never fully shed the taint of the transgressive and the offensive. As legitimate as their demand may be, it rattles those who represent the established political order in Washington. In Chapter 3, I discussed the most rogue of presidents: Claire Underwood. The ones I am turning to now can be seen in dialogue – both implicitly and explicitly – with her. Like *House of Cards*, the shows that will now be discussed also serve as a commentary on the state of American democracy, even though, in contrast to its Gothic sensibility, the genre is satire (*Veep*), conspiracy thriller (*Homeland*), or melodrama (*Scandal*). What each of these TV dramas leaves open, however, is whether these anti-heroines are truly self-absorbed (Selina Meyer), tyrannical (Elizabeth Keane), or unabashedly manipulative (Olivia Pope and Mellie Grant). Or does their rule come to be perceived as rogue precisely because they have been targeted as illegitimate by their peers?[4]

The serial format suggests that in each case the portrait of the first female president is open-ended. More is potentially still to come regarding the countersovereignty each of these anti-heroines embodies, even if the TV shows themselves have aired their final season. Seriality is, furthermore, at play in that, as in *House of Cards*, all the other TV dramas of the second wave continue to revolve around a *first* female president. As though cognisant of each other, they seem to be trying out different narrative variations on a thematic concern common to all of them. In that the first female president keeps returning, her serial bid for the Oval Office, however, also involves genre memory. The concurrent shows of the second wave are not only in dialogue with each other, when, for example, the politician played by Elizabeth Marvel fails to become a presidential candidate in *House of Cards* while her character succeeds in *Homeland*. As serial narratives, these shows also recall the previous series of TV dramas, repeating and refiguring the female presidents of the first wave. The resolute ruthlessness of Caroline Reynolds from *Prison Break* returns in a more nuanced shape in the female couple that uses both cunning and charm to win the Oval Office in *Scandal*. *Homeland* revisits the vulnerability of Allison Taylor's moral uprightness in the context of a stridently divided body politic. *Veep* uses satire to defuse the anxiety that female ambition engenders, exchanging Mackenzie Allen's capable command during a period of political interim for narcissistic incompetence.[5]

Whether they remain in power against all odds or are compelled to resign, the legitimacy of these *first* female presidents continues to remain unstable. Indeed, what this second wave of TV dramas also repeats is that the cultural ambiguity regarding their heroine's single-minded ambition is played out as a mixture of fascination and anxiety. If, in all cases, the rendition of their desire for power is exaggerated, it is also counterbalanced by their vulnerability. Our complicity in their fate is duplicitous. We are meant to enjoy the audacity of their aspiration and their opprobrium. Given this dramaturgically orchestrated tension, the following readings will return to the three positions sketched out in Chapter 3 regarding the typology of Shakespeare's queens. My cross-mapping proposes that *Veep* taps into the dark side of comedy and, as in *A Midsummer Night's Dream*, humiliation is the price the anti-heroine pays for her resistance against the men who try to keep her in her place. *Homeland*, in turn, borrows from Shakespeare's first tetralogy the quandary of a female ruler, calamitously caught up in internal political strife among her peers because she is a foreigner. Finally, *Scandal* offers a jubilatory spin on the villainess of tragedy, moving, as *Antony and Cleopatra* does, from the heroines' battle with male authority to the mythic restitution which this late Roman play offers.

To read these TV dramas in dialogue with these early modern plays is not meant to prove a solid intertextual relation between the two. Instead, as Stanley Cavell explains regarding the conversation he proposes between Shakespeare's romantic comedies and classic Hollywood comedies of remarriage, at issue is 'discovering, given the thought of this relation, what the consequences of it might be'.[6] Rather than reducing the problems regarding female rule as it has repeatedly come to be depicted in contemporary TV drama to Shakespeare's recognition that the exercise of power is always slippery, the question becomes, why have these concerns come to work themselves out in their particular shapes in TV dramas that both recall and reconfigure the shapings found in the early modern plays and their conflicted concern with queenship? While the crossmappings proposed in this chapter are predicated on the discovery of analogies between the two, drawing these similarities into focus also foregrounds the transformations that take place as the entanglement of fascination with anxiety regarding feminine countersovereignty is repeatedly reshaped. What are the consequences not only of a female president's inability to shed the rogue identity attributed to her but also, concomitant with this failure, what are the consequences of the erosion of political legitimacy this perpetrates? And what are the consequences of the repeated performance of such discrediting in serial drama?

What the serial circling around the *first* female president ultimately performs is a repetition compulsion on the level of the cultural imaginary, as though the anxiety attached to envisioning female countersovereignty cannot be repressed and must, instead, be played through and negotiated over and again. She remains the exception, even if repeatedly so. Even when the anti-heroine commands our sympathy, her authority is never self-evident. Comparable to the dramaturgic logic of the *fort-da* game, these TV shows repeatedly repudiate the legitimacy of a first female president, only to invoke it over and again as a possibility still to come.[7] Like the child in Freud's narrative, who throws away the reel representing his mother so as to master the painful experience of her absence by deciding himself when to retrieve her proxy, these shows repeatedly cast off the first female president so that her claim to becoming commander-in-chief can be posed over and over again.[8] The open-ended format of serial TV drama plays into a need to articulate the ambivalences attached to visions of female countersovereignty, even while the aim is not to resolve them. As unfinished business, the serial return of the first female president, however, not only draws attention over and again to the rogue kernel within democracy, to the included exclusion. The translation that each refiguration of this pathos formula produces also brings with it a subsequent ripening. Something is changed and something is gained in the process.

### Selina Meyer's charmed rule

The opening of each episode of *Veep* traces the trajectory of a red line, initially rising steadily to indicate a boost in the polls, only to suddenly plummet again, all the way to the bottom of the screen. Corresponding media images serve as the background for this curve of political luck, revealing the vicissitude involved in the American populace's response to the political ambition of Vice President (VP) Selina Meyer. The first in this series of images is her portrait on the cover of *Time* magazine, bearing the title 'Is This Meyer's Moment?' Then, other newspaper headlines pop up as a running commentary on the rising red curve – such as 'Senator's White House Run', 'Meyer Looking for Nomination', and 'Might It Be President Meyer?' They are accompanied by photographs of the radiant young politician, giving a thumbs-up to her audience. Once the ascending red curve arrives on the cover of *People* magazine, endowing this contender with the attribute 'Magic Meyer', a second series of headlines appears across the red curve that is now descending drastically. These document the striking turn her political fate has taken, declaring 'Selina's Un-super Tuesday', 'Selina Suspends Campaign', 'Meyer's Meltdown,' 'Nightmeyer'. The correlating images now record her defeat, portraying her as puzzled, wistful, and crestfallen. Finally, placed directly beneath an image of her pouting sullenly, a headline which, for the first time, uses white letters on a black background, reads 'Selina "Proud" to be Veep', satirically underscoring her ambivalent position. She is clearly everything but proud; and yet the final destination of the red curved line is its transformation into the letter 'V' beneath a portrait of Selina Meyer (Julia Louis-Dreyfus), placed within a star-studded blue circular frame, resting on the red, white, and blue stripes of the American flag, tied into a ribbon. This emblem of the *second* in command shows her dressed in a smart red suit, white pearls adorning her neck. She is sitting upright at her desk, a pencil poised in her hand as though she were about to sign a document, her pinched mouth offering up a forced smile.

After the fourth season, the opening changes slightly, adjusted to the narrative development that has taken place. Although the red line once again initially keeps rising only to ultimately plummet, some (though not all) of the media images have been exchanged. Corresponding to the logic of seriality, difference is inscribed in this serial repetition. The overall shape of the opening remains the same, even though it now documents the second round of a drastic change of circumstances in the life of this ambitious politician. While the *Time* magazine cover once more serves as the point of departure for this new polling curve, the first two headlines now remind us how our anti-heroine became the first woman president of the United States, albeit not yet elected by the people: 'Hughes Resignation: World Reacts', 'Nomination Race Intensifies', and 'Meyer Polls Higher'. The images accompanying this success capture her triumphant joy. Then, having reached the cover of *People* magazine announcing her magic, the red line once again plummets, moving along headlines that speak to the precarious situation of an acting president who must still be elected: 'Meyer Numbers Hit New Low', 'Meyer Loses Another Primary', 'Meyer: I Will Survive'. The last headline, once more in white

Figure 9  Selina Meyer's emblem of presidential power

letters against a black background, asks, 'The 8-month President?' while the portrait above it captures an expression of mournful dismay.

The opening to the fifth season draws the uncertain legitimacy of her presidency further into focus. While the headline announcing Senator Tom James as her running mate drives her polling curve up, the red line once more drops, accompanied by a series of devastating headlines that declare, 'Too Close to Call: Election Ends in Historic Deadlock', 'O'Brien/Meyer Refuse to Concede', and 'Congress Scrambles as Tie Forces House to Select President'. This serial repetition of a chain of media images, recalling Selina Meyer's bid for the presidency, now conducted from the Oval Office, draw into focus her confusion, her disappointment, but also her defiance. Even if the progression of headlines and portraits exposes her repeated loss of face, what remains constant is the visual emblem of her survival as a public figure, inserted inside its red, white, and blue frame. Despite all the fluctuations that her ambition is subjected to, Selina Meyer continues to look out at us from behind her desk. In the final season, she will make a second, this time successful, bid, going down in history as a one-term president, with her presidential library housed at Smith College.

In 'Frozen Yoghurt', this final destination of her serially fluctuating political curve is anticipated in all its ambivalence. Selina Meyer is suddenly called to the Situation Room in the West Wing because the president of the United States (POTUS), during a trip to South Africa, has an attack of severe chest pains.⁹ Flummoxed yet thrilled, she gathers the innermost circle of her staff around her. After a brief period of enjoying the seat at the head of the table, having been briefed on what she needs to know in her role as acting president in the case of an emergency, she is again asked to stand down. The relief she expresses over the speedy recovery of the president is visibly forced, and only reluctantly does she return the files and the pen that were given to her, unable to hide the disappointment she feels. Then, having already stepped out of the door, she meekly returns to take one last look at the room that she so desperately wants to inhabit, before slinking away.¹⁰ While this doubly unexpected turn of events – her ascent to and descent from power within one episode – foreshadows the narrative development of the serial drama as a whole, at this early point in *Veep*, she is back in the position of the ostracised VP whom POTUS ignores, incessantly undermining her wish for more leadership in their administration. He never visits her, nor does he call her to the Oval Office. Instead, he redacts her speeches, refuses to keep her informed, and even sabotages her policies in favour of his own bills.

Cockily, she assures her staff throughout the first season that President Hughes is a weak ruler, jealous of her popularity. Yet the fact that he is doing everything to keep her sidelined not only relegates her to the confines of the VP's office. In that she reigns there as a countersovereign, so prone to committing political blunders that she spends much time concerned with damage control, this can also be read as Selina performing the wounding lack of acknowledgement with which she is confronted daily. Not being taken seriously makes her unserious. Treated as the one who is not included in the actual political decision making, she assumes the habitus of the rogue implicitly ascribed to her, which is to say an attitude and incorporation of rogue power.¹¹ Despite her ruthless ambition, she repeatedly makes gaffes that are disastrous for her credibility, contradicts herself, and keeps shifting her position while giving in to the pressure of others. In contrast to Claire Underwood, who begins her own treacherous career in *House of Cards* the same year as Selina Meyer does, the corruption and cover-ups the latter is connected with pertain primarily to the image of herself she wants so desperately to project. Utterly self-absorbed, Selina responds, in everything she does, to her sense of not being recognised as the rightful ruler that she imagines herself to be, even while knowing of her own lack of authority. That throughout the show she is shown to be more interested in winning the Oval Office than in the policies she will try to implement once she achieves this goal can, thus, also, be seen as the collateral damage of her exclusion from real power.

Capricious and tempestuous, she draws her often incompetent staff into her charmed circle, enticing them to share in her vain ambition to become the supreme commander, as well as her glee when she manages to undermine one of her opponents. Yet she also abuses them, along with her daughter, Catherine, playing them off each other and punishing them with her tantrums when she has been thwarted. Given that, on the manifest level of this TV drama, her counter-rule is thought in terms of satire, *Veep* emphasises her arrogance, her insincerity, and, above all, her cruel narcissism. It has the playful quality of 'playing rogue'. Yet read against the grain, her vanity emerges as the counterpart to her radical uncertainty, given her lack of official legitimation. In the offices where, excluded from the centre of actual power, she holds court, she is, however, the absolute queen. Only her desires count, and everything revolves around manipulating the image of herself she seeks to project. Her power here resides in playing at being in command, not least of all because those surrounding her are willing to play their part in scenarios that conceive politics as carnivalesque theatre. As in *House of Cards*, we are made privy to the intrigues, the guile, and the deception at the heart of her rule when we listen in on the strategy talks she has with her team, sharing her disdain for those they seek to manipulate and dupe.[12] What is debunked is the double-faced nature of her charismatic self-performance. Beneath her beaming smile lies boredom, anger, and sometimes sheer exhaustion. The empathy she claims to have for those who seek her help or those she hopes to sway is disclosed as being unashamedly self-serving.

The charm Selina's wayward rule unfolds, not least of all because she does not hesitate to flaunt her erotic desirability, calls to mind the opening conflict in Shakespeare's *A Midsummer Night's Dream*. The quarrel the fairy queen has with her lord, Oberon, has also produced a separation in their sphere of rule. When they meet by moonlight, he calls her a proud and 'rash wanton', ascribing wilfulness and promiscuity to her as a way of chastising her for her refusal to meekly abide by his law.[13] The object of their dissension is a changeling boy he wants as his page, but whom she is unwilling to give up for the sake of his mother, a votaress of her order, who had died in childbirth. While, in contrast to Selina's POTUS, Oberon invades Titania's space with his brawls, the court she commands is also marked as a parallel world. Refusing to be intimidated by his claim to having sovereignty over her, she offers up a compromise: 'if you will patiently dance in our round/And see our moonlight revels, go with us;/If not, shun me, and I will spare your haunts.'[14]

The viciousness of Shakespeare's fairy king is that he, too, does not want to share his power with his lady and, instead, decides to torment her for this injury. He waits for her to fall asleep, and, because she is left unprotected by her attendant fairies, he anoints her eyes with the juice of a magic flower so that, upon waking, she will fall in love with the next thing she sees. He intends to 'make her full of hateful fantasies',[15] in which she will be so enthralled as to render up her page to him. The humiliation he intends is, thus, multi-faceted. Not only does he command her to wake when 'some vile thing is near',[16] so that while she is fully enamoured with the ass-headed artisan Bottom, the audience is called upon to read this as a monstrous 'dotage', the result of a deluded fantasy. It is also not enough that unwittingly she disgraces herself by sharing a night of erotic ecstasy with this disfigured mortal. She must also be made to recognise the wayward desire she has succumbed to. Oberon makes sure to lift this charm off her sight while her paramour is still lying by her side, forcing her to admit how she now loathes his visage. The new amity between the royal couple, with her now finally willing to meekly follow her fairy king, is thus predicated on the recognition of the folly of a fantasy of rapture, which her lord has enforced on her. As discussed in Chapter 3, Titania's humiliation serves as a serial repetition of the shame that Hippolyta endures in the first scene of *A Midsummer Night's Dream*. If, as has been suggested, the fairy queen performs the countersovereignty forbidden to the vanquished Amazon queen in her stead, she, too, must be contained before Oberon can bless the wedding bed of Theseus, his diurnal counterpart. Hippolyta, who enters Athens as a prisoner of its duke, has, as the vanquished lady by his side, only a passive, moral power. In the first act, her silence, while she witnesses her lord's decision to support a father's merciless insistence on curtailing his daughter's wish to determine for herself whom she will marry, compels Theseus to ask, 'what cheer my love'.[17] Hippolyta's implicit disapproval not only inspires Hermia's flight. As in a relay race, it is also picked up by Titania in a resistance to her lord, which, however, will prove to have been a temporary one. With the end of the night comes the end of the fairy queen's countersovereignty as well.

*Veep*'s Selina Meyer, the former lawyer coming from inherited wealth, could be seen as incorporating both – the Amazon queen, who wars against her adversaries, and the fairy queen, who rules over political revelling on an interim stage, especially when she becomes the forty-fifth president by default once POTUS resigns. It being election year, she must still be chosen by the people as the ruler of the demos. To underscore her sustained roguish appellation, she is sworn in as president during a small gathering in the Oval Office, but, owing to yet another misstep by one of her staff, she makes a mistake while taking the oath. When swearing to preserve the Constitution, she leaves out the second syllable, 'serve'. Because the Speaker of the House declares her oath to be illegal, and her, thus, not yet the rightful president, she is compelled to take it again, this time while on the campaign trail in New Hampshire. Unable to shed the taint of the included outsider, her rule in the Oval Office is, in serial repetition of the first three seasons, once more that of a charmed state of exception with the threat of an eight-month presidency hanging over her head. As acting president, she once more demonstrates an excess of the liberty and freedom that democracy associates with licence, while her 'veeple people', competing among themselves for her attention, play to her whims. Much like Titania's fairies, this silly entourage perpetrates a night-rule in the White House that undermines Selina's power in Congress as well as her approval by the American people. Conceived in terms of a satire sustaining a contemporary cultural suspicion about incompetence ruling in Washington, Selina's magisterial obsession with power, debunked as a delusion, remains the butt of the joke.[18] At the same time, the fact that she becomes more and more unlikeable in the course of the fourth and fifth seasons banks on the proximity between tyranny and comedy.[19]

One might be tempted to find comparable positions in *Veep* to those in Shakespeare's romantic comedy. The magically transfixed Bottom seems to resurface as her bag man Gary, to whom she is forever queen, regardless of how cruelly she treats him. The daughter, Catherine, whom she carelessly casts off whenever something more enticing comes into her field of vision, recalls the changeling boy who Titania renders up immediately to her lord once her enchanted eye has caused her to be enthralled with someone else. The fact that these distractions, in one shape or another, always pertain to her fantasy of presidency draws into focus the most salient point of connection between the two texts. While in *A Midsummer Night's Dream* a headstrong fairy queen is charmed into sexually doting on an ass-headed mortal, in *Veep*, ambition is the magic juice that charms this female politician's eye and lets her see everything distorted by a fantasy we might call hateful, owing to the ruthless narcissism it is predicated on. The object of contention with her lord, POTUS, is not a changeling boy but rather the seat behind the desk in the Oval Office.

As VP, Selina was meant, like the vanquished Hippolyta, to be the president's obedient lady, albeit not at his side and, instead, severed from his rule, residing in another office far away from his. Selina, however, comparable with Titania, instead asserts herself against male domination, which, in Washington's nocturnal fairy world, takes on several shapes.

There is her own VP, Tom James, who not only strenuously courts her voters on the campaign trail but continues to do so on election night. Selina finds herself compelled to make her appearance with her entire entourage so as to crowd him off the stage. Once it becomes clear that neither she nor her challenger Bill O'Brien will concede in this extremely close election, Tom James will convince his friends in the House to abstain their vote so that neither of the two presidential candidates can win there. Instead, the election moves to the Senate, where the choice is between the two VP candidates. There, Senator Doyle, whom Selina had previously allowed to dictate her moves in the hope of gaining the Oval Office, emerges as a most devious Oberon. Because she has promised to make him her secretary of state, he tips the election in favour of Laura Montez, who has been calling Selina a 'stand-in president' all along. This appellation, also, will prove to have been a virtual interpellation.

A final relation between *Veep* and Shakespeare's comedy of nocturnal confusion can, thus, be discovered in the humiliation Titania suffers upon awakening from fantasies that only appear hateful when seen in the sobering light of dawn. Forced to sit on a lawn within hearing distance of the parade for her victorious rival's inauguration, because the helicopter taking her from the White House malfunctioned, a medium shot of Selina's face captures her grimly frowning as she is forced to acknowledge how badly wrong her theatrics turned out. Then it begins to rain, and slowly a smirk passes across her face. With schadenfreude she assures her trusty bag man that the change in weather will at least ruin her successor's parade.[20] In contrast to *A Midsummer Night's Dream*, however, Selina does not meekly follow the congressman responsible for crushing her bid to power, as the sober-eyed Titania does her Oberon. Instead, staunchly resisting the paternal dominion that Shakespeare's comedy proposes, she will make a second, and this time successful, bid for office, becoming the first female president to be elected by the people. The fact that, in the final season of *Veep*, she will sacrifice everyone along the way marks a transition from a reckless dreamer to the vicious schemer of tragedy. Selina does not have the ability to see and stop. This, according to Stanley Cavell, would bring to an end a tragic cycle of repetition, in which the personal consequences of her blind ambition furiously hunt her down because she continues to do the thing which has produced them in the first place.[21] Despite, or perhaps because of, all her prior humiliations, she has neither the courage nor the prudence to abdicate.

In the finale episode, 'Veep', we see her once again in the Oval Office, impetuously ordering around her staff, though we will not see her actually rule there.[22] The point of this satire on feminine countersovereignty is, after all, that the fantasy she was enthralled with was garnering this political legitimacy, not what she would do once she had succeeded. She endures, yet her roguish predilection leaves her isolated from her entourage. Like Claire Underwood, she ultimately sits all alone behind her desk, and, during the last moments of the show, a sense of despair creeps across her face, although the comic satire has nothing to do with the Gothic sensibility of *House of Cards*. Then the telephone rings, and she falls back into her role as commander-in-chief. Freezing her into the figure of the lone tyrant, *Veep* passes as cruel a judgement on her, as does Shakespeare's comedy on both its queens.

## Elizabeth Keane's battle with her peers

In the credit sequence to *Homeland*'s season 7, we hear Hillary Clinton's voice-over speaking the words 'ridiculous lies and accusations', while the visual montage shows a car driving past the White House and then segues into a fisheye shot of President Elizabeth Keane. She is standing behind her desk in the Oval Office, both arms stretched out to express her own exasperation at a man positioned in front of her. Clinton's soundbite is taken from an interview with Trevor Noah, in which she talks about the way the media not only failed to pay attention to her policies throughout her campaign – entranced by the entertainment value of her challenger, she adds, journalists also did not stand up against all the allegations made against her.[23] Clinton is not the only ghost haunting the two seasons revolving around her fictional surrogate. Emily Nussbaum lauded the first season of this TV drama as an antidote to Jack Bauer's ends-justifying policies in *24*, the previous political thriller for which the showrunners Howard Gordon and Alex Gansa had written.[24]

*Homeland*, however, does not merely dramatise the opposite ideas as *24* did by replacing a rogue FBI agent, who cannot leave off the practice of torture he also feels guilty about, with the bipolar CIA agent, Carrie Mathison, who, suffering from the traumatic consequences of her actions, is prone to a paranoid vision of the world. Genre memory is also at work in the way the two seasons revolving around Elizabeth Keane's precarious administration recall the predicament of Allison Taylor in *24*, while rethinking in far harsher terms what it means for an initially upright female president to assert herself in the midst of rivalling political factions.[25] In both cases, the political crises the first female president needs to confront involve the collusion between American citizens and foreign intelligence agents. Elizabeth Keane, however, is from the start treated as an untrustworthy outsider not only by the military and the intelligence community, but also by members of the alt-right movement.

In contrast to *24*, the threat both to her administration and her life thus comes from within a deeply divided nation, even if this political disunity is also thought of in terms of an external attack on national security.

Given that, in the midst her being forced to fight on various fronts, she becomes the tyrant that her opponents claim her to be, she recalls Queen Margaret of the first tetralogy of Shakespeare's history plays. Defined primarily by her foreignness, she, too, must assert herself against the lords opposing her husband, the politically inept Henry VI, within the context of an ongoing war with France.[26] In Shakespeare's dramatic re-imagination of the Wars of the Roses, Suffolk decides to woo her for his king, hoping to gain political influence through her. Even before she arrives in England, Margaret, however, has a staunch adversary in Gloucester. As the king's uncle, he opposes a marriage with this impoverished Princess of Anjou, because, despite her beauty and eloquence, she brings neither wealth nor any advantageous alliance to the French royal family as dowry. Given, furthermore, that her unfamiliarity with the English court causes her to lean heavily on Suffolk for advice, Gloucester shrewdly intuits that she will curtail his own privileged position as protector to his unworldly nephew. York, in turn, emerges from the start as a second adversary because Margaret's marriage to Henry VI has robbed him of properties in France he felt entitled to after his military victories. The foreign queen is quickly deemed to be the perfect reason why York feels justified to pursue his own claim to the throne.

Equally decisive for the divisive power that Margaret assumes once she is crowned, is, of course, the political vacuum that Henry VI produces. Primarily interested in religious meditation, he longs to be a subject, not a king. In his stead, his queen inserts herself into the political disputes at court and disposes of lords who vex her. Indignant that as 'queen in title and in style',[27] she should, due to her husband's foolishness, be subject to the Duke of Gloucester, she briefly enters into an alliance with York, and, together with Suffolk, has her husband's uncle murdered. Once Gloucester is no longer there to overshadow her policies, York, however, returns to his initial conspiracy, using the populist insurrection by Jack Cade to further his claim to the crown. Although the rebel is also soon murdered, Henry VI, afraid of a further threat from the commoners, banishes Suffolk, and the isolated position into which this casts his queen finally unleashes York's true fury. While he merely accuses Henry VI of not being fit to govern and rule multitudes, he calls his queen a 'blood-bespotted Neapolitan', an 'outcast of Naples, England's bloody scourge'.[28] As the lords line up on the one or the other side of the dispute regarding who should be wearing the crown, the king, hoping to cease this civil war, makes a deal with his challenger. After

Parliament has debated the issue of legitimacy, he shows himself ready to allow York to succeed to the throne after his death, thus depriving his own son, Prince Edward, of his royal claim. Neither Queen Margaret, nor the lords whose allegiance she has procured, are, however, willing to accept the defeat of the House of Lancaster – instead, she declares war on York.

Initially her troops are victorious on the battlefield, and, after York has been captured, she is finally able to confront her infamous opponent. Mocking him for having led his riotous supporters into Parliament, she shames her prisoner with the futility of his dream of becoming England's king. To taunt him further, she offers him the napkin stained with the blood of his youngest son, Rutland: 'if thine eyes can water for his death,/I give thee this to dry thy cheeks withal'.[29] The mock coronation that follows, during which she places a paper crown on his head while her men tie his hands, parodies the deal he had sought to make with her husband. If Henry's death was to be tantamount to the removal of the royal succession from her son, she now declares, 'Off with the crown, and with the crown, his head'.[30] In the brief time left, York responds by returning her callousness in kind, calling her a 'she-wolf of France', an 'Amazonian trull', and 'false Frenchwoman'. What makes her most monstrous in his eyes, however, articulates a larger anxiety about female sovereignty. To him, she is a rogue because she has strayed from proper womanhood. Women, he claims, 'are soft, mild, pitiful and flexible;/Thou stern, obdurate, flinty, rough, remorseless.'[31] It is a harrowing scene, one in which even some of her followers can hardly check their eyes for tears. The fact that, just before his death, York continues to hurl defamations at her, however, also reveals how his appellation of this proud foreign queen has, throughout the play, been a virtual interpellation. In the utter mercilessness Margaret puts on display, she presents herself as the tyrant he has always declared her to be, and, true to this ascribed role, she is the one to inflict the third and fatal stab wound to his body.[32] The civil war continues, with York's eldest son, Edward, now claiming the crown for himself. He repeats the defamation of the queen in the spirit of the man she had executed, and, like his father, declares her pride to be the cause of all the terrible casualties of war still to come.

Assuming the role of a tyrant in the face of being slandered as a rogue is precisely the narrative trajectory of the first female president in *Homeland*. Elizabeth Keane, a widow, is to rule completely alone in the Oval Office. Her son, Andrew, who joined the military after 9/11, furthermore, died in action in Iraq, and for this reason, she wants to bring the troops home, reduce military operations abroad, forbid drone strikes, and demilitarise the intelligence community. As a result, officers within the National Security Agency (NSA) and the military invested in keeping the war in the Middle East alive plot to undermine her peace policies. She, thus, embodies both positions of Shakespeare's royal couple. On the one hand, her declaration to undertake a wholesale reform of American foreign policy, on which she successfully campaigned, recalls Henry VI in his desire to cease a civil war. On the other hand, her need to assert herself against the conspiracy brewing among her ranks, which already begins during her transition period, recalls Margaret's attack on the lords opposing her claim to power. Because, using her son's sacrifice for the country as justification, it soon looks as though she might win the argument in Congress against US military presence in Iraq, a second domestic front line opens up. The alt-right agitator Brett O'Keefe launches his own protest against her, and, supported by a CIA Black Operations director – much as Cade's populist uprising was by the Yorkists – he successfully uses his radio show to incite hate against her among his disgruntled listeners. During one of his broadcasts, O'Keefe even declares her threat to prosecute him for circulating disinformation to be an act tantamount to that of a dictator, opposed to a rule of the populace.

Although an assassination attempt on the president-elect, spearheaded by General McClendon, is thwarted, as in *Henry VI*, this insurrection also draws attention to how some of those serving under her command fatefully question the legitimacy of her rule. Comparable with Queen Margaret, faced with lethal insubordination among her ranks, Elizabeth Keane openly declares war on her own peers and their supporters. She has the renegade general tried for conspiracy against democracy and supports the death penalty as his sentence. She also stages a purge of the CIA and NSA and has all her alleged enemies arrested. Responding to the violent attack on her claim to the presidency with violence of her own, she has, indeed, become the embodiment of absolute power her adversaries have declared her to be. In 'America First', we see her sitting behind her desk in the Oval Office.[33] Through the closed door she can hear Carrie, appealing to her that innocent people are being arrested in her name, while the bodyguard prevents her advisor from entering. Elizabeth Keane does not respond. Instead, as the camera moves backwards into a long shot, we see her staring intently at her iPad, a glass of water in front of her. She is frozen into the symbolic body of the rogue ruler, completely alone, stern and obdurate.

In the following season, Elizabeth Keane finds herself fighting a domestic battle against several adversaries. Carrie, appalled at the arrest of her former colleagues, now sees in the politician, on whose transition team she had been working, nothing other than the embodiment of a ruthless

Figure 10 President Elizabeth Keane frozen in her symbolic body

political machine, and, in tandem with the populist resistance that continues among the alt-right, turns against her former boss. A new front line also opens up in Congress, where Senator Sam Paley, a maverick from Arizona, is leading the Senate Judiciary Committee in its investigation into possible collusion by members of Keane's administration with Russian intelligence. Comparable with York's riotous argument in Parliament, Paley manages to turn several of her cabinet members against her and then, invoking the Twenty-fifth Amendment, convinces Congress to declare her to be unfit to govern. Only late in the season will he realise that he has himself been manipulated into producing this political division by Russian agents. Trusting in his furious opposition to President Keane, they have used him to launch their own conspiracy to damage her presidency. Agent Yevgeny Gromov spearheads a wave of disinformation of his own regarding the alleged cover-up of the murder of the imprisoned general he, himself, had ordered. By falsely implicating her chief of staff, even while galvanising O'Keefe's alt-right protest, Gromov hopes to produce a situation of distrust in the context of which a president he finds too wayward to rule, will be compelled to resign.

Indeed, the remorseless precision with which this Russian agent pursues his goals allows one to surmise that by reading *Homeland* as a refiguring of Shakespeare's first tetralogy, Gromov takes on the shape of Richard, Duke of Gloucester, who also clandestinely has his brother assassinated in the Tower of London so as to cast the ruler he seeks to usurp in a bad light. And like Shakespeare's 'black intelligencer', the Russian agent will continue to manipulate those engaged in the domestic battle over the legitimacy of Elizabeth Keane's rule from behind the scenes. Even after Paley has realised that he has been nothing other than a useful idiot to Russian intelligence, the senator persists in his desire to hold his commander-in-chief accountable for what he perceives to be a national nightmare. Paley's attempt to cover up his entanglement with Gromov, is, however, exposed by her National Security advisor. Ultimately it is the senator himself who is arrested, brought before the Senate Intelligence Committee, and there found guilty on charges of compromising the president and pushing her out of office, while Elizabeth Keane, fully vindicated, is re-installed. Although the fact that she has to be sworn in a second time is further indication of the fallibility of her rule, with the man who had called her a tyrant himself cast in the role of the rogue, a further dramaturgic exoneration is underway. If, in *Richard III*, the eponymous usurper's devious conniving casts Queen Margaret's previous war-mongering in a more justified light, the more those who have conspired with Gromov show their true malice, the more the president's vindictiveness appears to be warranted.

This is most evident in a scene that corresponds to Queen Margaret's mockery of her most adamant opponent. In 'Paean to the People', Elizabeth Keane visits the man who sought to disempower her in prison, and she, too, having won her battle against him in Congress, uses her regained supremacy to mock him.[34] In contrast to York, the Arizona senator is fully contrite, and, while she stands before him, her face frozen into an expression of cold contempt, he admits to having let terrible things happen that have cost the lives of other people. She listens silently while he begs forgiveness, not for himself, but for his wife and sons, who, as he argues, are blameless. When she refuses to reply in any way to his plea that their claim to his pension be honoured, he goes on his knees before her, hoping this gesture of subordination might move her. Yet, after she has taken a step forward, still towering over him, she merely spits in his face. Then, without uttering a word, she turns away from him and leaves the room, while the camera tarries with the man whom she, too, has fatally stabbed, albeit in a figural sense. As in Shakespeare's history play, an ambivalence is at work, leaving us appalled by her remorselessness yet in sympathy with the woman who, having been so furiously cornered, can only respond to violence with violence.

Like her predecessor in *24*, she will ultimately emerge as a righteous, even if flawed, president. After this meeting, Elizabeth Keane drives through a nocturnal Washington, DC, looking forlornly at the illuminated architectural edifices of state power – the Thomas Jefferson Memorial, the Washington Monument – before turning her gaze away to signal that a self-meditation is underway. The following morning, she visits the cemetery and places a wreath on her son's grave, and, noticing that the American flag next to the headstone has begun to tilt to one side, she plants it more firmly into the ground so that it once more stands upright. At issue in the self-meditation that continues as she, touching the headstone, lingers awhile, is clearly the question of what it would mean for her to correct her own political stance. Only once she gets up, having reached her decision, does the camera catch her tearful face in a close-up.[35] While, in *Henry VI*, Queen Margaret comes to accept her banishment after her son has been stabbed to death by York's three sons, in *Homeland*, Elizabeth Keane is inspired by her dead son to abdicate her throne voluntarily. We are called upon to read her sacrifice in terms of what Elisabeth Anker calls a 'melodramatic political discourse'.[36] The maternal body natural and her symbolic body as the mother of the nation are fused in the pathos gesture of pain, which the close-up of her face encapsulates.

In her intention to put an end to the grave political division her presidency has unleashed, she has, again, assumed the traits of the peace-loving Henry VI. The way in which she decides to address the state of the nation in her abdication speech, however, also has recourse to the cursing which typifies Queen Margaret in the two last plays of Shakespeare's tetralogy. There, during the scenes of battle, the royal couple is usually split up. Margaret is a better warrior when her king is not at her side, and she continues to do battle even after he has been deposed and then assassinated on Richard's commands. Although she finally succumbs to the Earl of March (who will subsequently become King Edward IV) and accepts her banishment to France, she is still in England when the final play, *Richard III*, begins. Observing with a degree of schadenfreude how the royal women who once ousted her have themselves become the target of the tyrant who has usurped the throne, Margaret takes on the role of prophetess. Just before her final departure, she appears before the new queen to proclaim her warning. She first speaks to the fragile luck of the female sovereign, declining the word queen through a plethora of examples for how the course of justice can 'whirl about', transforming the happy wife into a distressed widow, first feared then herself fearing, first commanding then obeyed by none. Assuring this 'queen of sad mischance' that 'these English woes shall make me smile in France', Margaret offers a final piece of advice: 'Compare dead happiness with living woe;/Think that thy babes were sweeter than they were,/And he that slew them fouler than he is./Bettering thy loss makes the bad causer worse.'[37] A nostalgic enhancement of what has been lost as antidote to present misery is tantamount to seeing the past as a story of tragic deprivation. Margaret thus implicitly speaks to a seriality of violence, which makes use of a recollection of previous violence so as to ensure that an internal strife will continue.

Elizabeth Keane's abdication speech fuses her vision for what it might take to heal national wounds with her own warning of the serial nature of political struggle. Against the wish of her chief of staff, she does not address the American people from a podium in the East Room but rather from her desk in the Oval Office. As she explains to him, she wants to speak directly to them from the heart. For this reason, she has also decided not to read from the teleprompter and instead to let the spirit of the moment move her.[38] Although she appears conciliatory, she uses her own fallibility to point to the weaknesses and flaws of the body politic. As she emphatically points out, her concern is less that Russia was able to wage a covert war on her presidency and the country, given that this kind of attack has existed since the 1950s. Instead, what troubles her is that, as a deeply divided nation, they should have become such an easy target. The editing continually moves between a close-up of her face and shots of the reaction her words elicit in those in the White House (but also her opponents in Russia), who are watching her on live TV. While she is willing to share some of the blame, she invokes the image of democracies dying not only in the face of revolutions, of military *coups d'état*, of armed men in the street, but also 'when we're not paying attention'. The end, she warns, does not come in an instant but arrives slowly, like twilight, with our eyes at first not noticing.

Elizabeth Keane continues to look intently into the camera as she admits that her own fallibility as president brought the country to this crisis point, while also – and therein lies her implicit debt to Shakespeare's queen – giving voice to a veiled curse. Turning the prejudices brought to bear on her female sovereignty to her own advantage, she insists that she was only able to become part of the problem that has thrust the country into an existential conflict because too many were willing to accuse her of lying the minute she opened her mouth. Realising that this unacceptable response to her as a leader is not likely to change, she finally accepts her interpellation as rogue. Her resignation is the logical consequence of this acknowledgement.

The camera, circling around her face, captures a full moon shining through the drawn curtain of the window behind her desk as she assures her audience that, while no single leader can save a democracy, without a leader in whom the demos is willing to trust, no democracy can be saved. Then, once more looking directly into the camera, she explains with utter resolve: 'People will say I'm stepping down [...] because I'm a woman. Well, if it takes a woman to shock this country back to its senses then so be it.' As the camera moves into an extreme close-up of her face, she assumes a more menacing gaze. Her final words call for a counter-interpellation, now directed at those who had been calling her a rogue: 'Let's make a promise here tonight, an American promise, to each other, that instead of scorching the earth between us, we will try every day to find common ground.' Her appeal is that they help and pray for the new president, who will take her place as of midnight because their future depends on this support. Her final words, 'God bless America', remain ominously tinged.

If her prophecy thus comes with a warning, which involves a recollection of the political violence on which attaining a more peaceful tomorrow is predicated, this rhetorical gesture also recalls the end of Shakespeare's tetralogy. Richmond, about to ascend the throne as Henry VII, evokes a similarly ambivalent vision of the sustained peace he hopes to have attained with the death of the tyrant, Richard III. His declaration that the civil wounds of the Wars of the Roses are, finally, stopped is introduced by a recollection of the violence that preceded the peace that now, hopefully, lives again: 'Abate the edge of traitors, gracious Lord/That would reduce these bloody days again/ and make poor England weep in streams of blood./Let them not live to taste this land's increase/That would with treason wound this fair land's peace.'[39] The words Richmond chooses to give voice to this vision point to the possibility of a repetition of bloodshed. His appeal to a divine force not to allow traitors to take the stage again broaches in the negation what it seeks to avert. It is this double-voiced appeal which Elizabeth Keane's resignation speech taps into when she, too, invokes a repeated scorching of the earth as that which is to be prevented at all costs.

What is gestured towards implicitly is that the cycle of violence inherent to power is not stoppable. The positions in this political theatre are simply cast with new players. Even the disappearance of a female sovereign, over whose rogue rule this internal conflict came to be negotiated, does not change this cultural repetition compulsion. Decisive about *Homeland*, however, is that it thinks about what it means for the first female president to abdicate in terms of dramatic genre as well. In contrast to Selina Meyer in *Veep*, Elizabeth Keane is able to do what, according to Cavell, is tantamount to averting, or perhaps overcoming, tragedy. She has, as he puts it, 'the courage, or plain prudence, to see and to stop'.[40] She articulates a conditional hope when she shares with the American people her recognition that one must not close one's eyes to a threat to democracy that is of one's own making. This renders her resignation far less tragic than Selina Meyer's desperate survival behind the desk in the Oval Office. Elizabeth Keane's promise is the possibility of restitution afforded in Shakespeare's oeuvre not by the romantic comedy, nor by the tragedies, but by the late romances.

### Fixing a female presidency

Discovering a way out of the tragic impasse of feminine countersovereignty is precisely what is at issue in Shakespeare's historical re-imagination of the last queen of the Ptolemaic Kingdom of Egypt. As Jyotsyna Singh notes, 'to suggest that Cleopatra is a performer and playmaker has become a critical commonplace', which views both her charismatic self-dramatisation and her sexual sway as a source of empowerment.[41] By shaping her own self-representation, Cleopatra contradicts the name 'foul Egyptian' applied to her by the Romans; a virtual interpellation of her as a rogue queen who must remain outside their society. In Shakespeare's drama, the infinite variety of feminine seduction she consummately puts on display, however, emerges not only as her idiosyncratic expression of political authority. Her ultimate challenge to Rome's humiliating exclusion also leads to her final self-creation as a myth. Dressed in full royal regalia, she chooses the mortal asp's bite to stage a carefully crafted suicide inside her monument. As she lies down on her bed, convinced that Antony is calling to her from beyond the grave, her immortal longing lets her reply: 'Husband, I come!'[42] Her lavishly exposed marble-constant body so effectively transforms the wayward warrior queen into the eternal lover that even her victorious opponent, Octavius, is not only compelled to admit, 'she levelled at our purposes'. He also reads her corpse as an eternal embalmment of an erotic power to which he, himself, is not immune: 'she looks like sleep/As she would catch another Antony/In her strong toil of grace'. Thwarted in his wish to exhibit her in his triumphal procession in Rome, he instead has this quasi-mythic remarriage commemorated, commanding his men, 'She shall be buried by her Antony./No grave upon the earth shall clip in it/A pair so famous.'[43]

While, throughout the play, the erotic allure that Cleopatra has over the Roman triumvir is conceived in terms of her power as rogue Egyptian queen, Antony's fatal sexual infatuation with her, as Jonathan Dollimore has argued, is used as an antidote *against* but also an expression *of* his political ineffectiveness in Rome.[44] Equally significant for the mutual implication of power and seduction negotiated over Cleopatra's body from the onset, however, is the ambiguous declaration she makes to her attendant, Mardian, in the first act: 'Think on me/That am with Phoebus' amorous pinches black/And wrinkled deep in time?'[45] While her blackness casts her, as Ania Looma puts it, 'as a sexually active non-European female ruler', who is unique in Renaissance drama in that she commands her own sphere, this is a precariously constructed autonomy: 'as the ruler of Egypt her space is threatened by the expansionist designs of the Roman empire, and as a woman by the contradictions of heterosexual love'.[46] A further gendering of power is brought into play in that there are two Roman women who serve as her counter-image in the site of official power. Antony's first wife, the politically ambitious Fulvia, who wages war on Octavius while her husband is in Egypt with his paramour, emerges as her double. 'Observing Antony's indifferent response to the news of Fulvia's death', as Barbara J. Baines notes, allows Cleopatra to see her former rival as a reflection of herself: 'Now I see, I see,/In Fulvia's death how mine received shall be', and, indeed, in his 'excellent falsehood', the weak politician-general, Antony, will betray both women deemed rogue by the Roman senate.[47] To reassert his allegiance to Octavius, he agrees to marry his adversary's sister, the sober-eyed, obedient Octavia, who, in her unequivocal acceptance by Rome's society, assumes the opposite position to both warrior women.

To crossmap Shonda Rhimes' *Scandal* with Shakespeare's *Antony and Cleopatra* draws on the way Olivia Pope (Kerry Washington), running a crisis management firm, also uses flamboyant self-dramatisation as a way of asserting her political power in Washington. Although she calls the members of her team 'gladiators in suits' and self-righteously claims that she is the one wearing a white hat, she can be seen as a feminine figure of illegitimate power, given that in battles she deems righteous, she often oversteps the law. Furthermore, she, too, is unique as a black female powerbroker among the anti-heroines in contemporary TV drama vying for control of the Oval Office. Skilfully commanding her peers, she is a shrewd talker who either bullies or cajoles them into doing her bidding.[48] And, like Cleopatra, she, too, uses her sexual allure to sway President Fitzgerald Thomas Grant III, whose election, as we discover in flashbacks, she helped rig. While, during the campaign, she had told him to repair his marriage to his wife, Melody (Bellamy Young), because he requires a first lady by his side, his infatuation with Olivia continues throughout the seven seasons.

Fitz Grant, thus, recalls the triumvir Antony. He, too, is a flawed president because of his emotional and political dependency on Olivia. While several congresswomen challenge the president for his erotic licence, members of his own party see Olivia, to whom he grants illicit power in his Oval Office, as a threat to national security. This unofficial black female ruler is, however, a further liability because the romantic desire that Fitz harbours for his fixer also makes him repeatedly want to leave the political game in Washington, comparable with Antony's flight to his paramour's palace in Alexandria. Though he will not step down and, instead, will govern for two terms, Fitz will divorce his wife and, throughout the show, continue to pursue his dream of making the charismatic seductress, who is more obsessed with political power than domestic bliss, his wife.

In Cyrus Beene, the president's chief of staff, Olivia has her most ferocious opponent inside the official government. Single-minded in his desire for absolute power, this contemporary Octavius is not only willing to battle against the man he had made president. Like his Roman predecessor, he knows how to manipulate his allies in the Senate and in the public, even changing party affiliation when it seems opportune to do so. His deep suspicion and jealousy of the woman who has the president's ear also compel him to repeatedly wage a war against Olivia, using his populist instincts to counter her own hold over the media. As the president's legitimate wife, Mellie, in turn, initially resembles Octavia, fully accepted as first lady in Washington's political circles. In response to her husband's rebukes she will, at times, even strike an alliance with Cyrus. Yet in her fierce ambition to become president herself, she bears traces of Fulvia as well. After she has been elected as a junior senator for Virginia, Mellie sets herself against the dirty-hands politics Cyrus commands, much as she asserts herself against her husband, who, throughout this serial drama, only half-heartedly supports his wife's political endeavours.

Mellie begins to re-evaluate her other rival, however, once she begins meeting Olivia in the basement corridor of the White House to forge clandestine plans of her own. As she explains during one of these meetings, 'I had a realisation about you. You are my way to freedom. You are going to make me President.'[49] Olivia, realising the new power she can have through Mellie, accepts the role of manager of her campaign, and the two warrior women do, indeed, emerge as doubles. Early on, they begin to assure each other that they deserve the Oval Office because they have earned it. The decisive difference to *Antony and Cleopatra* which this serial TV drama thus brings into play is that Cleopatra's notorious autonomy has been distributed among these two women. Indeed, in a less cynical manner than Claire Underwood's resuscitation of Lady Macbeth, *Scandal* makes use of this alternative political couple to offer its feminist refiguration. What if, rather than competing with each other, two ambitious women who are kept apart from official political decision making, albeit for different reasons, joined forces? What if, rather than accepting defeat, they managed to take over the site of legitimate sovereignty?

There is, however, a second correspondence between *Scandal* and Shakespeare's late Roman play, dramaturgically mirroring the infinite variety Cleopatra stands for. By making use of widely different perspectives through varied repetition, the play not only anticipates the parallel editing that serial TV drama deploys. Rather, as Janet Adelman argues, its 'insistence upon scope, upon the infinite variety of the world, militates against the tragic experience'.[50] Much as Cleopatra resists containment, the play undermines its own binary opposition between Egypt as a feminine site of politics dominated by theatrical passion and Rome as the site of rationality and masculine rulership, precisely by moving among comic, satiric, and tragic versions of this dramatic tension. Able to embrace this simultaneity of competing visions only through a generic impurity, the play, Adelman concludes, 'is essentially a tragic experience embedded in a comic structure'.[51] *Scandal*, in contrast to the other serial dramas revolving around a first female president discussed so far, also thrives on a genre hybridity that fuses a political revenge tragedy with melodramatic comedy. By doing so, it not only draws into focus the mutual implication of erotic and political power. Rather, *Scandal* ultimately also undermines the very opposition between legitimate and illegitimate power, which the TV drama negotiates in relation to its African American anti-heroine.

By season 6, when Mellie Grant will be elected as the first female president, a 'deep state' within her husband's administration has been revealed, and with it the black agent Eli Pope who, along with Fitz and Cyrus, emerges as the third member of this contemporary triumvirate. Indeed, if *Scandal*'s Washington resembles Rome after Julius Caesar's death, with an infinite variety of power games being played out, Olivia's father Eli, the founder of a covert government agency named B613, occupies a further rogue position in the ongoing political conspiracies, devised and fought for what he repeatedly calls the good of the Republic. The binary tension between Cleopatra's feminine theatrical politics and Rome's masculine state power thus evolves into a fluid and shifting opposition, with Fitz acting both as the official commander-in-chief of the nation and, in his alliance with Olivia's father, as a member of the secret government working independent of Washington's rule. Bringing gender into the equation, *Scandal*'s contemporary Cleopatra, in turn, at times works with this clandestine network, indeed wants the command of B613 for herself. Yet in her bond with Mellie Grant, who, throughout, remains firmly grounded in the official politics of Congress and is ignorant of the activities of this covert agency, Olivia also sometimes finds herself pitting her interests against those of both her father and her paramour, while they, as often as not, work to undermine her authority.

In Shonda Rhimes' conspiracy narrative, rogue rule, driven by two powerful black players, is thus conceived as a marginal power that is also at the very heart of democracy. As Derrida notes, while rogue rule is a principle of disorder, posing a threat against public order, 'it represents something more than a collection of individual or individualistic rogues. It is the principle of disorder as a sort of substitute order.'[52] The idiosyncratic twist *Scandal* offers to this definition is that it conceives of a rule by those deemed wayward in terms of both gender and race. Furthermore, while, in his histories and tragedies, Shakespeare does not think of any power as being legitimate, what is specific to *Antony and Cleopatra* is the way the slipperiness of all power relations is conceived in relation to the distinct resilience of the eponymous couple. While Antony at time sides with Octavius against the rogue Egyptian queen, at times leads her army against her Roman adversary, he also plays the role of husband in the quasi-mythical couple she stages in her court in Alexandria to override all earthly politics. In a comparable manner, Fitz and Olivia's oscillation between legitimate and illegitimate politics at times pits this interracial couple against Washington's official politics, at times against each other, while the constancy of their erotic bond also serves to illustrate that which holds the Republic together is that which transgresses legitimated institutions, be they public or private. As the alternative same-sex couple, Olivia and Mellie, in turn, embody the tension between a charismatic individual clandestinely claiming absolute power, on the one hand, and the ordinary politician, officially representing the institution of the presidency, on the other.

Given that the uncertain legitimacy of the first female president is an issue in *Scandal* as well, the penultimate season of *Scandal* keeps circling around the night Mellie initially loses the election to her democratic challenger, Francisco Vargas. In contrast to the shows discussed so far, however, this defeat is the result of yet another rogue queen suddenly emerging on the scene. Luna Vargas taps into the secret network around Eli Pope to have her husband assassinated while he is on stage, giving his acceptance speech. As she later confesses to Olivia, she wanted to make sure Mellie would win, in part because she did not want to be relegated to the role of first lady, in part because she had wanted to make a statement with his death, having deluded herself into believing that this would ensure the survival of his political vision. Pressured by Olivia, she will commit suicide by taking poison, thus performing the death scene which, in Shakespeare's play, the Egyptian queen designs for herself. The assassination Luna ordered, however, leaves a political power vacuum in its wake, in which it is unclear who the next president is to be. In this interim, a battle breaks out between those vying for sovereignty comparable to the battle fought in a plethora of sites in the last two acts of *Antony and Cleopatra*. Fitz, displaying his own version of excellent falsehood, betrays Olivia by siding with her father, who is unwilling to relinquish his command over B613. Olivia, for her part, seeing this fraught election as her second chance at the Oval Office, is willing to do whatever is necessary, no matter the consequence, to claim the presidency for Mellie. The couple ultimately come together, however, in the final battle that Fitz and Olivia must fight against Cyrus and his peers in the Senate.

In the midst of these sustained conspiracies, Mellie emerges as an infinitely varied figure. We see her pouting when she cannot get her way and smiling radiantly when she does. A Rhodes Scholar, she is initially perceived as being too smart and aloof to be popular, yet once she shows herself willing to put her personal suffering on display, she proves her likeability. She can be rambunctious, as when she begins dancing in Olivia's office, once it becomes clear that she will most likely be POTUS 45, forcing her fixer to reluctantly join in.[53] Yet her trusted advisor, the African American Marcus, who joined her husband in the White House after having been part of Olivia's firm, repeatedly reminds her and her peers that she is a leader; clear-headed, patient, and exacting. Mellie is, however, also positioned as an onlooker to the clandestine power network run by Olivia and Fitz, and although she is not in charge, she will be implicated by the consequences of the actions they undertake. When she sits at her desk in the Oval Office, her symbolic embodiment of the presidency thus serves as a counter-image to the rogue couple operating inside her administration, from the basement space which had once been Franklin D. Roosevelt's swimming pool.

That Mellie, though above board, is everything but innocent is anticipated in the scene showing her alone in her office while watching a broadcast on TV of the Electoral College, about to appoint her as the next president of the United States. Once she is sure that the tally is in her favour, she gets up to look at herself in a mirror, as though gauging whether she looks the part. As her gaze travels to her face, she notices a streak of blood on her chin. Minutes earlier she had been forced to witness two of Luna's agents kill one of her adversaries to make her recognise the secret power that made her election possible. It remains unclear whether the dismay she evinces at seeing this trace of blood pertains to the fact that she is now an accessory to this particular crime, or to the fact that her entire claim to the presidency is tainted.[54] Indeed, precisely because she is implicated in conspiracies not of her making, her reign remains endangered. Although Eli Pope is able to stop the sniper who takes aim at her during her inauguration, the fact that she must be saved further illustrates not only the fragility of the Republic but also the fallibility of her position as its official leader.

At the same time, Mellie's conquest of the Oval Office, with Olivia as her chief of staff, rewrites the defeat Cleopatra imagines for herself at the hands of Octavius and his victorious Roman army. *Scandal* asks us to imagine, what if the 'foul Egyptian', having joined forces with her Roman counter-image, Fulvia, and vanquished their opponents together, assumes a Janus-faced rule? The telling feminist transformation that this TV drama offers is that in this portrait of the *first* female president as an interracial, same-sex couple, both women deserve but also depend on each other. If Mellie is the public face of this presidency, Olivia is its rogue lining. To consolidate this double body of female countersovereignty, she gets Mellie to sign an executive order re-installing B613, with her, finally, in command. Drawing into focus the slipperiness of power relations, 'Transfer of Power' ends with Olivia sitting on the steps of the Lincoln Memorial, drinking from a bottle of expensive red wine with Cyrus.[55] In the most devious boundary shifts in this TV drama, a pact is made between these two rivals. Olivia, realising it was he who planted the idea of the assassination in Luna's head, promises to give him the VP position he had hoped to gain by this move. He, in turn, realising that Mellie has, by virtue of her executive order, made Olivia the true commander-in-chief, calls her, in yet another virtual interpellation, the most powerful person in the world. Neither feels jubilatory at this moment, only justified. The last shot captures them from behind, frozen in their pose, looking out at a nocturnally lit Washington Monument.

As though the spirit of Octavius had been reawakened in the final season of *Scandal*, Cyrus spearheads an investigation in Congress, hoping for an impeachment of the first female president so that he can assume what he believes to be his rightful position in the White House. While his efforts initially show signs of success in so far as a rift opens up between Mellie and her chief of staff, when Olivia announces her resignation in the episode 'Army of One', she reconfirms their bond, listing what she and Mellie have achieved, while praising her as a leader with vision and courage later on.[56] Her loyalty to dismantling the patriarchal gang of male politicians who, once again, seem to gain the upper hand remains part of her idiosyncratic feminist vision of politics. Once Mellie, in turn, realises that she cannot stand up against Cyrus alone, Olivia will, again, become her command in what the two women see as a war against both of them, the Oval Office, and democracy. Jake Ballard, who has served as Eli Pope's henchman throughout the show, emerges as part of the newly regrouped male counter-alliance, hoping for a pre-emptive strike against Olivia, whose power he has grown to resent. Cyrus, however, overconfident that his less overt conspiracy will be significantly more effective, assures him, 'we have the chessboard set up exactly the way we want it. The queen is in check, impeachment is nigh', adding that the president 'is a prisoner in her own house'.[57]

Yet Mellie, cornered in the Oval Office, much like the Egyptian queen in her mausoleum, offers a histrionic self-performance that welds sexual allure with regal haughtiness worthy of Cleopatra. In 'People Like Me', aware of the surveillance camera planted in the ceiling, she leaves her desk, a glass of gin in her hand.[58] Having begun her monologue, she takes off her shoes, coyly climbs on to a couch, then glides back to the floor and circles around the seal on the rug in front of it. All the while she speaks directly into the camera, taunting the man who is surveilling her. She disdainfully calls Jake a man easily duped by each of the masters he has chosen to follow, even while assuring him of her supreme domination. The reverse shots reveal how her monologue, which ends in the threat that she is coming after him, does, indeed, rattle him.

Contrary to Cyrus's prediction, what is nigh is not Mellie's downfall but rather a move beyond the revenge tragedy he is leading. In the face of their imminent appearance before the Senate Select Committee investigating B613, the political remarriage between this first female president and her double is emphatically reaffirmed. In their last meeting in the basement beneath the White House, Olivia urges Mellie that they should not adopt violent means just because this has been the way the men who have been leading the country since its inception have operated.[59] If refusing to continue in this vein means being more just, then putting an end to the serial politics of illicit violence *Scandal* has drawn into focus requires, as she argues, a further change in the scenario: 'the only way we can win this is if our bond is stronger than theirs. If we hold fast together no matter what comes.' In a moment of mutual acknowledgement, each woman assures the other that she is with her. For a moment the camera catches the two women in a close-up, nodding silently to each other. Then, though still facing each other, they look past each other in opposite directions, visually reunited as the Janus face of female countersovereignty.

In the ensuing discussion with Fitz, they will, indeed, seek to stop the repetition compulsion of serial violence on which both presidencies were predicated. They have gained a moral insight into the consequences of their actions and, like Elizabeth Keane in *Homeland*, they are willing to take responsibility for the Republic by acknowledging the rogue nature of their rule. In their case, however, to stop and to see emerges as an ingenious chess move, meant to checkmate their mutual adversary. Any cover-up of their clandestine network, while protecting their legacy, would enable Cyrus; their willingness to go over the cliff, in turn, will take him down as well. Dramaturgically, the move beyond tragedy,

Figure 11 The Janus face of female countersovereignty: Mellie Grant and Olivia Pope

however, requires a *deus ex machina*, which banks on yet another outing of a rogue.[60] Unexpectedly, Eli Pope is called as a witness and, while admitting that he created the clandestine agency, he proceeds to accuse the white men sitting on the Senate Select Committee of a complacency that left the Republic in a state of neglect. After these legitimate representatives of the demos proceed to point him out as having played by rules that are outside those of the community, namely terrorist activity, election rigging, and assassination, he responds by listing how his rogue rule was, in fact, an organised force that has been part of American democracy for the past thirty years.

In a monologue that turns the courtroom into a stage where he is fully in command, Eli brazenly takes responsibility for 'every decision to go to war, every president sitting in office, every soldier brought home in a casket', only to add, 'I kept the stock market afloat, the dollar where it needs to be, our shores at peace. I am responsible for the fact that this nation still stands. I wake up every morning and I make America great. That is my legacy.' Yet in his rhetorical finish, delivered with a self-confident twinkle in his eye, he defies them to make public 'that a black man has been running the country', while all the white men only wield their power 'because his black power allows them to'. The wink to the president of the Senate Select Committee that accompanies his closing words, 'God bless America', serves to underscore the quandary facing them. Fully aware that they cannot expose a secret to the public that will debunk their own power, he offers as proxy his surrogate son. Jake Ballard is subsequently arrested as commander of B613, tried, and sentenced to prison. With the shadow government shut down, so, too, is all talk of impeaching President Mellie Grant. When Cyrus is called to the Oval Office, it is not her he finds holding his letter of resignation. Instead, Olivia stands in front of her desk, handing him the document he has no other choice but to sign. This will have been her last act as chief of staff. Along with the shuttering of B613, the unofficial face of this dual feminine rule, complementing its official face, must also be dissolved. The couple can now part on amicable terms. As Olivia explains to Mellie, sitting on the balcony behind the White House, they no longer need each other.

The final montage sequence strings together vignettes of restitution that celebrate the move beyond a fascination with the illegitimate, the clandestine, and the rogue on which this TV drama has thrived, and, with it, a move beyond tragedy. Two African American girls walk past the paintings of former white male presidents. Interpolated into their passage through the National Portrait Gallery are brief scenes showing how life will go on for the key players of *Scandal*: Olivia walks past the White House in flamboyant strides. Mellie, having just signed a new law, poses for the news cameras in the Oval Office with her new partner, Marcus, by her side. Fitz helps unveil his own presidential portrait. Olivia has dinner with Eli in his home. Then we see Fitz, stopping Olivia on a street in the Washington Mall. The open door of his car indicates the second mixed-race couple to be reunited. Then the sequence returns one last time to the two girls in the gallery, who have now stopped in front of a portrait of Olivia. Whether it is hanging next to all the other commanders-in-chief or in a room apart is left undecided. The words 'we the People' running along the right-hand side, however, recall Cleopatra's final self-creation as a myth. If the closing scene in *Antony and Cleopatra* celebrates her eternal remarriage beyond self-sacrifice, *Scandal* also ends with a commemorative representation of its heroine, not her marble-constant corpse, but a close-up of her face in a painting, asserting her marriage with the demos.

As Gérard Wajcman suggests, if history takes shape only in the stories which a culture chooses to tell about itself, then contemporary TV drama can be conceived as a symptom, giving shape to the ambitions and hopes but also the malaise currently preoccupying America as a nation. In contrast to other storytelling, however, in this new media format, the narrative no longer sets in when a crisis disturbs an initially calm world, only to produce a new situation of serenity once the crisis has been resolved. Specific to contemporary TV drama is, instead, that its serial narratives move from one crisis to the next. The world depicted, thus Wajcman's claim, 'shows the world of the crisis in series. The crisis is serial, the serial drama is its aesthetic form.'[61] If, then, seriality is a particularly adequate aesthetic form to articulate the worries and the fantasies that contemporary culture harbours, each of the TV dramas discussed in this chapter self-consciously deploys this mode of narration as a comment on the crisis that a *first* female president poses. Each of the women in the Oval Office needs a sequence of crises to prove something – be it resilience in the face of failure, moral strength in the midst of domestic insurrection, or a consorted effort to defy male detractors. The resolutions that each serial drama comes up with vary. *Veep* ends by staging Selina Meyer's incorrigible compulsion to repeat her blind self-absorption. *Homeland* imagines an inspired ceremony of resignation for Elizabeth Keane as she takes a deep breath after finishing her address to the nation. *Scandal* finds closure with a string of images that put official politics on Mellie Grant's side and personal self-fulfilment on Olivia Pope's. In dialogue with each other, their stories about what it means for ambitious women to want and to execute power offer a serial response to a cultural malaise, which remains a question of unfinished business.

## Notes

1 Jacques Derrida, *Rogues. Two Essays on Reason* (Stanford: Stanford University Press, 2005), p. 63.
2 Derrida, *Rogues*, p. 64.
3 Derrida, *Rogues*, p. 67.
4 In comparison to Jed Bartlet in *The West Wing*, whom they see as the earlier television president with integrity, Kaklamanidou and Tally see Olivia Pope as a warrior and Selina Meyer as a frustrated striver as two of the multi-faceted female characters dominating the contemporary political world of TV drama, *Politics and Politicians*, p. 25 and p. 125. Another important distinction is that the serial dramas discussed in this chapter feed on the suspicion towards Washington, as discussed in Chapter 3. *The West Wing* served to restore a trust in politics after Nixon and Watergate by casting Jed Bartlet as an unequivocal embodiment of civil religion, and, as such, as an example for a moral compass regained. The climate of mistrust that began after 9/11 under George W. Bush and continued through the Obama administration into that of Trump is reflected in this return of rogue politicians. Though Elizabeth McCord is less unambiguous, her transition into the Oval Office in the final season of *Madam Secretary* (CBS 2014–19), in turn, speaks to a different political sentimentality, namely the desire for the return of trust in the presidency.
5 Though initially, Elizabeth McCord has no ambition to become a first female president herself, and only decides to run in the fifth season, *Madam Secretary*, from the start, not only recalls the political level-headedness displayed by Mac Allen in *Commander in Chief*. As noted in Chapter 3, this TV drama also uses a similar episodic emergence of crises as narrative proof of her skilful command while repeatedly overcoming all obstacles. The show's focus on a heroine who advises the president on critical issues of foreign affairs, in turn, is paralleled

by the figure of Charleston Whitney Tucker, who briefs the president daily on vital security issues in the TV drama *State of Affairs* (NBC 2014). Given that President Constance Payton is also the first black woman to be elected, she can be seen in dialogue with the far more ruthless Olivia Pope in *Scandal*, who insists that she, too, is entitled to the Oval Office. In the second season of *Quantico* (ABC 2015–18), the first female president, Claire Haas, ultimately calls off an air strike in a hostage situation because she is not willing to act like every male president who came before her. This dramaturgic twist suggests another resurgence of the exploration of an independent female sovereignty already rehearsed in *Commander in Chief*.

6 Stanley Cavell, *Pursuits of Happiness. The Hollywood Comedy of Remarriage* (Cambridge, MA: Harvard University Press, 1981), p. 145. See also Elisabeth Bronfen, 'Rethinking Genre Memory', in Hunter Vaughan and Tom Conley (eds), *The Anthem Handbook of Screen Theory* (London: Anthem Press, 2018), pp. 193–208.

7 In the eight shows discussed in Chapters 3 and 4, four female presidents are compelled to resign, four are able to move into this position only because of the premature death or resignation of the president, only two are actually elected by the people, and one is elected only after two prior attempts have failed.

8 See Chapter 2 in Sigmund Freud, *Beyond the Pleasure Principle* (1920), *The Standard Edition*, volume XVIII (London: Hogarth Press, 1955), pp. 12–17.

9 *Veep*, 'Frozen Yoghurt', season 1, episode 2, dir. Armando Iannucci, writ. Armando Iannucci and Simon Blackwell, m22.40 (HBO 2012).

10 As Marc Edward Shaw puts it, 'she is weighed down with the desire to have the crown upon her head', isolating this scene as a salient example for the tragicomic tone informing Iannucci's political satire, *Politics and Politicians*, p. 144.

11 For a discussion of the term, see Pierre Bourdieu, *Habitus and Field. General Sociology, Volume 2. Lectures at the collège de France 1982–1983* (London: Polity Press, 2019).

12 Joe Conway, coining the term 'satire verité', suggests in 'After Politics/After Television: *Veep*, Digimodernism, and the Running Gag of Government', *Studies in American Humor*, 2 (2016), that as serial drama, revealing to us behind-the-curtain politics, *Veep* can be positioned between *The West Wing*, with its professionally and morally competent backstage team of political players, and *House of Cards*, in which the Shakespearean asides of both Frank and Claire Underwood foreground self-interest, self-advancement, and a more sinister mode of image-making, pp. 182–207.

13 William Shakespeare, *A Midsummer Night's Dream*, Sukanta Chaudhuri (ed.), *The Arden Shakespeare*, third series (London: Bloomsbury, 2017), 2.1.63.

14 Shakespeare, *Midsummer*, 2.1.140–2.

15 Shakespeare, *Midsummer*, 2.1.258.

16 Shakespeare, *Midsummer*, 2.2.38.

17 Shakespeare, *Midsummer*, 1.1.122.

18 The linguistic transgression and extensive use of tabooed language that Dorothea Will discusses in her article suggest a further connection to the bawdy language in Shakespeare's comedy; see 'The Human Face of Politics? Political Representations, Power Structures and Gender Limitations in HBO's Political

Comedy Veep', in Birgit Däwes, Alexandra Ganser, and Nicole Poppenhagen (eds), *Transgressive Television. Politics and Crime in 21st-Century American TV Series* (Heidelberg: Universitätsverlag Winter, 2015), pp. 127–41.

19 The fine line between tyrannical conspiracy and comedy's scapegoating is most visibly at issue in 'Testimony', where Selina and her team appear before the House Judiciary Committee to explain the lobbying in Congress against her own Families First Bill, and, to save their skin, they all collude to designate Bill Ericsson as their fall guy; *Veep*, season 4, episode 22, dir. Armando Iannucci, writ. Sean Gray and Will Smith (HBO 2015).

20 *Veep*, 'Inauguration', season 5, episode 10, dir. Becky Martin, writ. Jim Margolis, m26 (HBO 2016).

21 See Stanley Cavell, 'The Avoidance of Love: A Reading of King Lear', *Disowning Knowledge. In Seven Plays of Shakespeare*, updated edition (Cambridge, Cambridge University Press, 2003), p. 81.

22 *Veep*, season 7, episode 7, dir. David Mandel, writ. David Mandel, m50 (HBO 2019).

23 *Homeland*, season 7, all episodes, m2.30 (Showtime 2018). See Matthew Dessem, 'Hillary Clinton Talks with Trevor Noah about Trump, Weinstein, and People Who Wish She'd Go Away', *Slate*, 2 November 2017.

24 Emily Nussbaum, '"Homeland": An Antidote for "24"', *New Yorker*, 29 November 2011.

25 Lindsay Steenberg and Yvonne Tasker argue for a symbolic dichotomy between the Bush administration's *24* and *Homeland* as a reflection on the Obama administration regarding issues of national security and an inherited war on terror, '"Pledge Allegiance": Gendered Surveillance, Crime Television, and Homeland', *Cinema Journal*, 54:4 (2015), p. 138. See also James Castonguay, 'Fictions of Terror: Complexity, Complicity and Insecurity in Homeland', who, in the same issue, sees *Homeland* less as an antidote, exorcising the ghosts of *24*, and instead as reflecting the Obama administration's continuation of a Cold War paranoid style of politics; pp. 139–42.

26 As Patricia-Ann Lee, 'Reflections of Power: Margaret of Anjou and the Dark Side of Queenship', *Renaissance Quarterly* 39:2 (1986), pp. 183–217, suggests, if, faced with the weakness of her husband, Queen Margaret came to be regarded as the leader of the royal party, the negative queenship attributed to her by historians subsequently recording the Wars of the Roses may have been Yorkist propaganda. By the time Shakespeare wrote his history plays, however, this also served as a contrast to the 'royal icon of triumphant and compelling brilliance' of Elizabeth I, p. 217. One the one hand, his portrait of Queen Margaret as a less acceptable form of feminine power was possible because it belonged to the historical past. On the other hand, as an example for illegitimate queenship, it also, albeit obliquely, addressed the anxieties about the Tudor queen's rule.

27 William Shakespeare, *King Henry VI. Part 2*, Ronald Knowles (ed.), *The Arden Shakespeare* (London: Bloomsbury, 2004), 1.3.49.

28 Shakespeare, *King Henry VI. Part 2*, 5.1.117–18.

29 William Shakespeare, *King Henry VI. Part 3*, John D. Cox and Eric Rasmussen (eds), *The Arden Shakespeare* (London: Bloomsbury 2001), 1.4.82–3.

30 Shakespeare, *King Henry VI. Part 3*, 1.4.107.

31 Shakespeare, *King Henry VI. Part 3*, 1.4.140–1.
32 In *House of Cards*, this pathos gesture is refigured as well, when, in the final scene of the TV drama, Claire, kneeling in front of her desk in the Oval Office, stabs her husband's murderer, Doug Stamper, to eliminate her last adversary.
33 *Homeland*, season 6, episode 12, dir. Lesli Linka Glatter, writ. Alex Gansa and Ron Nyswaner (Showtime 2017). Genre memory is at work in that this closing shot recalls Mac Allen, who, in *Commander in Chief*, is repeatedly shown returning to her desk to figure out how to deal with yet another crisis, as well as Allison Taylor, sitting in the Oval Office alone, waiting to hear how the unfolding crisis is playing itself out. It can also be seen in dialog with the emblem of Selina Meyer at her desk, at the end of each opening sequence of *Veep*.
34 *Homeland*, season 7, episode 12, dir. Lesli Linka Glatter, writ. Alex Gansa, m39 (Showtime 2018).
35 *Homeland*, 'Paean to the People', m44.
36 See Elisabeth R. Anker, *Orgies of Feeling. Melodrama and the Politics of Freedom* (Durham, NC: Duke University Press, 2014). See also Diane Negra and Jorie Lagerwey's discussion of the female centrality in *Homeland*'s presentation of debates 'around the securitization of American life' in 'Analyzing *Homeland*: Introduction', *Cinema Journal*, 54:4 (2015), p. 131.
37 William Shakespeare, *Richard III*, James R. Siemon (ed.), *The Arden Shakespeare*, third series (London: Bloomsbury, 2009), 4.4.105, 4.4.115, and 119–22.
38 *Homeland*, 'Paean to the People', m50.30.
39 Shakespeare, *Richard III*, 5.5.35–9.
40 Cavell, 'Avoidance of Love', p. 81.
41 Jyotsyna Singh, 'Renaissance Anti-theatricality, Anti-feminism, and Shakespeare's "Antony and Cleopatra"', in John Drakakis (ed.), *New Casebooks Antony and Cleopatra* (Houndmills, Palgrave Macmillan, 1994), p. 309. See also Katherine Eggert, *Showing Like a Queen*, who suggests that she transmutes '"feminine" moodiness from a simple spell of changeability into a complex act of re-creation', p. 149.
42 William Shakespeare, *Antony and Cleopatra*, John Wilders (ed.), *The Arden Shakespeare*, third series (London: Bloomsbury, 1995), 5.2.286.
43 Shakespeare, *Antony and Cleopatra*, 5.2.335, 5.2.345–7, and 5.2.357–9.
44 See Jonathan Dollimore, *Radical Tragedy. Religion, Ideology and Power in the Drama of Shakespeare and his Contemporaries*, reissued third edition (Houndmills, Palgrave Macmillan, 2010).
45 William Shakespeare, *Antony and Cleopatra*, John Wilders (ed.), *The Arden Shakespeare*, third series (London: Bloomsbury, 1995), 1.5.28–30.
46 Anita Loomba, 'Theatre and the Space of the Other', in Drakakis, *New Casebooks*, p. 288. Loomba also suggests that Shakespeare may have imagined Cleopatra as dark in association with mystery and sexual lasciviousness, but, given her Greek descent and the fact that Ancient Greece was ethnically diverse, it is, in fact, not clear what 'black' in this play means, *Shakespeare, Race, & Colonialism* (Oxford: Oxford University Press, 2002).
47 Shakespeare, *Antony and Cleopatra*, 1.3.66. See Barbara J. Baines, 'Girard's Double and *Antony and Cleopatra*', in Nigel Wood (ed.), *Antony and Cleopatra* (Buckingham: Open University Press, 1996), pp. 26–7.

48 See Simone Puff, 'Another Scandal in Washington: How a Transgressive, Black Anti-Heroine Makes for New "Quality TV"', in Däwes, Ganser, and Poppenhagen (eds), *Transgressive Television*, pp. 103–26.
49 *Scandal*, 'Get Out of Jail, Free', season 5, episode 6, dir. Chandra Wilson, writ. Chris Van Dusen, m21 (ABC 2015).
50 Janet Adelman, *The Common Liar. An Essay on Antony and Cleopatra* (New Haven: Yale University Press, 1973), p. 49.
51 Adelman, *Common Liar*, p. 52. Regarding the infinite variety of dramatic perspective, Linda Charnes notes that more than any other Shakespeare play, *Antony and Cleopatra* is filled with messengers and reporters from a panoply of locations. See *Notorious Identity. Materializing the Subject in Shakespeare* (Cambridge, MA: Harvard University Press, 1993).
52 Derrida, *Rogues*, p. 66. See also Patrick Jones and Gretchen Soderlung, 'The Conspiratorial Mode in American Television: Politics, Public Relations, and Journalism in *House of Cards* and *Scandal*', *American Quarterly*, 69:4 (2017), pp. 833–56.
53 *Scandal*, 'The Belt', season 6, episode 4, dir. Tom Verica, writ. Paul William Davies, m2.30 (ABC 2017)
54 *Scandal*, 'Trojan Horse', season 6, episode 11, dir. Jann Turner, writ. Jess Brownell and Nicholas Nardini, m42.10 (ABC 2017).
55 *Scandal*, season 6, episode 16, dir. Tony Goldwyn, writ. Matt Byrne and Mark Fish, m 41 (ABC 2017). As Christopher J. Gilbert argues in 'Return of the Ridiculous, or Caricature as Political Cliché', *Communication, Culture and Critique*, 7 (2014), by staging post-truth politics, shows like *Scandal* produce what he calls an uncanny viewing effect. By disclosing public figures as supposed puppet masters, they do not efface political reality. Instead, they efface the distinction between this reality and imaginations of a politics of post-truths.
56 *Scandal*, season 7, episode 11, dir. Allison Liddi-Brown, writ. Austin Guzman, m39 (ABC 2018).
57 *Scandal*, 'People Like Me', season 7, episode 16, dir. Joe Morton, writ. Chris Van Dusen, m2.40 (ABC 2018).
58 *Scandal*, 'People Like Me', m16.33 (ABC 2018).
59 *Scandal*, 'People Like Me', m34 (ABC 2018).
60 *Scandal*, 'Over a Cliff', season 7, episode 18, dir. Tom Verica, writ. Shonda Rhimes, m30 (ABC 2018).
61 Gérard Wajcman, *Les séries, le monde, la crise, les femmes* (Paris: Verdier, 2018), p. 25, translation by the author.

# 5
# All the frontier's a stage: *Deadwood*

### Doest thou know Dover

In the third and last season of *Deadwood*, Jack Langrishe, who has been touring the frontier between Denver and San Francisco with his theatre company, appears in the gold-rush town Deadwood. While he is soon able to begin the refurbishment of a former brothel, he keeps postponing the opening night of the theatre because one of his actors is fatally ill. Chesterton, who upon being carried out of the stagecoach had confided in him that this would be his last camp, nevertheless wants to see the place where he knows he will never perform, and so, one evening, he is conducted there in a wheelchair. The scene, lit only by a kerosene lamp, begins with Jack sitting next to the dying man in the front row of the auditorium, holding his right hand. Invoking for him what the stage will look like, he tells him that the names Thalia and Melpomene, the Ancient Greek muses of comedy and tragedy, have been embroidered in gold on the tabs of the curtain. Chesterton responds by calling the masks a big lie, only to add, 'Same damn thing, Jack, comedy and tragedy.'[1] This is one of several self-reflexive moments in this nocturnal conversation between the two actors. As I am going to show in this chapter, Shakespeare's implicit re-surfacing throughout David Milch's TV drama is predicated on a blurring of these two genres.

Once Jack has called upon his friend (both minor characters in the show) to imagine that the curtain rises and the stage is set before them, the camera, as though to support the spectral performance he is about to undertake, briefly moves to a shot that captures the two men from behind. Then it returns to the previous alternation between close-ups of the two men, with rack-focus shots sustained throughout the scene. After a brief pause, Jack begins to speak the words the blinded Gloucester addresses to Poor Tom in *King Lear*: 'Doest thou know Dover'.[2] Attentively watching his partner, Jack adds, 'there is a cliff whose high unbending head looks fearfully on the confined deep. Bring me back to the brim of it and from that place I shall no leading need', abbreviating the original text slightly.[3] In Shakespeare's tragedy, the desperate man, not realising he is speaking to his disguised son, Edgar, wants to throw himself off that cliff. Jack, banking on an analogous desire for death on the part of his friend, yet nervous whether he will take the bait, momentarily moves into an improvisation pertaining to what he should do while mounting. The dying man, however, initially remains almost immobile, staring silently at the floor, so that Jack, unnerved, is close to abandoning his role completely.

Then, finally willing to adapt Shakespeare's words to his own situation, Chesterton jumps to the next scene in *King Lear* in which these two characters appear and quietly asserts, '[h]ere's the place'. Jack, astonished and relieved, finishes for him the passage in which Edgar pretends to his father that they are standing above an abyss: 'How fearful and dizzy it is to cast one's eyes so low'. More befitting the part he is playing in this eerie dialogue, Chesterton, in turn, slips into the role of Gloucester, about to jump. Condensing his lines, he whispers, 'Set me where you stand. Let go my hand.'[4] If, in this theatre in the real, Jack had used Shakespeare to gently prod his friend onwards in his passage from life to death, he, at this point, indeed cautiously removes his hand. Having recourse once more to Edgar's words, yet also speaking as the one directing the old actor, he assures him, 'you are now within a foot'. In other words, while, in this macabre performance, the theatre director can seamlessly move between the role of the blind father and that of the disguised son, at the moment of his death, Chesterton has become completely identical with his dramatic part. The word 'line', uttered twice, is the last thing he will say, as though, for this actor, not knowing the rest of the script were tantamount to having come to the end of his life. Being alive and playing a part are shown to be inextricably entwined.

Chesterton has, of course, revised the Shakespearean text. While, in the tragedy, Gloucester survives his jump, his words have been severed from the original and repurposed to provide the old actor with an exit in keeping with *Deadwood*'s most prominent debt to Shakespeare, namely his serial engagement with the world as theatre. Chesterton has, indeed, leapt to a death long desired. Frozen in his last role, his corpse remains seated upright on the chair while the other members of the troupe suddenly appear out of the darkness from where they had been watching this scene. The magic suspension of disbelief has been interrupted, and, exhausted by his efforts, Jack, declaiming the Lord's Prayer, puts an end to his own role-playing while his friends assure him that they will now see to the body of the dead man.

Jack's choice of this particular tragedy, however, has yet a further self-referential purpose in this scene. In Shakespeare's tragedy, the old king's decision to divide his kingdom among his two daughters, Goneril and

Regan, results in an interregnum marked by lawlessness and civil war, at the end of which a new political order under the sovereignty of the King of France will begin.⁵ The gold-rush town where Jack is about to open his theatre is also in a state of interregnum, and throughout the three seasons of this serial drama, those in power forge ever-shifting alliances in a world where there is no law at all. Built on Sioux territory, Deadwood is not only an illegal settlement but also considered to be outside the jurisdiction of any laws made in Washington. At the same time, because the government has just signed a treaty with the Sioux, they have given up their claim on these hills, and a competition between Montana and Nebraska has erupted as to who will annex this territory. Throughout the three seasons of *Deadwood*, the transformation of the camp town into a community is accompanied by the impending change in governance once, having gained statehood, they, too, will have joined America. Jack's private performance of the fourth act of *King Lear*, anticipating the end of disorder (albeit at the price of the extinction of the king's entire lineage), thus mirrors and reflects on the historical moment of transition in which the many storylines of Milch's serial drama are positioned. The semi-regulated lawlessness prevailing in the camp town Deadwood at the beginning of the TV drama will also come to an end.

While we never see the Langrishe troupe perform on the stage inside the theatre, Jack does put on an amateur night outside, explicitly in memoriam of the passing of his colleague. He opens the display of talent by the townspeople with what he claims was Chesterton's favourite epithet, 'all the world's a stage, and all the men and women merely players', only to finish by invoking a seminal reversal of roles: 'Tonight, we will be the audience to you'.⁶ While the fact that the theatre people never perform can, as Paul Stasi and Jennifer Greiman note, be seen as a subversion of the Shakespearean trope of the play-within-the-play, it also points to the way that not only the show *Deadwood* but also the eponymous town are, from the start, permeated with theatre. Indeed, 'putting the theatre of the camp on an actual stage makes explicit what is already implicit in its theatrical relations'.⁷ As will be developed in more detail in this chapter, what happens on the thoroughfare, in the public spaces, and in the private rooms is not just conceived as a plethora of scenes in a serial chamber drama. Rather, what the interweaving of diverse storylines draws into focus is that the town Deadwood is a stage, where everyone is merely a player in the larger political forces drawing this lawless territory into the Union.

Though they never actually quote Shakespeare, the cast of characters at the heart of this serial TV drama, in a manner deeply indebted to his trope of the world as stage, interact and deliberate on how they might act, and comment on actions that have occurred or actions they anticipate as happening. If, as Alexa Huang and Elizabeth Rivlin suggest, 'the affiliations between "act" and "acting" underscore the point that the theatre stages ethics', part of the debt to Shakespeare also entails thinking of Milch's serial drama as taking on his discovery of theatricality as one of the most effective instruments of power.[8] In the course of the three seasons, the town of Deadwood emerges as a medial space where, caught up in shifting constellations, its characters pit their deliberations regarding the degree of freedom and agency available to them against the equally histrionic assertion of political authority, with the roles they play in part sustaining and in part subverting this power.

It has, of course, not only become a critical commonplace to call *Deadwood* a Shakespearean western, but also to locate its influence primarily in the language spoken by the characters.[9] David Milch himself has pointed out that while his characters generally use language that is not their own but rather gleaned from their reading, their historical counterparts would, if they had any learning at the time, have read a lot of Shakespeare.[10] It is also useful to recall that the presence of the Bard in frontier literature has a long tradition. Both James Fenimore Cooper in his *Leatherstocking Tales* and Catharine Maria Sedgwick in her novel *Hope Leslie* privilege quotations from his plays as their chapter mottos, suggesting Shakespeare's quotes to be the common cultural reference for readers interested in novels about the frontier.[11] At the same time, the way in which *Deadwood* repeatedly layers the theatricality of Shakespearean dialogues and soliloquies on to recognisable plot motifs of the western genre also recalls a similar rhetorical move in John Ford's classic western films, where characters repeatedly recite famous speeches from Shakespeare's plays.[12]

It is a particular scene in *My Darling Clementine*, however, which Jack Langrishe's appropriation of bits and pieces of dialogue from *King Lear* most clearly references.[13] A British travelling actor, Granville Thorndyke, who is meant to perform in the Birdcage Theatre in Tombstone, has failed to show up. The marshal, Wyatt Earp, who has gone in search of him, finds him standing on a table in the saloon, reciting Hamlet's monologue, 'To be or not to be'. Doc Holliday, of whom it is said that he has left his mark in Deadwood, has accompanied his friend and, drawn by the recitation, is able to intervene when raucous members of the audience try to put an end to a performance they find tedious. Although he renews his recitation, Thorndyke, admitting it is a long time since he last played this role, has forgotten the remaining lines of the monologue and asks Doc to carry on for him. Seamlessly, the gambler picks up where the other man left off, speaking with great intensity about death as the undiscovered country, until, having reached the moment when Hamlet claims that conscience makes cowards of us all, his cough prevents him, too, from finishing. With Jack Langrishe's nocturnal performance in the dimly lit theatre in *Deadwood* in mind, we note a similar movement of the Shakespearean text from one speaker to the next, with the one picking up where the other left off, to signal that this is the language they share. One might also note that both in Ford's film and in Milch's TV drama, the actors are also not able to finish their recitation.

If, as Peter Babiak argues, allusions to Shakespeare are integral to John Ford's vision of the frontier because they point to the imminent transformation of this lawless world into a part of the nation, this is applicable as well to the overarching narrative situation in which Jack's own explicit citation of Shakespeare is embedded. Like Doc's reference to the undiscovered country of death, Chesterton's passage from life also serves as a parallel to the way a particular feudal form of governance is about to end. The fact that his death is followed by an amateur night, furthermore, anticipates that the ordinary business of the town will continue, albeit in a somewhat more democratic manner. It is, after all, by popular vote that the political leaders of the town will be legally installed for the first time as a result of the elections in the last episode of this serial TV drama.[14] As David Milch claims, 'we are at our best, I think, as people, when that benign impulse towards community expresses itself in the impulse for order'.[15] The density of the language, enmeshing the ornate lofty speech of the 'high' with the profanity of the 'low', which critics have consistently seen as the key feature of *Deadwood*'s debt to Shakespeare, thus itself speaks to the relationship between lawlessness and political order throughout the show's three seasons. The low registers pertain to the comic enjoyment gained from a carnivalesque inversion of hierarchies, as is evidenced by the proclivity to profanity and bawdy utterances. But it also applies to the violence with which the authority of the law imposes itself on both legitimate and unjustified subversion of this order, often also invoking crude and derogatory modes of expression.

By treating *Deadwood* as a serial chamber drama, which draws into focus the relation between power and theatricality during a period of political transition, this chapter will trace the spectral presence of Shakespeare over and beyond any direct citation. I am less concerned with the way we believe we hear Shakespeare in dialogues and monologues that are not actual quotations. Instead, what I propose to explore is the way we sense a Shakespearean dramaturgy even if there is no explicit reference to any of his plays. In his highly stylised re-enactment of a gold-rush town in South Dakota in the 1870s, Milch taps into similar constellations of power and subversion of authority we find in *Hamlet*, but also particularly in Shakespeare's problem plays, not least of all because in these, comedy and tragedy prove to be very much the same thing. My point, in other words, is that while the ornateness of the dialogues and monologues draws attention to the fact that his characters have recourse to someone else's language, when they deliberate on what action they should take or the consequences of actions already undertaken, they are also performing a script appropriated from the set of dramaturgic constellations that comprise Shakespeare's theatricalisation of power relations (itself an unhinging of temporalities). In the series of parallel storylines revolving over and again around dramatic crisis and resolutions, they act, and interact, like Shakespearean characters, although – in contrast to Jack and his dying friend – they do so severed from any explicit reference to any one of his plays. Indeed, many of Milch's characters not only self-consciously undertake their dramatic actions as theatrical acts. In what might be thought of as the cut-and-paste technique of collage, some characters even appear to tap into the dramaturgic devices of several plays so that, in a thoroughly idiosyncratic condensation of Shakespearean elements, these come to be scattered and recombined over the entire three seasons.

Given the lack of fidelity in Milch's approach to appropriation, the question *Deadwood* raises thus also involves asking what it means to read this serial TV drama as a Shakespearean re-imagination of this particular historical moment of transition. The question at issue is not how an unfaithful adaptation such as *Deadwood* matches up with or deviates from the Shakespearean texts, and whether this is, indeed, really to be counted as Shakespeare – it is not, of course. Yet, because Shakespeare implicitly hovers over the entire TV drama, the discovering of dramaturgic correspondences instead raises questions pertaining to which particular elements in the Shakespearean oeuvre is *Deadwood* in relation, and in what relation? How does *Deadwood* reshape or extend our conception of what constitutes the essential dramatic aspects of the Shakespeare plays it can be shown to reuse? As Douglas Lanier puts it, 'In what ways does attributing the label "Shakespeare" to a particular work change the cultural formation that goes by the name "Shakespeare"'.[16] The question, thus, is not only what is gained by identifying *Deadwood* as a Shakespearean western but also how our understanding of the plays from which dramaturgic elements are appropriated, reassembled, and repurposed changes when we revisit them through the lens of this subsequent reworking.

In contrast to my discussion of *Westworld* in Chapter 1, this is not, however, a question of certain characters being unwittingly haunted by passages from Shakespeare's plays. Rather, if he is what Jack Langrishe explicitly draws on to help his friend die, it is more a question of taking possession again of a common text, accepting it as a shared legacy and as a gift. What, in turn, connects the two TV dramas is the way that, in both cases, Shakespeare is shown to write America at a critical foundational moment – in *Deadwood*, this involves the forging of a community about to achieve statehood; in *Westworld*, the creation of a new world of artificial humans modelled on a frontier town like Deadwood. While, in the latter show, this regeneration plays itself out as a correlation between violent desires and violent ends, in the former it takes the shape of a creative if ambivalent enmeshment of violence and the law.

Befitting Milch's decision to stage his historical re-imagination of Deadwood's gradual transformation into a community as a chamber drama, the dramatic action only rarely occurs in the Black Hills outside the camp town. In contrast to the classic western, we hardly ever see anyone riding through the open prairie, while the importance of the stagecoach is that it introduces new characters to the story. By primarily limiting the locations for the dramatic action to the thoroughfare and the houses lining it, *Deadwood* instead draws into focus the theatricality at play in the shifting constellations of power and its subversion. At the beginning of this serial TV drama, Al Swearengen, who founded the camp, is the sole sovereign in this lawless town, an orphan from Chicago, wanted there on murder charges. Yet legend has it that he is British nobility and, indeed, he rules like a feudal lord, holding court in his office on the first floor of the Gem saloon. His two loyal henchmen, Dan and Johnny, either stand behind those who have been granted an audience, or attentively watch from the bar below, deliberating on what is going on behind the locked door. To demonstrate his superiority, Al is often shown looking down over the balustrade outside his office at the saloon below. In an even more histrionic fashion, he also often stands on the balcony of the Gem, looking out over the thoroughfare to survey the business being conducted there. Indeed, the balcony is itself a stage-like setting, on which he makes declarations as if speaking a monologue.

When Cy Tolliver arrives in Deadwood to transform what had formerly been a hotel into a second saloon, he comports himself as a rival lord, as corrupt and violent as Al, and he, too, uses the balcony on the first floor of the Bella Union to put his own prominence on display. The third lord to arrive is the historical George Hearst, insatiable in his desire to transform his company into the largest private mining firm in America. To demonstrate that he is willing to take up both the political

Figure 12 Al Swearengen's balcony stage

and the theatrical challenge of his two rivals, he purchases the Grand Central Hotel and not only breaks down walls to produce his own headquarters for clandestine meetings; he also breaks a hole through the front of the building leading to a landing on the first floor so that, directly facing the Gem, he, too, can make his claim to a visual higher ground. Fully in line with the dramatic interplay between the high and the low in Shakespeare's comedies (and, as in these plays, supporting a subversion though never an obliteration of hierarchies), the thoroughfare below serves as the public space where all those characters deployed by these three lords in their power play interact. Intermittently emerging and then again disappearing from the field of vision of their superiors, they perform the parts that those standing above them, both literally and figuratively, command them to play. Yet part of the comic spirit ruling over the thoroughfare is that it proves to be the stage where, as Langrishe's amateur night amply puts on display, the less powerful characters can also showcase their talents by improvising.

The different locations below are all sites of passage where some characters not only put into question or even deviate from directions given to them from above. Much of their everyday dealings also falls outside the three lords' line of vision. On the thoroughfare and in the rooms in houses lining it, storylines take shape which, while influenced by the struggle between the three power brokers, are also independent of them. At the same time, the thoroughfare is a zone of diverse encounters, connecting the prostitutes to all the small shop owners of diverse ethnicities along with their wives and children, to the labourers and miners, as well as the Chinese immigrants living in Chink Alley. Thus, what *Deadwood* takes from Shakespeare's dramaturgy is not so much the carnivalesque logic of comedies like *A Midsummer Night's Dream* or *Twelfth Night*, in which, for a clearly limited period of time, official law is suspended, giving way to a play of transgressions.[17] Instead, making full use of the serial logic of TV drama, it draws on Shakespeare's combination of parallel storylines, where those involving characters deemed socially lower are used to mirror and comment on those revolving around their superiors. The dramatic traffic on and around the thoroughfare not only offers a counterpoint to the violence the three lords unleash, at times with tragic results. Because the overarching narrative of this serial TV drama privileges the perspective from below as much as the intrigues that come from above, what is forged is a diverse theatrical space, entangling a plethora of perspectives. The characters whose designated position is politically below may be impacted by the patriarchal power hierarchy ruling the town from above. In that the narrative, however, keeps oscillating between the top and the bottom, it also draws into focus that there is no one unequivocal centre. The actions that play themselves out below thus trouble (though never directly challenge) the political triumvirate not only because it is here that certain characters are shown to interfere with their authority. The parallel editing also puts into question the omnipotence of their visual regime.[18]

For yet another reason, Chesterton's claim that comedy and tragedy are the 'same damn thing' applies to the stage Deadwood offers up. In both theatrical genres, the dramatic action is performed in what is marked as a staged interim outside the ordinary every day. Both negotiate and play through concerns which, in the opening scenes, are shown to require a resolution of sorts. The difference, in turn, pertains to the question of whether a completely new order is about to begin, as is the case in Shakespeare's tragedies such as *King Lear* or *Hamlet*; or, whether the disruption of the political order which got the action going in the first place has come, once more, to be regulated, as is the case in his comedies. The distinction, of course, is always blurred. In Shakespeare's plays, comic elements are often inscribed into a tragic drive towards a violent end that will bring with it a new beginning, while comedy's return to the ordinary distribution of power invariably bears tragic traits. Applied to the narrative development over the three seasons of *Deadwood*, one might say that the annexation of the Dakota Territory corresponds with a new beginning, and yet this implies an end of precisely the lawlessness which makes the frontier so enticing in the cultural imaginary of

America. The benign impulse for order is tragic for all those whose creative if also violent vitality no longer has a place in the community it has forged. At the same time, in Milch's historical re-imagination of this period of transition, tragic nostalgia for a world which, in retrospect, we know will have ended meets comedy's hope. In this period of interregnum, everything is still possible. Characters can disappear from and return to this stage at will; they can even challenge and reconceive the roles imposed on them. They have been resuscitated from the past as figures working towards, and for, the future.

## Speaking with the dead

As Susan Cosby Ronnenberg points out, *Deadwood*'s persistent concern with themes of surveillance, deception, disconnection, and interpretation suggests parallels to *Hamlet* and *Much Ado About Nothing*, 'both of which focus on these same ideas but in very different ways given their respective genres of tragedy and comedy'.[19] Indeed, Al Swearengen has in Shakespeare's Danish prince a fitting analogue, but not, however, in his melancholic self-doubt regarding how to undermine his uncle, King Claudius, who he is convinced usurped his father's throne. Rather, what the original founder of Deadwood has inherited is Hamlet's deft use of theatre as an instrument of discovery and revenge. Like Hamlet, whose histrionic self-display stops neither at feigning madness nor at abusing his distraught beloved, Ophelia, when he thinks this will compel his adversaries to show their hand, Al self-consciously stages his sovereignty as an act meant not only to intimidate and manipulate others. The self-reliant prowess he exhibits publicly – when standing on his balcony, when striding down the stairs to the saloon, and on the rare occasion when he confronts people directly on the thoroughfare – is also meant to screen out the personal fallibilities he admits to in private.[20] Though he never lacks resolve, he, too, is constantly contemplating his next moves and evaluating possible options in dialogues with all those whom he has convinced to be the accomplices in his shady machinations. While action in theatre always encompasses speech-acts, as Ewan Fernie argues, in the case of Hamlet, 'his action is preconditioned, counterpointed, filled out by speech'.[21] For Al, one could make a similar claim, given that he, also, tends to exchange deeds for words. Though in the first episodes of *Deadwood*, the saloon owner is introduced as a man of excessive violent action, his verbal exchanges with all those under his command are evidence of an equally forceful linguistic action in its own right.

Furthermore, like Hamlet, who transforms Elsinore Castle into a stage where all the members of the court unwittingly play the part he has designated for them, Al also draws everyone into the drama of discovery and rivalry he has designed. In his case, however, it is a serial performance, meant not only to constantly reassert his power against all opponents who threaten it, but also to negotiate the terms most favourable to him regarding the impending political annexation. In Shakespeare's tragedy, Hamlet, to prove that what his father's ghost whispered to him was true, even convinces a troupe of travelling players to put on a play he calls 'The Mousetrap'. Because the plot is something like the murder of his father, he hopes that this performance will allow him 'to catch the conscience of the King'.[22] Al, in turn, is not only the one who directs all those around him in a script of his own devising, but also the one who repeatedly has the real stage director intervene as well. Jack Langrishe has been Al's friend since long before he arrives in the town. While *Deadwood* does not make use of an actual stage performance that publicly puts on display George Hearst's murderous intrigues, when the battle with him becomes acute, Al asks the theatre director to monitor his thinking. His advice is particularly useful, as Daniel Salerno puts it, owing to 'his facility with the complex moral questions of Shakespearean drama'.[23]

What both characters also share is the network of intermediaries they require to perform their drama of surveillance. In Shakespeare, Hamlet not only gathers his intelligence from the reports made by the sentinels but also uses his fellow student, Horatio, to observe his adversaries and report back to him about their activities. Al, in turn, has set up a complicated network of intelligence gathering and infiltration, which extends over the entire location of the camp town and beyond. His favourite prostitute, Trixie; the hotel manager, E.B. Farnum; and the ruler of Chink Alley, Wu, are his most trusted spies, engaging in clandestine encounters, eavesdropping on others, and then reporting back to him what is happening in places to which he has no direct access himself. While the fact that he needs these go-betweens draws into focus the limit of his visual regime, it also supports his position as director. Though his perspective on the unfolding of his drama of surveillance is restricted and his position of sovereignty decentred, standing on his balcony or sitting behind his desk in his office, Al is the figure around whom everything circles. The fact that he is not only the one who incites the dramatic action but also the one who must deal with the consequences once the performance is done is encapsulated in his most histrionic self-display. More often than not, Al is the one to scrub the bloodstains off the floor in his saloon.

The most sustained parallel between Al and Shakespeare's prince, however, is the idea that self-meditation is particularly encouraged in the face of death. After the gravedigger has pointed out the skull of the king's fool, Yorick, Hamlet addresses it while pondering how mortality puts into question all human action. Although the apostrophe to the dead man initially prompts his recollection of the happy childhood he shared with him, seeing him thus transformed soon makes Hamlet shudder. At the same time, the prince's words bring with them a performative magic. For a brief moment, he makes present again a man of whom there is nothing left but a skull. In *Deadwood*, Al, too, in a gesture of self-reckoning, speaks to a dead man – to be more precise, to the severed head of a Sioux chief, rotting away yet also preserved in the wooden box in which it is stored in his liquor cabinet. In contrast to Hamlet, however, Al does so repeatedly, so that these soliloquies produce an internal dramatic serialisation, which, by offering an insight into his intentions, underscore over and again his role as director. These soliloquies allow us to be privy to the decision making behind his drama of surveillance, revealing that this is also one of self-discovery in the face of impending danger. However, rather than breaking the fourth wall by speaking directly to the camera and making us his accomplices, Al instead justifies his actions to a dead man, whom he needs in order to formulate his thoughts before arriving at a particular decision.[24]

We learn that the head had initially been brought to Al by a bounty hunter. When he asks Johnny to get rid of it, the latter hesitates and, having inspected the head that is bundled up in a sackcloth bag, suggests that he might put it on display in the bar, given that 'it's a nice conversation piece, if it's handled the right way'.[25] Al initially ignores this macabre recommendation, and the head seemingly disappears from the cast of characters, until, like those who leave Deadwood only to return many episodes later, Al remembers that he never disposed of it. Repurposing this conversation piece, he now makes the Sioux chief his silent interlocutor. Sitting alone at night in his office, a glass of whisky in his hand, he confesses to him that his rival, Cy Tolliver, has knowledge which he needs to keep secret to preserve his power. Yet 'the world being the world', as Al puts it, someone else is in the know, putting the plans of this 'dimwit nobility' at risk.[26] To verify his suspicion, he needs a reason to seek out the deputy sheriff, Charlie Utter, who runs the freight office, and make him divulge what he knows. Walking towards the box and then sitting down next to it, he explains the dramatic action about to happen: 'You, Chief, will be my prop and ploy.' Then, having congratulated himself for having kept him around, Al ends their talk by assuring him, 'I've no plans of us parting company'. He has inscribed no address on the package and will, once he has the information he needs, return it to its place in his liquor cabinet, explaining to the dead man's head, in one of many adages to follow, that every fracas counts as a small victory.

# All the frontier's a stage: *Deadwood*

Figure 13 Al Swearengen's conversations with a dead Sioux chief

Milch self-consciously draws attention to what is at stake in this act of self-meditation in the following episode, as though to give a lesson in dramatic technique. When Dan, who has been overhearing these soliloquies, challenges Al about speaking to himself, the latter confides in him that he has been talking to the severed rotting head. His henchman's bemusement prompts him to explain that he is doing so in order to vocalise 'thoughts best kept to yourself'.[27] Then, after Dan leaves, Al takes the package with him as he steps out on his balcony to watch Tom Nuttall ride his brand new bicycle – a novelty for the townspeople – down the thoroughfare for the first time. Having explained to his silent confidant that even the decapitated deserve recreation, he places the package on a barrel, opens it, and removes the severed head to take a close look at it before returning it to the box.

In contrast to Hamlet, gazing directly at the work of death does not put human action into question for Al. Rather, it reassures him in the role he has chosen for himself. Though invisible to those below, who see only Al towering over the thoroughfare, the dead Sioux chief literally has his back. In his position as an ironic onlooker, Al can enjoy the human frivolity playing itself out on the stage below precisely because he knows of the transience of all human action. The fact that he continues to share his thoughts on what is happening below with the dead man behind him allows him to articulate his awareness that the 'standing in the camp' he enacts by virtue of so prominently displaying himself on the balcony is nothing other than a performance. Once Nuttall has successfully completed his ride, Al once again closes the box and sheepishly carries it back in. If no one but he is meant to see this prop, then it is because these soliloquies draw their effect from the fact that they entail a shared secret. Along with the dead man, only we are privy to his clandestine thoughts.

Al will not only continue to confide in the dead Sioux chief, primarily regarding his worries about the developments that are happening in the camp in preparation for the electoral process, which, as he notes in one of these conversations, is 'fraught with contingencies'.[28] He will also again take him along as his inauspicious companion while watching another celebration on the thoroughfare – Alma Garret's wedding to the prospector Whitney Ellsworth. In this instance, the prop is used as a vanitas symbol, reminding us of the inevitability of a change in luck. Tapping into the logic of serial repetition, Nuttall's first ride on his bicycle had anticipated the second one, during which he inadvertently caused a runaway horse, frightened by the movement of this unknown vehicle, to trample Sheriff Bullock's son William to death. To Nuttall, the bicycle will subsequently become an unwelcome symbol of fate turning what had initially been a joyful experience into a luckless one. In the scene of the wedding celebration, Al and his dead companion looking down from the balcony together at a spectacle of frivolity again anticipate a premature death. In this case, however, it is not an accident but a premeditated murder. George Hearst will have one of his hired Pinkertons kill Ellsworth, so that, in hindsight, this wedding celebration will also have been overshadowed by fatality.

As the pressure which the ruthless businessman exerts continues to grow, the package will, indeed, become ever more a proxy of the fragility of Al's own position. At one point, Al even tries to imagine which move the Sioux chief would have chosen in a similar situation of attack. To underscore that, as for Hamlet, speaking to this insignia of death allows Al to ponder the fragility of his enterprise, the last soliloquy makes use of shot-reverse shot editing. Hearst has issued him, as will be discussed in detail further on, an ultimatum. He insists that Trixie, who took aim at him with her pistol, must be sacrificed if he is not to unleash his Pinkertons on the town. Al, however, has decided to kill Jen, another woman working for him, in Trixie's stead. Desperately in need of confessing the quandary he is in, he opens his liquor cabinet and looks at the package sitting on its shelf.[29]

While Al, in the process of explaining his indebtedness to Trixie, recognises his own abuse of her as one of the reasons for his own guilt, the camera position shifts and now captures him from the perspective of the dead man. Then, once he takes himself to task for his inability to use any other weapon but a knife, the camera once more shows the package looming above him, only to return, in a final reverse shot, to the position of the severed head. Suddenly Al moves towards the Sioux chief, accusing him of being slow to adapt himself, before he slams the cabinet door shut, leaving us, for a brief moment, in the dark with the dead man. If, throughout *Deadwood*, the words directed at the disarticulated head perform an intimacy Al shares with no one else, facing this externalised double one last time not only allows him to meditate on his own fallibility. Speaking to the package is also a sustained performative action that keeps the Sioux chief alive in precisely the fragility of power they share. In contrast to Hamlet, it is this self-discovery that makes Al resolute in his final ploy against his enemy.

### Theatre of lawlessness

In *Measure for Measure*'s Duke Vincentio, Al has another fitting analogue in that he, too, is at the centre of a drama of surveillance. In this case, however, the dramatic constellation at issue revolves primarily around the disclosure of transgression at the heart of the law. While, in contrast to the camp town, Shakespeare's Vienna is not a place where there is no law at all, what compels the duke to stage his own absence is the licentiousness that has become rampant because, under his watch, he has allowed the strict statutes of his city to slip. Under the pretext of travelling to Poland, he installs Angelo as his deputy, so that he may, as he explains to the friar, the only figure in on this ruse, 'in th'ambush of my name strike home,/And yet my nature never in the fight/To do in slander'. The duplicity that the duke is performing is, however, even more perfidious. Not only does he appoint a deputy so that the fallout of any punitive action Angelo undertakes may be in his name but not touch his personal standing. As he also explains to the friar, 'to behold his sway,/I will, as 'twere a brother of your order,/Visit both prince and people'.[30] In this disguise, seeking to discover those responsible for all the corruption, he will subsequently wander along the streets of Vienna, asking people their opinions on what is amiss in the city. Then, once the overzealous Angelo, who seeks to implement harsh punishment of all illegal sexual activities, himself displays his own transgressive desire, the disguised duke will actively intervene. He will seek out those his deputy has imprisoned and come up with a plot in which all those in need of his help will play the parts he assigns to them.

The goal of this theatricalisation of his power – and therein lies the analogy to *Deadwood* – is to undermine the unremitting harshness of his proxy so as to re-install his own power. It will subsequently be regarded as more sustainable in its moral flexibility, even if it is now tarnished not only by laxness but also by the deviousness he deployed to regain it. In this dramatic constellation, the ruler's underhanded battle with a deputy is necessary to not only draw out into the open the mutual implication of law and transgression, but also negotiate the terms for containing a political obscenity which can never be fully obliterated. Applying this constellation to *Deadwood*, we find that, in contrast to the duke, Al never puts on a disguise to influence others. Instead, he sends out his lackeys and spies to eavesdrop on others for him. Yet the power he wields is also veiled, given that most of the plotting takes place in the privacy of his office, while even his trusted henchmen watch from below, wondering what is being discussed. These clandestine conversations, in which the panoply of transgressions that his rule is predicated on are revealed only to those he involves in his shady machinations, serve as a counterpoint to his histrionic self-display on the balcony.

Also, in contrast to Shakespeare's duke, Al is not compelled to install a deputy to disclose the corruption that reigns in Deadwood. Instead, he does so under the pressure that, in the process of gaining statehood, the law decided upon in the capital of South Dakota will be imposed on his rule of the camp town. Befitting the logic of serial narration, the TV drama *Deadwood* offers two variations for Al's confrontation with a deputy whose strict interpretation of the law includes its transgression. The first is the historical Seth Bullock, who gave up his post as sheriff in Montana to open up a hardware store with his Jewish partner, Sol Star. Swearengen quickly realises that he would be in a better position to negotiate the terms for Deadwood joining America if they were allies. As a favour to Tom Nuttall, with whom he founded the camp, he had allowed one of his cronies to be made sheriff, seeing this merely as a ceremonial position. When Seth comes to challenge this choice, Al describes to him the bribery involved in his dealings with the politicians in Yankton, telling him 'I give you the law'.[31]

Seth's assertion that the law can be honest makes Al suddenly realise that this tempestuous former marshal would be someone who would not be a whore to corruption. Although Seth at first turns down his proposition, once he witnesses the man who claims to be representing the law commit a racist murder on Cy Tolliver's command, he changes his mind. Confronting the newly named sheriff on the thoroughfare, Seth vehemently removes his badge and tosses it into the mud. Because Tom Nuttall will also no longer stand by a man who has allowed himself to be bought out, the badge remains there until Seth, after hesitating briefly, picks it up, thereby taking the law into his own hands. All the while, Al watches from his balcony, smiling. In his office, in an act of self-declared sovereignty, Seth will later pin the tin on the lapel, while Al, toasting him with his whisky glass, expresses his approval. Comparable to Shakespeare's duke, he hopes that with a man more fanatic about a vengeful law than he as his proxy, he can play the mastermind behind the scenes.

In Shakespeare's *Measure for Measure*, the transgressive kernel inhabiting Angelo's stern law reveals itself in his illegitimate desire for Isabella, a nun, whose religious vows to chastity are as severe as his vow to punish all immorality in Vienna. Having been enlisted by her imprisoned brother Claudio to speak for him, she finds herself confronted with a false choice. Either she gives in to Angelo's sexual demands or her brother will be executed for his transgressions. Once she confesses the quandary, she finds herself cast as the bait connecting the two men representing the law of the city. While Angelo has chosen her to enjoy in secret a lecherous desire he scorns in public, the duke has chosen her as the main player in the drama of deception he comes up with to uncover the duplicity of his deputy. He directs her to acquiesce to Angelo's demand and meet him in a secluded garden house at night. In the darkness, Angelo will not realise that Mariana, the betrothed woman he has repudiated, has taken her place.

Appropriating this triadic constellation, *Deadwood* casts Alma, the widow of Brom Garret, in the position of Isabella. Early in the first season, Al orchestrates a fatal accident for her husband, hoping to pressure her into selling a claim that unexpectedly proves to be one of the richest in the camp. The furious passion which Seth, in turn, develops for Alma is transgressive not because of a vow of chastity on her part, but because he is married. Furthermore, in his role as her self-proclaimed protector, Seth reveals as violent a kernel to his understanding of the law as does Angelo. When Alma's father, Otis Russell, a wily conman, appears in camp, himself interested in her gold, Seth, blinded by his adulterous desire, imposes his version of a death sentence on him. To demonstrate his interpretation of justice, he publicly beats Otis to a pulp, thereby unwittingly undermining his own moral superiority as representative of the law, and with it, Al's unofficial authority.

Alma thus also finds herself positioned between the sheriff and the man pulling the strings behind the scenes, though not because Al is the one directing her. Rather, the love-stricken Seth is so distracted by his passion that he, as sheriff, has become an unreliable asset in Al's political negotiations regarding the impending annexation. This draws the two men into an adversarial confrontation that, too, revolves around disclosing his deputy's duplicity. In 'A Lie Agreed Upon', Al, conversing with Dan, who is standing with him on his balcony, compares Seth, who he sees leaving the Grand Central Hotel, to 'some randy maniac bishop'. Annoyed at what he sees as a betrayal of their previous pact, he publicly challenges the civic duty which the sheriff puts on display, calling out to him clear across the thoroughfare, 'Luck trouble didn't jump out earlier, huh, Bullock? Might have found you mid-thrust at other business.'[32]

In the private confrontation that begins shortly after in Al's office, Seth takes off his badge first before beginning *mano a mano* battle, in the course of which both men go over the balcony and continue their bloody fight as a brutal public spectacle. Only the astonished gaze of the sheriff's son, who has just arrived in the camp town in a stagecoach with his mother, stops Al from using his knife to stab the sheriff in the back. The superiority he has reclaimed by sparing Seth's life leads to a re-installation of his deputy. When he returns the next night to reclaim his gun and badge, all those who have gathered to witness this renewed challenge expect Al to execute him. Instead, he shows mercy, emerging from the Gem unarmed, offering him the accoutrements of law he has come for, and assuring him of his renewed allegiance.

This bond will hold. In the sanitised report Al gives to the newspaperman, Merrick, for his article, he proclaims, 'that purveyor for profit for everything sordid and vicious, Al Swearengen, already beaten to a fare-thee-well earlier in the day by Sheriff Bullock, has returned to the sheriff the implements and ornaments of his office. Without the tawdry walls of Swearengen's saloon, the Gem, decent citizens may pursue with a new and jaunty freedom all aspects of Christian commerce.'[33] In *Measure for Measure*, disclosing the transgressive desire subtending his deputy's merciless interregnum rule allows Shakespeare's duke to cast his resumption of power in a more generous light. Publicly accused by him of having grossly slipped 'both in the heat of blood and lack of temper'd judgement', Angelo can only fulfil the wishes his sovereign imposes on him and, as a sign of his penitent heart, accept the betrothed Mariana he had previously scorned.[34] *Deadwood* offers a similar dramaturgic move. Having demonstrated that his strategy of appeasement is superior to Seth's uncontrolled rage, Al has produced a situation in which the sheriff is under an obligation to him in their mutual concern with preserving his law in the camp town.

Befitting the logic of seriality, once the two men are again allied, Hearst assumes the position of Angelo to Al's duke. His interpretation of financial capitalism is as fanatic as Seth's notion of justice.[35] While he is not installed by Al, the law of consolidation he imposes on the town by buying up all the claims also challenges the previous rule of habitual moral laxity. As he explains to Cy Tolliver, who will become his confidant, the small-mindedness and self-interested behaviour so pervasive in Deadwood is what his operations must work against. The constellation of adversarial power his arrival brings with it again finds Al working behind the scenes, sending out his intermediaries to discover his opponent's schemes and making use of theatrical ploys to assert himself, while Hearst demonstrates the force of his regime openly. Like Angelo, he, too, uses the death penalty to make a public spectacle of his law, having all those who hinder the implementation of his goals killed by the Pinkertons he has engaged as his private army.

At the same time, the transgressive kernel to his law also reveals itself in a dangerous desire, only in his case this involves his blind love for gold and the power it confers upon anyone who has it. As he explains to the grifter Odell, son of his black cook, seeking the colour would be a collective drive that transcends race. Were everyone to agree on its value uniformly, animosities could be contained and people could instead organise to seek it together. As such, like Angelo, Hearst sees his enterprise in terms of a quasi-religious mission, yet one so radical that his fellow men are not yet prepared to accept it. As he confides in Odell, working himself into a fit of tears, 'the truth that I know, the promise that I bring, the necessities I'm prepared to accept make me outcast'.[36]

In this constellation, Alma again emerges as the bait in the battle between the two men over whose law will rule in the town. In contrast to Isabella, she is not the object of Hearst's sexual desire, but only the means to fulfil his lust for the gold her claim yields. Yet the two meetings she has with him to negotiate the sale both entail a form of sexual abuse. Like Isabella in *Measure for Measure*, Alma is compelled to go to her adversary twice, because, during the first meeting, Ellsworth, who had previous dealings with Hearst in the Comstock Lode, calls him a murderer and interrupts the negotiation. It is during the second meeting to which Alma goes alone to his rooms that he (like Angelo to Isabella) makes an indecent proposal. While he does not require of her to lay down the treasures of her body to him, he uses bawdy imagery to scorn her proposal as being absolutely offensive, comparable to asking a man to use his jack-knife to make himself a capon before her.[37] Once she has risen from her chair, he hurls his counterproposal at her, asking her to hear the amount he is willing to pay to buy her out. To bar her way out of this ugly encounter, he approaches her and, having first whispered into her ear that she is reckless, accuses her of indulging herself, intimidating her by suggesting that he is about to rape her.

Alma can only turn away her face, frozen in fearful anticipation of what is to follow, until Hearst steps back and lets her leave. He will first stage a feigned shooting and then have one of his Pinkertons murder her second husband, to corner her after all into finally signing a contract of sale on his terms. Even during this last meeting, at which both Seth and Sol are present to protect her interests, he cannot resist the temptation to harass her once more, lasciviously commenting on the change of her

Figure 14 Jen's lethal bed trick

perfume as she once more walks past him to leave what has again turned into an ugly encounter.

The bed trick, so seminal to the duke in catching the conscience of his deputy in *Measure for Measure*, is refigured in *Deadwood* in line with Hearst's sexualised violence. Upon seeing Ellsworth's dead body being driven into town on a wagon, Trixie, as has already been noted, pulls out the gun she has tucked away in her stocking. Baring her breasts, she resolutely walks up the stairs of the Grand Central Hotel, knocks on Hearst's door, and, pulling up her skirt to reveal her genitals, shoots him. She manages to escape undetected by the Pinkertons who are mingling on the ground floor, but because she merely wounds him in the shoulder, Hearst insists on a blood sacrifice. Although he has already made plans to move on to another camp, he will not leave Deadwood until he has visual proof that the woman who shot him is dead.

In his most adroit theatrical ploy, Al not only directs but also plays the major part in the spectacle he puts on to satisfy Hearst's desire for retribution. He will use his knife to cut Jen's throat, another prostitute working for him, let a tearfully guilty Trixie dress her in the clothes she had worn, before having her boxed in a coffin next to the pool of blood on the floor. Aware of how fallible this dramaturgic device might be, he assigns to himself the most dangerous part. Downstairs in the saloon, he gives his directions to his allies in this last scene of battle. 'We show united in the prelude when he's making his entrance', he explains, 'Comes to viewing the body, I stand for virtue alone. The deception failing, I'll make a pass at him with my blade. In the aftermath, play the lie as mine.'[38] Once Hearst has arrived, he leads him to his office, where, rather than having illicit sex, the businessman inspects a corpse which he takes to be that of another woman. To satisfy his sadistic lust, he touches not the genitals that had briefly distracted him when Trixie took her aim, but the slit on the throat of her substitute. Convinced by the spectacle, he wipes his bloody hand on his handkerchief and tosses it at the head of the sacrificed woman before leaving the room without saying another word. Comedy and tragedy are, indeed, the same damn thing in this instance. Trixie's survival, and with it the possibility of marriage which the comedy genre demands, is bought at the expense of her friend's tragic fate.

In Al's chief go-between, E.B. Farnum, we find a further tragi-comic correction to the distress and destruction that Hearst unleashes in Deadwood. Although early on in the TV drama, he proclaims himself mayor, he is a figure of perpetual ridicule. Often, the other men running the town exclude him from their clandestine deliberations. Kept in the dark regarding their schemes, he has no real authority in Deadwood, so that the self-importance he persistently puts on display can be thought in terms of the classic Fool's debunking of political authority. Yet, in so far as this self-serving meddler seeks to ingratiate himself with anyone whom he deems important, he can also be seen as a resuscitation of *Measure for Measure*'s Lucio. The *dramatis personae* lists him as a fantastic to indicate that he is an extravagant, foppish young nobleman, known primarily for his fanciful ideas. To help his imprisoned friend, he is responsible for getting Isabella to intercede on her brother's behalf. He is also the one who spreads slanderous gossip about the absent sovereign to the disguised duke himself, only to later claim that it had been the meddling friar who had libelled him. It is precisely his loose tongue (for which, in Shakespeare's dark comedy, he is almost whipped and hung at the end) which E.B. has inherited from this figure of absurdity. In Milch's serial TV drama, he, too, not only spies on those who frequent his hotel through a hole in the wall of his office, only to convey what he has overheard to Al; he is also fundamentally indiscreet, spreading slanderous gossip about those who treat him with contempt.

It is, however, particularly his own idiosyncratic penchant for holding soliloquies that mark him as a fantastic, who lives primarily in the world of his wild ideas. In contrast to Al's calm self-meditations, these are rants during which he lets his tongue run loose against those who abuse him but also against his own frailty. In the first of these, he speaks about himself as though he were Al, while scrubbing the bloodstains off the floor in one of the rooms in his hotel, where his boss had a man killed. He is not only angry at being used as go-between whom Al is not willing to recompense adequately for his effort, but also that he has allowed himself to be terrified into doing his every bidding. When he is subsequently sent on yet another errand by his boss, he offers an accurate comical critique of the power relations he cannot extricate himself from. As he indignantly crosses the thoroughfare, roughly pushing those who get in his way aside, he mutters to himself, 'no deceit too prolonged, no errand too demeaning, no rebuke too vile. Al Swearengen's a cue and Farnum merely his billiard ball.'[39] Ridiculous as he may be, in his insight into how deplorably he is being played by Al, E.B. also emerges as the subversive spirit of comedy. When he calls the thoroughfare 'quagmire and bullshit', he is perceptively debunking the very network of surveillance he is embroiled in.

There is self-awareness here, and yet, as though to underscore that there is no outside to Al's drama of discovery and revenge, Farnum remains implicated in the plotting. Unlike Lucio, he never openly spreads slanderous gossip about his boss, yet like Shakespeare's fantastic, he will sometimes work for the other side, carrying false news around the town for Hearst because he feels there might be some financial gain in it for him. Indeed, because he cannot keep his exasperation – and with it his tongue – in check, E.B.'s perpetual trading in gossip at times produces mischief unwittingly, as when he shares with Hearst information about the drug addiction of the woman whose gold claim he wants to acquire at all costs. When he defends himself to Al, claiming he meant no disloyalty, he is oddly honest. Living primarily in the ceaselessly thwarted fantasy of his own self-importance, it belongs to the fantastical side of his character to pass information on to everyone indiscriminately. It is his *modus operandi*. Yet by conveying messages for everyone, he subverts the idea that any one side has a clear gain on intelligence in this mutually shared drama of surveillance. Instead, like Lucio's, his dramatic function consists in making certain that the storyline moves from one intrigue to the next, with each new cycle accompanied by more clandestine information being trafficked across the thoroughfare.

The last of his soliloquies takes place in his private office. In the previous episode, Hearst, angered that Al had once again gained the upper hand, vented his fury on Farnum by spitting in his face. To reassure himself that he does have supreme power over someone, he had forbidden the hotel manager to clean this stain of humiliation off his face. Now, an extreme close-up of E.B.'s distressed eyes accompanies the beginning of his most painful rant on the ridicule that others subject him to: 'That I have not wiped his expectoration from my cheek is understandable. I'm threatened with death if I do.'[40] Functioning as the comical counterpart to Al's conversations with the dead Sioux chief, there is, nevertheless, a tragic note in this awareness of utter dependency on the violent whims of his superiors. The camera moves into a medium shot to accentuate the accusation E.B. now hurls at himself, 'That I stand immobile these hours later speaks of a flaw in my will.'

To visually underscore that the anagnorisis he is about to vocalise involves his rejection of the role of peon which Hearst has imposed upon him, the camera begins to shift between exhibiting his entire figure and close-ups of his face. After Farnum imagines further indignities involving other bodily excretions from his tormentor, he asks himself whether he would then still stand stoic. Finally, he resolutely pulls a handkerchief from his pocket and, while wiping the spit off his face, addresses his imaginary tormentor in the spirit of defiance: 'I am going to fuck you up'. This declaration of revolt, even if it will not come to fruition, is the epitome of the inversion of the high and the low celebrated by comedy. For a brief moment, the spirit of revolt is articulated by the very character who, throughout, had cultivated the pose of the obsequious subaltern.

## Serial subversions

The most effective blurring of tragedy and comedy in *Deadwood*'s appropriation of Shakespearean dramaturgy is, thus, effected through the combination of enmeshed storylines that not only make use of a tension between the high and the low. Offering multiple perspectives on the drama of discovery and resistance which Al stages in this frontier camp town, the serial narration combines individual vignettes into a chain of small windows that open one after the other on a hierarchical system of power that, though shown in all its fallibility, remains intact. While individual characters experience sorrow and fatality, and several festive celebrations, like Alma's wedding, are followed by a new crisis, tragedy, nevertheless, is averted. The theatricalisation of power is played out against a backdrop of ordinary lives touched by but also exceeding it. The multi-perspectival narrative renders visible a plethora of chance events that are not part of the main drama, and, in so doing, undermines any all-encompassing tragic necessity by showing what is not drawn into its thrall. This is, however, also the dramatic logic of serial narration in general. As Gérard Wajcman argues, by making use of fragmentation, dispersion, rupture, and decentring, serial TV drama tells a world, but not all of that world, because the world it calls forth is not whole. The interruptions and partitions on which serial sequencing is based ruptures narrative linearity and privileges the loss of a unique centre. It foregrounds fortuity and unrealised potentialities instead.[41]

Thus, if E.B. Farnum incessantly intervenes with his snooping and gossip, or if Trixie poses a disruption of the grand schemes into which she has been co-opted to participate by taking revenge into her own hands, the disturbance these characters pose finds, in the parallel editing that serial TV drama deploys, a formal correspondence. If their actions deconstruct any claim to absolute power, especially the power to see and thus to control everything, so, too, does a narrative that keeps interrupting the main storyline. Indeed, many characters inhabiting the thoroughfare draw us into aspects of their lives to which Al and his adversaries are not privy. As in Shakespeare's plays, where scenes jump from the aristocratic players to the commoners, who reflect and reflect on the actions of their superiors, the cross-cutting in *Deadwood* develops narrative trajectories that either lead beyond the power struggle over the impending annexation or have little to do with. They render visible to us many particular positions, which, though connected by a common concern, are not fully consumed by it. As such, they break up the serial drama into a plurality of stories, a skein of loosely connected narrative threads that can come undone again. As has already been noted, some characters disappear completely; some leave, only to reappear again later; and some are constantly on the stage that is this camp town. While their stories run parallel to each other, they are sometimes conjoined, but they are never fully tied together. Rather, this plethora of individual positions is connected at certain moments, only to break up again and then, at a later point, be temporarily joined once more.

At the same time, there is a larger ideological agenda to this serial form, given that, in *Deadwood*, it corresponds to a specific understanding of what makes up a political community. As Caroline Levine suggests, when characters in serial TV drama are loosely and unevenly brought together in 'a makeshift order rather than a coherent system', this draws attention to the radical potential that resides in acts of rearrangement.[42] The incessant encounters, collisions, and alliances of the characters on the horizontal line of the thoroughfare thus not only serve as a counterpoint to the vertical axis of power and its subversion in relation to the battle between Swearengen, Bullock, and Hearst. They can also be seen as a self-reflexive comment on the way the serial narrative form entangles parallel storylines to offer the aesthetic unfolding of a multiple and diverse community. If the order which the serial form veers towards is never all-inclusive, it is also never complete and never resolved.

In *Deadwood*, Trixie is the figure who best exemplifies comedy's privileging of potentiality over a fate that is only accidentally averted even while leaving its traces. Like E.B., she works as a spy for Al, secreted and listening in for him in private spaces where he cannot go, and yet, in contrast to him, she is headstrong where he is obsequious. She also meddles, in her case primarily in relation to the schemes in which others involve Alma Garret. Initially, she changes the course of the widow's fate by helping her with her opium addiction, undermining her own boss's desire to swindle her out of her gold claim. Later, to undercut rumours regarding her adulterous relation with Sheriff Bullock, she forges the marriage between the widow and Ellsworth. Trixie is, furthermore, the one character in this TV drama to transform her social position dramatically. If she is introduced as Al Swearengen's favourite prostitute, she soon not only begins to learn accounting in Sol Starr's hardware store, she later also moves into rooms next to the house he has bought, to dedicate herself exclusively to being the mistress of the man running for mayor against Farnum.

The playfully aggressive verbal sparring that characterises her romantic relation with the Jewish store owner, in turn, suggests a correspondence to another one of Shakespeare's dark comedies. In *Much Ado About Nothing*, Beatrice is introduced as waging a merry war of wit against Benedick, using her words as her sword to fend off his courtship. The bawdy and even cruel comments these two characters toss at each other, though manifestly deployed to keep them separate, exchange an erotic intercourse for a linguistic one. That this battle of words also serves as a comic counterpart to the fateful misunderstanding between the other romantic couple is another one of the dramaturgic ploys that *Deadwood* appropriates from Shakespeare. While Trixie retaliates against everyone with her foul mouth, the banter she entertains with Sol is a mark of their growing intimacy. For her, too, words are intended as deeds, only in contrast to Swearengen or Hearst, the cruel things said do not anticipate ruthless actions. Instead, as expressions of a tenderness that can only be articulated through a degree of resistance to it, her vehement scolding not only anticipates the sexual pleasure that follows but is also an expression of her ambivalent desire. Though more steadfast than clever, Sol, in turn, fully plays along in the repartee, realising that this merry war of wit is his best ploy to overcome the wariness Trixie exhibits at the thought of giving up her profession. He adroitly transforms their lessons in accounting into his successful courtship.

There is, however, a further correspondence between Trixie and her loose-tongued Shakespearean predecessor. The dramaturgic consequence of the merry battle of wit on the part of the sparring lovers is the resilient bond it forges in the face of calamity. In *Much Ado About Nothing*, Beatrice is compelled to stand by while her cousin, Hero, is slandered by her bridegroom on her wedding day. Duped into believing that she was unfaithful to him the night before, Claudio publicly repudiates her and storms out of the church with his companions. That this is an implicit act of killing becomes evident when Hero, realising that her voice is not being heard, faints. It is at the body of her scorned and dishonoured kinswoman that Beatrice asks Benedick, who alone has remained in the church, to kill Claudio for her. Yet it is also in the heat of her lust for revenge that she can acknowledges their love for each other for the first time.

*Deadwood*'s reworking of feminine retaliation has Trixie, outraged at the perfidious killing of Ellsworth, take the law into her own hands and deviously pay Hearst back in kind. Rather than asking Sol to do her killing for her, she herself goes to Hearst's rooms and shoots him. In contrast to *Much Ado About Nothing*, and therein lies the significant transformation that the TV drama offers, death cannot be averted. If it was the sight of Ellsworth's corpse that provoked her manly behaviour, Jen's corpse is required to resolve the crisis. In Shakespeare's dark comedy, the fainted woman not only regains consciousness, but, rehabilitated in the eyes of the public, Hero will ultimately exchange marriage vows with a remorseful Claudio. What *Deadwood*, however, appropriates from Shakespeare is the consequence that facing an imminent danger has for the forging of a romantic bond between characters conceived as witnesses, not participants, in the fateful turn of events. In a last violent quarrel, Trixie, tired of hiding from Hearst's Pinkertons in Sol's home, informs him that she will go back to her trade to get him votes at the polls. Furious at what he understands to be recklessly selfish, Sol shoves her out of his front door, exclaiming, 'At least I can say I threw you out if you'd rather die than live with me?'[43] The camera tarries with him as he sits down in despair over his own tempestuous action, until, interrupted by a knock on his door, he lets her back in. Their tearful embrace signals their consummate acknowledgement of each other. The spirited bantering they have shared throughout has established the 'meet and happy conversation', which, according to Stanley Cavell, is what a viable couple is predicated on, fulfilling the promise of marriage demanded by comedy.

Conceiving the stage which the camp town Deadwood provides in terms of the topsy-turvy freedom of a world on the periphery of the nation brings yet a further comedy to mind. As a site where official law has not yet taken hold, and, as such, as a space of utopian possibility not yet realised (though also perhaps never to be achieved), it also recalls the Forest of Arden of *As You Like It*. Less sombre than interregnum Vienna, this green world is, after all, the place where aristocrats, banished by a tyrannical duke and dressed as outlaws, have set up an alternative community beyond political envy and intrigue, into which their children, themselves seeking freedom from the political oppression ruling at court, flee. It is, however, also the place where a melancholic gentleman, Jaques, speaks out against the hunt, weeping for the wounded animals and chastising a young lover for marring the trees by writing love-songs on their barks. In *Deadwood*'s Calamity Jane, who wanders along the thoroughfare, drunk and perpetually cursing, his deep sadness at the ephemerality of the world is resuscitated. With a bottle in her hand more often than not, she becomes the companion to all those who, like her, are not part of the ordinary everyday business being carried on around them, or who, if only momentarily, have abandoned their business to grieve the ill fate of the world. If she is often found crying over her own fallibility, she is also the one to protect the most vulnerable from the hunger for prey, rampant in Deadwood, though in her case this pertains not to wild animals but to the children and those who have fallen ill.

At the same time, in her frontiersman costume, Jane also appears on this stage as the cross-dressed Shakespearean heroine par excellence. As in the comedies, she assumes male attire not only as a form of protection during her journey through dangerous territories. It also serves as a cover for her shame regarding her own erotic desires. The intimate bond that is forged between her and Joanie Stubbs, who has set up her own high-class brothel, the Chez Amis, could be seen as a variation on the close friendship which Celia and Rosalind have for each other in *As You Like It*. In Shakespeare's comedy, despite the fact that her father has banished her cousin, Celia insists that they shall not be sundered because 'thou and I am one'.[44] Out of love for Rosalind, Celia accompanies her friend, who, in turn, dons male clothes and chooses a rapier as her weapon, to perform a swashing and martial masculinity to all they might encounter as they wander through Arden forest. Like these two runaway women, who establish their new home in a cabin bought from a shepherd, Joanie will also share her home with Jane after a crime of passion forces her to close down her business. In this forlorn space, the curtains drawn to keep out a threatening world, Joanie and Jane comfort each other, drink together, and talk about the friends they have both lost.

Sometimes Jane, though intoxicated, will hold watch with her rifle to defend her friend, and, although she keeps wandering off, Joanie is able to draw her back repeatedly, not only into this transient home but also into the one she temporarily settles in after selling the space to Jack Langrishe. In the tender, if fragile, love between two women, who have cast themselves out from ordinary everyday business, *Deadwood* dramatically explores a lesbian desire that Shakespeare's comedies only gesture towards. Looking back at these, we are called upon to wonder, what if Rosalind, rather than allowing herself to be drawn into the courtship drama of others, had chosen to remain in the cabin with Celia, exploring with her an alternative affective union to the marriage expected of them at court? We are given an intimation of what that might have been like when, in 'A Constant Throb', the two return to Joanie's lodgings one evening. While undressing, Jane relates a dream where she fuses together a series of scenes in which her account of the humiliation she repeatedly feels when making cowardly moves segues into a proud recollection of moments of having shown courage. Twice, she interpolates into this series a different scene, reminding Joanie of an intimacy that combines both a sense of shame and deep satisfaction: 'and then you kissed me'.[45] The passionate caress that follows may bespeak to a shared happiness that will only prove temporal, and yet, the repeated confirmation of this unlikely couple is also an example for how tragedy can take a turn into comedy.

## Unsettled endings

The potential for repetition written into the narrative closures of serial drama is a final debt that *Deadwood* pays to Shakespeare. *Hamlet* ends with Horatio, the friend of the prince who has survived the domestic massacre, asking of Fortinbras, who has arrived from the Polish war front, to speak 'to th'yet unknowing world/How these things came about'. As in so many of his plays, the report he promises to give is one made offstage. Assuring the survivors that it is 'from his mouth whose voice will draw no more', he claims there is urgency to his account, 'lest more mischance/On plots and errors happen'.[46] Although a new political rule under the Prince of Norway is about to begin, so, too, could a new series of fatal discoveries, betrayals, and violent acts of retribution. In the three comedies, in turn, couples are formed which reconfirm the political rulership, the instability of which had brought about the dramatic traffic in the first place. In *As You Like It*, the deity of marriage, Hymen, appears to 'make conclusion/Of these most strange events',[47] joining the hands of four couples, including the daughters of the banished duke and his usurper brother, before the rustic revelry begins, at the end of which he and his entourage will return to the court, once more fully installed in his power.

In *Much Ado About Nothing*, Benedick and Beatrice, though 'too wise to woo peaceably',[48] finally agree to marriage, alongside Claudio and Hero, who can finally complete the vows so cruelly interrupted in the church in the previous act. The schemer has been caught and will be punished once the festivities are over, but we are left to wonder how plausible the happiness of these couples is, and, thus, how secure the peace they are meant to ensure. The re-established sovereignty of the duke in *Measure for Measure* is the most uncertain of the three. Disclosing Angelo's duplicitous rule may have shifted the focus away from his inability to control the corruption rampant under his rule, yet it has not brought with it an enhanced trust in the laws of his city. His own marriage, also meant to reassure that all is once more well, is not predicated on consent. To his proposal, 'what's mine is yours, and what is yours is mine', Isabella, who has so staunchly defended her vow of chastity throughout, says nothing. It is open to question whether all the misdoing that has been discovered can safely be forgiven and forgotten. Something remains deeply amiss.

The tricky balance between dramatic resolution and an inbuilt drive for a relaunch is at the heart of all serial TV drama. If, when the first episode opens, the overarching storyline has already begun, so too, when the last episode finishes, things will continue even if we are no longer witnesses to this repetition of events. As already noted, the entire dramatic traffic of *Deadwood* occurs under the auspices of an impending end to this interregnum. Like any other historical drama, all that was possible in this period of transition has been re-enacted in the full awareness of its inevitable end. At the same time, although statehood is about to come, no definitive resolution to the hierarchical constellation of adversarial power and its subversion has been reached. Instead, the theatricalised power struggle that is acted out over the three seasons moves serially from crisis to crisis, with brief interpolations not of calm but of celebrations.[49]

If, in what could be thought in terms of a serial drama in three acts, the first season of *Deadwood* opens with the arrival of Cy Tolliver and the threat this poses to Al Swearengen's absolute rule, it ends on a note of containment that preserves the violence of this rivalry even as it is restrained. Al has not only installed Seth Bullock as sheriff of Deadwood, but the military troops, which Cy had hoped to deploy in his favour, are leaving the camp town. Those primarily involved in this first critical confrontation watch the departure from above – Alma Garret from her window in the Grand Central Hotel; Al's new associate from the balcony of the Gem; his loyal henchmen, along with Trixie, Sol, and E.B. Farnum, from below on the thoroughfare. But inside the saloon, Doc Cochran is mirthfully dancing with Jewel, whom he has fitted with a new boot. While Al hovers at the balustrade looking down, Trixie returns to the bar, and, briefly, her gaze meets his, smiling, before both once more turn their attention to the two unlikely dancers. Everyone is held in suspension in this festive moment of time-out, waiting for the next season – and with it the next cycle of power struggles and schemes – to begin.

The second act also ends in a communal dance, this time to celebrate Alma Garret's wedding. As already noted, Al stands on his balcony with his silent interlocutor, the dead Sioux chief's severed head. He greets his henchmen, who have returned from a successful tussle with one of George Hearst's representatives, fought to re-install Wu as lord over Chink Alley. The camera leaves him to capture Merrick, carrying a copy of his newspaper among the dancing crowd on the thoroughfare and calling out his newest headline: 'Elections are coming.'[50] While the bride and bridegroom, together with her adopted child, Sofia, climb on to their wagon and drive off, Seth emerges from the saloon. Trixie and Sol note in anticipation the brief exchange of forlorn gazes between the bride and the sheriff before he walks away towards the home where his wife is waiting. The scene, however, is not over yet. An ecstatic Jane calls out, 'we ain't done fucking dancing', and the music strikes up again, bringing with it what *As You Like It* and *Much Ado About Nothing* anticipate – more revelry. This time, all those touched by the standoff between Al and his new adversary are not onlookers. Doc is not the only one dancing with Jewel. The transformation inscribed in internal serial repetition is such that Trixie and Sol, Joanie, Jane, and Charlie Utter have all joined them on the dance floor. Al, once again, is the onlooker, yet this time, in his role as clandestine director, he nods his head to the rhythm of the music before the screen goes black. This would be the utopic resolution comedy promises.

The closure at the end of the final season, in turn, is most pointedly inconclusive. There is no character who offers to recapitulate the things that came about. Instead, the closure to all dramatic traffic consists of dismissing the characters from this stage. As George Hearst, guarded by two Pinkertons, walks towards the stagecoach that will finally take him away from the town that has bonded against him, he notices Wu's troops, standing armed in Chink Alley. Having assured Merrick that he is about to start his own paper in Deadwood, 'to lie the other way', he climbs on to the seat next to the driver so that he can 'take a last look around' from a visual higher ground.[51] All those involved are taken into focus one last time by the camera as well. Seth walks out onto the thoroughfare, glaring at the departing man. As Alma Garret passes Hearst in her wagon, he scornfully tips his hat at her from on high, compelling Seth to approach him. In his fury, he commands Charlie, his deputy, who has already got his rifle, to stay behind, while Jack Langrishe emerges, equally anxious to witness the spectacle. Cy, looking down from his balcony, has also drawn his revolver to protect the departing man who has appointed him his deputy in Deadwood.

Once Seth has approached the coach, surrounded by armed Pinkertons, he taunts Hearst from his inferior position, 'You're done tipping your

# All the frontier's a stage: Deadwood

Figure 15  E.B. Farnum re-installed in the Grand Central Hotel

fucking hat. Get out of here or I'll drag you out by the ear.' Alma, who has briefly asked the man driving her wagon to stop, looks back in fear at her former lover. While he and Hearst exchange taut glances, the others look on nervously. For a brief moment, everything could erupt in violence. Then Hearst haughtily signals the man sitting next to him to drive on. One might think of Malvolio, who, at the end of *Twelfth Night*, leaves the stage, assuring those who have taunted him, 'I'll be revenged on the whole pack of you.'[52] As he drives out of the camp town, Cy lowers his gun and walks back into his saloon. Although Hearst is gone, we know that together with this proxy and all the men he has left behind, his influence will remain. Seth exchanges one last tender gaze with Alma before she drives out of the camp in the opposite direction, then Jack also turns away and enters the house he had emerged from.

During the conversation with Utter that follows, Seth refuses the role of hero and instead contemplates his own failure, should he have lost the election. His gaze briefly wanders over the thoroughfare, where Sol is leading Trixie away from the Gem, his arm gently protecting her. She has covered her head with a scarf so that none of the Pinkertons will recognise her. Then, as Seth walks away from Charlie, he walks towards us, and, looking directly into the camera, signals as though in a tacit understanding that he is abdicating his position as player before passing by the camera and walking, now with his back to us, out of our line of vision. He is replaced by E.B. Farnum, gingerly emerging from the hole in the front of the Grand Central Hotel, to stand where Hearst used to, looking down on the thoroughfare in mimicry of his haughty gaze, his arms akimbo. He foolishly believes that he has claimed the higher visual ground as well. The only ones to remain on the thoroughfare are all the anonymous townspeople. It is now just an ordinary road leading through the town.

A tragic crisis has been averted, but the community, for which peace has been preserved, is as fragmented and discontinuous as the series of vignettes with which these characters are dismissed from what had been their stage. When the camera returns, as in the previous closing sequences, to Al, he is once again cleaning the blood off the floor in his office. Johnny enters to ask about Jen's death, having been fond of the woman who died in Trixie's stead. Only after he has left does Al offer the last of his soliloquies, not, however, to the severed head of the Sioux chief. This time the line 'wants me to tell him something pretty' is addressed to the murdered woman, lying in the coffin next to her own pool of blood. All that is left for him to do, as the director of his most sombre dramatic ploy, is to clean the floor for a new cycle in the struggle over power to commence. His briefest soliloquy is, however, also a gesture towards the Shakespearean epilogue in which a character, appealing directly to the audience for their applause, also puts an end to all theatrical illusion.

## A second open ending

If the logic of serial drama is that everything has always already begun, this also means that everything could begin again. *Deadwood: The Movie* follows this principle, returning to the camp town ten years later, for the South Dakota Statehood celebration of 1889. In so doing, David Milch offers a self-reflexive comment on the need to return to a re-enactment of the past, not only out of curiosity about what has happened to his players in the wide gap of time that we were separated from them, but also because some unfinished business remains. Much as Shakespeare in the late romance *Cymbeline* recycles his own works, taking bits and pieces from previous plays and reassembling them into a collage, so, too, David Milch falls back on dramaturgic constellations familiar to us from the previous episodes. Jane, once more drunk, again rides into town on her horse; only now, purposely seeking out Joanie, she is the one more active in this second round of courtship. Alma, who subsequent to her departure from Deadwood has made a fortune in banking, arrives with Sofia, her adopted daughter, on the train. She still harbours a passion for Seth, who has remained with his wife and has three children with her. His partner, Sol, is still carrying on a merry battle of words with Trixie, who, however, is now pregnant with his child. E.B Farnum, still mayor, is as obsequious yet overlooked by the others as ever, even while he continues to spy and report back to Al what he has discovered. Though dying, the owner of the Gem, in turn, continues to survey the traffic on the thoroughfare from his balcony, offering his commentary on the action below.

The arrival of George Hearst, now junior senator for California, sets a series of dramatic actions in motion that recall the previous crises, even while these self-reflexive dramatic repetitions involve some seminal differences as well. Hearst once more takes recourse to murder in the hope of getting a plot of land, now, however, to build telephone poles, and once again, he and Al stare at each other from their respective balconies across the thoroughfare as a sign of their sustained rivalry. The funeral for Seth's son, accidentally trampled to death by a runaway horse, which was depicted at length in the previous serial drama, has now transformed into the burial of the murdered Charlie Utter. At the same time, again as a counterpoint to Hearst's ominous business dealings, a marriage is celebrated, with Trixie as the bride. During these festivities, Seth, as tempestuous as ever in his interpretation and enforcement of the law, again arrests Hearst, who, having suddenly realised the trick that Al had played on him, once more demands punishment for the prostitute that sought to kill him ten years earlier.

These narrative recyclings are, however, complemented by a series of flashbacks, revolving around the violence on which joining the nation was predicated, most prominently the deed for which Hearst seeks revenge. Two forms of serial repetition are thus deployed. As the characters once more engage in interactions and exchanges dramaturgically familiar to us, our attention is drawn to the difference between this new TV drama and the previous one. Sharply drawing into focus how they have all aged also foregrounds that in the spirit of comedy, something has changed. The flashbacks, in turn, not only literally montage fragments from the past seasons into the narrative flow of the film, presenting the characters' earlier selves as doubles of their current selves. These flashbacks also draw attention to the tragic sense of fallibility that has not changed, troubled as Al and Trixie are by the ghost of the woman they sacrificed to Hearst. The film repeatedly resuscitates Jen as a phantom presence, the visual fragments from the previous seasons deployed as a staged embodiment of their guilt, along the lines of the return of the ghost of Banquo in *Macbeth*. Jen cannot be laid to rest because at her dead body, deployed by the film's narrative as a shared secret that binds Al and his accomplices together, all the violence on which the serial regeneration of this community in the face of crisis was predicated has come to be condensed.[53]

Figure 16 Trixie accepts Al Swearengen's legacy

There will be no end to this haunting, drawing these players back into the past over and again, even as the serial repetition of their ordinary lives pushes them forward into the future. Because what *Deadwood: The Film* also takes from the dramatic resolution that Shakespeare's comedies offer is the idea that the ending is a new beginning, though not a radically new foundation of the community. While the constellation of power has been re-established, important differences have been included in the repetition. Although it is as yet uncertain how things will play out, something has changed. In a final confrontation with her abuser, Alma outbids George Hearst for the plot of land he had murdered for. Not only has Joanie inherited the Bella Union from her former employer; in his will, Al also names Trixie the new proprietress of the Gem. The property has passed on to the women, and with it, if not a completely new kind of political power then at least an opportunity for self-determination.

The sequence of vignettes with which the film closes draws this into focus. While Al is dying, Trixie walks onto the balcony, the striped jacket he had worn throughout this TV drama draped over her shoulders. This is the first time we see her there, claiming her possession of his former visual regime along with his costume. Below she sees Jane proudly leading Joanie down the thoroughfare. Across the way, Alma is once more looking out of her hotel window, her gaze directed at Seth, returning home to his wife. Trixie's gaze, however, is reserved for Sol, standing at the open door of their home, tenderly holding their newborn child in his arms. After sharing a smile with him she returns to Al, who, once again, with his dying breath, has the last word, challenging her appeal to a divine power. The last image, however, is a close-up of his dead hand finally resting in her living one. As the closing shot, this visual emblem, condensing the gesture of passing away with that of passing on a legacy, also speaks to the potentiality in serial narration.

## Notes

1 *Deadwood*, 'Leviathan Smiles', episode 8, season 3, dir. Ed Bianchi, writ. Kem Nunn, m44.18 (HBO 2006).
2 William Shakespeare, *King Lear*, R.A. Foakes (ed.), *The Arden Shakespeare*, third series (London: Bloomsbury, 1997), 4.1.58.
3 Shakespeare, *King Lear*, 4.1.76–8, 81.
4 Shakespeare, *King Lear*, 4.6.11–12, 24, 27, 25.
5 The notion of an interregnum is taken from Antonio Gramsci, who, in his *Prison Notebooks* (1926), uses this term to speak of a moment of crisis, when an old world order is dying and a new one has not yet been born. In this interim, he adds, a variety of morbid symptoms make their appearance; trans. Joseph Buttigieg (New York: Columbia University Press, 2011).
6 *Deadwood*, 'Amateur Night', season 3, episode 9, dir. Adam Davidson, writ. Nick Towne and Zack Whedon, m 35.06 (HBO 2006). William Shakespeare, *As You Like It*, Juliet Dusinberre (ed.), *The Arden Shakespeare*, third series (London: Bloomsbury, 2006), 2.7.138.
7 See Paul Stasi and Jennifer Greiman's introduction to *The Last Western. Deadwood and the End of American Empire* (London: Bloomsbury, 2013), p. 15.
8 Alexa Huang and Elizabeth Rivlin's introduction to *Shakespeare and the Ethics of Appropriation* (London: Palgrave Macmillan, 2014), p. 6. See also Stephen Greenblatt's discussion of the poetics of power and the poetics of theatre in his chapter 'Invisible Bullets', in *Shakespearean Negotiations* (Berkeley: University of California Press, 1988), pp. 21–65.
9 Early on, Mark Singer noted in his review 'The Misfit: How David Milch Got from *NYPD Blue* to *Deadwood* By Way of an Epistle of St. Paul', that the Elizabethan-like language on this show ranged from ornateness to profanity, *New Yorker*, 14 February 2005, pp. 192–205. John Mack Faragher, also noting the unfamiliar mixture of floridity and swearing, understands the 'almost Elizabethan syntax and cadence' as an effective way for the series to establish historical distance, 'HBO's Deadwood: Not Your Typical Western', *Montana: The Magazine of Western History*, 57:3 (2007), p. 61. Brad Benz, offering a detailed analysis of the soliloquies and dialogues which separate *Deadwood* from other westerns, suggests that when critics laud these for their Shakespearean qualities, they are referring to the artistry of the language and less to the minutia of the syntax or the historical accuracy of the swearing, '*Deadwood* and the English Language', *Great Plains Quarterly*, 27:4 (Fall 2007), p. 249.
10 See Alan Permagent, 'Milch Breathes Life into Characters on Deadwood', *Buffalo News*, 21 July 2005, C7.
11 See also F.O. Matthiessen, *American Renaissance. Art and Expression in the Age of Emerson and Whitman* (Oxford: Oxford University Press, 1941) for a

discussion of Shakespeare's influence on nineteenth-century American literature in general, but Herman Melville in particular.

12 See Stasi and Greiman, *The Last Western*, p. 11. They also isolate the show's peculiar thick, poetic, and obscene dialogues, in their combination of a density of expression with a variety and nuance of profanity as what makes this show an idiosyncratic Shakespearean western.

13 *My Darling Clementine*, dir. John Ford, 20th Century Fox, 1946, m31.30.

14 Peter E.S. Babiak. *Shakespeare Films. A Re-evaluation of 100 Years of Adaptations* (Jefferson, NC: McFarland & Co, 2016), p. 12. See also Hans Richard Brittnacher, 'Western als Drama und Theater: Deadwood', who reads Shakespeare's trope of the play-within-the-play as a reflection on how theatre was originally conceived as helping the polis understand itself. The amateur night, taking place on the thoroughfare, performs the coming together of the community over and against the violent intrigues in the two main sites of power, Al Swearengen's office in the Gem and George Hearst's headquarters in the Grand Central Hotel.

15 David Milch, 'The New Language of the Old West', supplementary material on DVD release of *Deadwood*, disk 6, HBO (2008); in '"I Will Have You Bend": Language and the Discourses of Power in Deadwood', *Literary Imagination*, 12:2 (2010), Daniel Salerno makes a similar point. Taking issue with a reduction of the Shakespearean aspect of this TV drama to the linguistic style, he suggests that the hybrid discourse of the show, making use of multiple linguistic registers, explores the social and political questions involved in a discourse of power, in which the few must govern the many, p. 193.

16 Douglas Lanier, 'Shakespearean Rhizomatics: Adaption, Ethics, Value', in Huang and Rivlin (eds), *Shakespeare and the Ethics of Appropriation*, p. 33.

17 This will be explored in Chapter 6, which reads the espionage system around which the TV drama, *The Americans*, in terms of a carnivalesque transgression of official laws.

18 As Susan Cosby Ronnenberg notes in her study *Deadwood and Shakespeare. The Henriad in the Old West* (Jefferson, NC: McFarland & Co), while exploring how order is established out of disorder, the community that is formed in this serial TV drama not only brings together individuals with competing personal interests. Because it presents multiple perspectives on events, 'the idea of a single, unified perspective is challenged and resisted', p. 35. Similar to my own discussion of the resuscitation of comedy's enmeshment of the high and the low in *Deadwood*, she, too, finds a seminal correspondence between the fragmented nature of Milch's multi-perspectival TV narrative and Shakespeare's juxtaposition of court scenes featuring the aristocracy and those of the tavern or street scenes featuring commoners. Michael J. Shapiro, 'HBO's Two Frontiers: *Deadwood* and *The Wire*', *Geopolitics*, 20:1 (2015), makes a similar point about the polydiegesis of Milch's TV drama, arguing that the plurality of positions shown, produced through cinematic montage, undermines all notions of a central sovereign power.

19 Ronnenberg, *Deadwood and Shakespeare*, p. 31. Although she, too, is interested in making connections between this serial TV drama and Shakespeare's work, her focus is on how parallels can be found between the motivations and behaviours of protagonists both in the Henriad and in *Deadwood*. Salerno, 'I Will

Have You Bend', suggests yet another correspondence. Focusing on the way Al Swearengen is a master in achieving the power he seeks through violence acted but also the force of his language, see in Falstaff and Iago his closest analogues, p. 197.
20 As Mark L. Berrettini notes in his essay 'Messages from Invisible Sources: Sight in *Deadwood*'s Public Sphere', Al is uncomfortable at not being able to rely on his own sight alone for the information he needs to rule and for this reason maintains his spy network. The balcony scenes offer a theatrical counterpoint in that he reveals himself to be 'acutely aware not only of how visual aspects of power work, but also of the fact that he is the subject of the visual power he so clearly prizes', *The Last Western*, p. 162. One might add, he is so in the double sense of the word 'subject', both the focus of the attention and the one in command of the performance.
21 Ewan Fernie, 'Action! *Henry V*', in Hugh Grady and Terence Hawkes (eds), *Presentist Shakespeares* (London: Routledge, 2007), p. 97.
22 William Shakespeare, *Hamlet*, Ann Thompson and Neil Taylor (eds), *The Arden Shakespeare*, third series (London: Bloomsbury, 2006), 2.2.540.
23 Salerno, 'I Will Have You Bend', p. 208. See also Jason Jacobs' discussion of Al Swearengen as a director in *Deadwood* (London: Palgrave Macmillan, 2012).
24 These soliloquies can also be read in terms of psychoanalytic sessions. In 'Uploading Hamlet: Agency, Convergency and YouTube Shakespeare', *Anglistica*, 15:2 (2011), Stephen O'Neil notes that the soliloquy was used to give the audience an access to a character's motivations and thoughts. By giving 'the suggestion of a deeper self, of "that within"', he finds a retrieval of this dramaturgic device in YouTube vlogs, p. 69. Regarding the choice of a Native American as the one to whom these soliloquies are addressed, Stasi and Greiman, *The Last Western*, suggest in their introduction that they can be taken as 'an allegory for our own perpetual return to those narratives that repeatedly resurrect such figures in order to kill them all over again', p. 12. It is also worth noting that while Al reserves his soliloquies for the Sioux chief's head, he does have monologues addressed to the living as well, above all repeatedly to Dolly while she is giving him a blow-job. As Diane Cook, 'Moral Relativism in David Milch's Deadwood', points out, these give us an insight into the abuse he experienced during his childhood, illuminating another aspect of the fragility of his current authority; in Sorcha Ni Fhlainn (ed.), *Dark Reflections, Monstrous Reflections. Essays on the Monster in Culture* (Oxford: Inter-Disciplinary Press, 2006), p. 12. See also Stephanie Mueller's examination of the discussions he has with the Sioux chief's head, 'National and Economic Incorporation in HBO's Deadwood', in Christl Buschendorf, Stefanie Mueller, and Katja Sarkowsky (eds), *Violence and Open Space.: The Subversion of Boundaries and the Transformation of the Western Genre* (Heidelberg: Universitätsverlag Winter, 2017), pp. 167–86. Finally, these soliloquies can also be seen as anticipating the breaking of the fourth wall in *House of Cards*, discussed in Chapter 3.
25 *Deadwood*, 'The Trial of Jack McCall', season 1, episode 5, dir. Ed Bianchi, writ. John Belluso, m21.15 (HBO 2004).
26 *Deadwood*, 'E.B. Was Left Out', season 2, episode 7, dir. Michael Almereyda, writ. Jody Worth, m36.29 (HBO 2005).

27 *Deadwood*, 'Childish Things', season 2, episode 8, dir. Tim Van Patten, writ. Regina Corrado, m25.20 (HBO 2005).
28 *Deadwood*, 'Boy-the-Earth-Talks-To', season 2, episode 12, dir. Ed Bianchi, writ. Ted Mann, m46.45 (HBO 2005).
29 *Deadwood*, 'Tell Him Something Pretty', season 3, episode 12, dir. Mark Tinker, writ. Ted Mann, m29.57 (HBO 2006).
30 William Shakespeare, *Measure for Measure*, A.R. Braunmuller and Robert N. Watson (eds), *The Arden Shakespeare*, third series (London: Methuen, 1965), 1.3.41–5.
31 *Deadwood*, 'Jewel's Boot is Made for Walking', season 1, episode 11, dir. Steve Shill, writ. Ricky Jay, m35.40 (HBO 2004).
32 *Deadwood*, 'A Lie Agreed Upon (Part 1)', season 2, episode 1, dir. Ed Bianchi, writ. David Milch, m11.50 (HBO 2005).
33 *Deadwood*, 'A Lie Agreed Upon (Part 2)', season 2, episode 2, dir. Steve Shill, writ. Elizabeth Sarnoff, m47.09 (HBA 2005).
34 Shakespeare, *Measure for Measure*, 5.1.470–1.
35 For a discussion of Hearst as the embodiment of economic self-determination, seeking to impose the law of financial capitalism on the camp's economic sovereignty and the spirit of frontier freedom this stems from, see Kyle Wigins and David Holmberg, '"Gold is every man's opportunity": Castration Anxiety and the Economic Venture in *Deadwood*', *Great Plains Quarterly*, 27:4 (2007), pp. 283–95.
36 *Deadwood*, 'Unauthorized Cinnamon', season 3, episode 7, dir. Mark Tinker, writ. Regina Corrado, m21.29 (HBO 2006). There is tragic irony in his speech to Odell. Though the young man is blinded by his own desire for money, Hearst has seen through the grift and will have him murdered by one of his men, while keeping from his mother his role in the demise of her son.
37 *Deadwood*, 'True Colors', season 3, episode 3, dir. Gregg Fienberg, writ. Regina Corrado and Ted Mann, m37.09 (HBO 2006).
38 *Deadwood*, 'Tell Him Something Pretty', m37.12.
39 *Deadwood*, 'Plague', season 1, episode 6, dir. Davis Guggenheim, writ. Malcolm MacRury, m9.15 (HBO 2004).
40 *Deadwood*, 'The Catbird Seat', season 3, episode 11, dir. Gregg Fienberg, writ. Bernadette McNavara, m6.15 (HBO 2006).
41 See Gérard Wajcman, *Les séries, le monde, la crise, les femmes* (Paris: Verdier, 2018).
42 Caroline Levine, *Forms. Whole, Rhythm, Hierarchy, Network* (Princeton: Princeton University Press, 2015), p. 17.
43 *Deadwood*, 'Tell Him Something Pretty', m19.09.
44 Shakespeare, *As You Like It*, 1.3.94.
45 *Deadwood*, 'A Constant Throb', season 3, episode 10, dir. Mark Tinker, writ. W. Earl Brown, m43.37 (HBO 2006).
46 Shakespeare, *Hamlet*, 5.2.363–4, 376, and 378–9.
47 Shakespeare, *As You Like It*, 5.4.124–5.
48 William Shakespeare, *Much Ado About Nothing*, Claire McEachern (ed.), *The Arden Shakespeare*, third series (London: Bloomsbury, 2006), 5.2.67.
49 As Wajcman notes where the historical cycle used to move from a situation of calm, through a crisis, on to return to a resolution that brought with it a

new situation of containment, the cultural mood that contemporary TV drama reflects is one of permanent crisis, without stasis or moments of repose, and instead performing a sequence that leads from crisis, to crisis, to crisis in rapid succession, *Les séries*, p. 22, my translation.
50 *Deadwood*, 'Boy-the-Earth-Talks-To', m51.12.
51 *Deadwood*, 'Tell Him Something Pretty', m45.
52 William Shakespeare, *Twelfth Night*, Keir Elam (ed.), *The Arden Shakespeare*, third series (London: Bloomsbury, 2008), 5.1.371.
53 See Richard Slotkin's book on the trope of regeneration through violence, *Gunfighter Nation. Myth of the Frontier in Twentieth-Century America* (Norman: University of Oklahoma Press, 1998). See also my own discussion of the shared secret of collective violence fundamental to the building of frontier community in John Sayles' film *Lone Star* in Elisabeth Bronfen, *Home in Hollywood. The Imaginary Geography of Cinema* (New York: Columbia University Press, 2004).

# 6
# Carnival of spies: *The Americans*

### Nothing that is so is so

In the midst of a series of riotous misunderstandings in *Twelfth Night*, Viola, cross-dressed as the page Cesario, engages the clown Feste in a conversation about how, owing to its malleability, language can readily be subverted and thus used to sow confusion. Picking up on his witty subversion of meaning, she wants to know why he, being Olivia's jester, should also frequent the court of the Count Orsino, whom she is currently serving. Feste, insisting that he is 'indeed not his mistress's fool, but rather her corrupter of words', explains that it actually belongs to his role to be present in both places: 'foolery, sir, does walk about the orb like the sun, it shines everywhere. I would be sorry, sir, but the fool should be as oft with your master as with my mistress.'[1] In this performer of verbal duplicity, who openly acknowledges that he has no fixed place in Illyria, Viola has discovered a confrère. Having herself arrived there after a shipwreck, she had decided to conceal her sexual identity by dressing herself as a eunuch. The captain, whom she has entrusted with the women's attire that would reveal her true social status, had, in turn, promised, 'your mute I'll be'.[2] While these are, in fact, the last words he will speak, disappearing from the stage entirely, Viola, left to her own devices, soon finds herself in a tricky engagement. Commissioned with wooing the countess for her master, she, like Feste, is also shuttling back and forth between these two houses. However, while he can disappear and reappear with impunity because this goes with the meandering of his words, her employment is far more precarious. As a stranger in Illyria, who, to boot, is not what she purports to be, Cesario/Viola is constantly running the risk of being discovered.

There is, however, a further resemblance between the two. Because both are aware that they are merely performing roles with which they are not identical, they are simultaneously actors and observers. As Viola notes once Feste has left her, it requires intelligence and practice to play the fool effectively: 'He must observe their mood on whom he jests/The quality of persons and the time', and, like a hawk, react to everything he perceives.³ By assuming a role aimed at fooling others, at issue for both the jester and the cross-dressed page is that they are displaced in more than one sense. Having no proper place in Illyria matches the instability of identity their disguise brings with it. Furthermore, though participants in a game with mistaken identities, they also repeatedly comment on the dupery they perpetuate. The two sides to their role-playing also distance them from the very foolery they embody. Not only do they know that they are not identical with the part they enact, they also know that the two rulers, for whom they carry messages back and forth, want to be fooled. There is, however, a difference in effect. While Feste's corruption of words offers a meta-comment on the folly of love-sick royalty, Cesario's ability to enthral both Orsino and Olivia is the result of the cross-dresser Viola's ability to play to a self-deceiving desire on the part of both of them.

We might, thus, surmise that what Shakespeare's last festive comedy offers is a theatrical rendition of early modern spy work. After all, Viola repeatedly visits Olivia's court not only to deliver the tokens of love Orsino sends as part of his romantic conquest. In the process, Viola is also supposed to find out what this lady's intimate desires actually are and, having discovered her secrets, to relay this secret information back to the count. Furthermore, given the need for such clandestine traffic, it is worth recalling that Olivia resists Orsino's courtship not only because she is mourning her dead brother. As her kinsman Sir Toby notes, 'she'll not match above her degree, neither in estate, years nor wit';⁴ which is to say, she will not be relegated to the inferior position in any marriage contract she signs. At stake for Olivia in this courtship battle is maintaining her sovereignty over her estate. That she should become entangled with the page Cesario, allegedly below her degree, speaks to this fantasy. She needs him to protect her against Orsino's onslaught.

At the same time, *Twelfth Night*'s romantic espionage is predicated on a destabilisation of identities in which all the involved characters partake together.

In the encounter with the countess that follows upon her conversation with Feste, Viola can only use coded language to berate Olivia for forgetting herself in loving someone beneath her rank: 'you do think you are not what you are'. Olivia, admitting that she thinks the same of her, ultimately prompts Viola to declaim outright, 'I am not what I am'.⁵ Whether the countess has, indeed, seen through the disguise that covers both Cesario's rank and gender, or whether it is the frisson of secrecy that excites her, remains undecided. The dramatic effect of this exchange, however, is that we are meant to take pleasure in the cleverness of the cross-dresser, who, having discovered the intimate desire of the one she has been sent to spy on, continues to deceive her because she is allowed to do so.

To further draw into focus the mutual implication of spy work and a self-deceiving desire on the part of those who are entrapped, *Twelfth Night*, much like contemporary serial drama, offers a parallel storyline. Olivia's waiting-gentlewoman, Maria, joins Sir Toby in the boisterous festivities to which the play's title alludes. As Keir Elam notes, if the play has long been associated with carnival, then it is because it shows a world turned upside down, in which the rational hierarchy of the ordinary has come to be replaced with 'revels associated in early modern England with the last day of the Christmas season, and in particular with the election of a "Festus" or "Lord of Misrule" to preside over the maskings'.[6] The target in Maria's storyline is Malvolio, whose stern puritanism she claims to be a pose. Like Viola, she also plays to her victim's self-delusion, even if her goal is to humiliate Olivia's steward. Given that the treacherous trick she will play on him occurs in the context of a courtship battle, it is noteworthy that Sir Toby calls her Penthesilea, ascribing to her the role of a combative Amazon queen.[7] Her opponent in this carnivalesque skirmish, in turn, is frameable because, prodded by her into believing that Olivia is secretly attracted to him, Malvolio has allowed his imagination to be blown up. While Maria's troops, hiding in a box tree, spy on him, Malvolio, ignorant of their presence, performs a scene from his daydream of being Olivia's husband.

If Maria's spy-like deception is aimed at shaming her adversary and thus provoking his expulsion from this charmed world, this finds its most potent instrument in the letter she drops just before Malvolio appears. She is not only certain that he will pick it up. Because she can write very much like her lady, she can also count on the fact that he will take this fake letter to be a missive from his secret love. To enhance the confusion that misrule engenders, the disguised handwriting also corrupts Olivia's language, offering up the fake news of her desire for Malvolio in the encrypted language of riddles. Precisely because Maria is cognisant of Malvolio's clandestine amorous and social ambitions, she can be sure that he will be able to decode the letter according to her intention and perform the script she is proposing. When, obeying every point of the letter, he subsequently appears before his adored lady in yellow stockings and cross-gartered, this, too, is a form of cross-dressing, even if the effect is the opposite of Viola's. Exclaiming, 'Why, this is very midsummer madness', Olivia repudiates his advances unequivocally.[8]

In both storylines of *Twelfth Night*, disguising one's appearance or one's handwriting, assuming a role that is not identical to one's actual social status, spying on others and setting them up, draws attention to the cruelty inscribed in the carnivalesque jest. It is shown to violate those who fall for it. At the same time, it also discloses that the very desire which makes the dupery possible in the first place entails an imaginary relation these characters entertain with their world. However, if, like spy work, carnivalesque misrule does its work primarily on the level of fantasy, it nevertheless has consequences; it cannot be sustained forever. The fact that the comedy's title refers to the twelfth night of revelling also means that it is to be taken as the last official holiday. The enjoyment of misrule put on display is enhanced by virtue of the knowledge that it must come to an end. All the disguising culminates in discoveries that conclude the revelling while also imposing recognition on all who have either duped others or duped themselves. In the final act, the sudden appearance of Viola's twin brother allows Orsino to give a name to the duplicity that had caused all the confusion: 'One face, one voice, one habit and two persons'.[9] Faced with this division of herself, Viola finally admits that her masculine attire is only a usurped appearance. Once Olivia assures Malvolio that the letter that got him to put on his silly attire is not her writing, though much like it, Maria, in turn, is compelled to confess that she and Sir Toby conceived this as a vicious jest.

Yet, as Keir Elam points out, Shakespeare's last festive comedy is a play 'that promises an epiphany – a secret or encoded transcendental signified waiting to be revealed – but strategically withholds it'.[10] The reunion of the twins may anticipate a double marriage, which will use these two foreign intermediaries to unite the two houses. Such resolution, however, is suspended. Orsino insists that Viola will only become his 'mistress and his fancy's queen' once he sees her in her woman's weeds.[11] The captain she gave them to has, however, been imprisoned, and Malvolio is the only one who knows what has become of him. Olivia's steward, furthermore, has quit the scene in anger, promising revenge, so that all Orsino can do is send someone to find him. In the 'meantime', as though to counter the spirit of disenthralment which the end of carnival heralds, he prolongs the disguise of his future wife.[12] If Viola is still cross-dressed, he insists on treating her as though she were Cesario, postponing the wedding. What begins again, off stage, is revelling in a different key.

While *Twelfth Night* is never directly cited in *The Americans*, Shakespeare is gestured towards in a few tossed off quotes, severed entirely from their original context. During an elegant dinner at a political convention, a KGB operative invokes *Hamlet*'s Queen Gertrude. When the Polish dissident he is trying to entrap refuses another glass of red wine, he exuberantly counters, 'the priest doth protest too much, methinks'.[13] In the same episode, Elizabeth Jennings tries to make a deal with a man to whom one of her accomplices owes money. He initially refuses, claiming 'I prefer my pound of flesh'.[14] Her attack on his private parts compels him to change his mind. Later in the season, when her husband Philip suggests that he can get the woman he is having an affair with to place a bug in the office of the head of counter-intelligence at the FBI, Elizabeth taunts him, saying 'no knock on your charms there, Romeo'.[15] He will prove her wrong, committing bigamy by marrying Martha to make her go for this ruse.

The point of departure for the crossmapping this final chapter explores is not, however, any actual Shakespeare citation. Instead, the correspondence it proposes is that the topsy-turvy world of festive comedy has an analogy in the equally carnivalesque world of Cold War espionage. While I will place *A Midsummer Night's Dream* in conversation with *The Americans* in the second part of this chapter, my opening exploration of these correspondences pertains to *Twelfth Night*. Like Illyria, Washington, DC, in the decade which culminated in the fall of the Berlin Wall in 1989 offers a stage for mistaken identities and strange licence which, in this case, is both sexual and violent. The cruelty contained in, but also contained by, the jests that Shakespeare's characters play on each other breaks through the surface unconstrained in *The Americans*. The similar structure of performance, in turn, resides in how, as in Shakespeare's comedy, these two Soviet undercover agents, working for a KGB programme called 'Directorate S', use masquerade and revelling to perform secret missions predicated on the fact that they are not what they seem.[16] Like Feste and Viola, they, too, have no fixed place in this world. Although they successfully pass as Americans, and Philip periodically even toys with the thought of defecting, in their minds they also belong to Russia. They not only perceive all the places they inhabit in the United States through the lens of the cultural values of the country they are spying for. The flashbacks they have from their previous life interpolate the homeland they left many years ago into their current one. Aliens in America and purporting to be ordinary American citizens although they are the very opposite, they, like Viola, live under the constant threat of their identity being discovered.

There is yet a further dimension to their lack of a proper place that aligns this TV drama with Shakespeare's festive comedy. Repeatedly sent out to discover the secret desires of the US government in the ongoing nuclear arms race, the Jenningses also find themselves caught in a feud between two houses in Washington – the KGB Rezidentura and the FBI. Indeed, one might liken the Soviet position to that of Olivia, equally unwilling to match above her degree. Parity with the strategic power of the United States – whether at the negotiating table or in the case of war – is the argument that drives the illegals in their escalating spiral of subterfuge. At the same time, in *The Americans*, Cold War patriotism also takes the shape of a self-deluding desire. Although, in this case, the two love-sick aristocrats have been exchanged for two war-hungry superpowers, the violent confusion the Jenningses cause also raises the question of who the true fool in this power struggle is. Indeed, in this dark rendition of carnival, Washington is the stage for a destabilisation of both the American and the Soviet rule. In this case, of course, the Jenningses are not separated like the twins in *Twelfth Night* and, instead, operate together, following commands given to them by the Center, in a play whose subtitle might read 'Make the world a safer place'.

If, like Viola, the play with mistaken identities that the Jenningses repeatedly stage is predicated on the concealment of their actual social status, cross-dressing in *The Americans* is not in regard to a blurring of gender and class designations. Instead, by donning costumes, wigs, and glasses, the two undercover spies successfully perform a wide array of American citizens. In so doing, they are not only able to play parts that allow them to enjoy acts of transgression, even if, as this serial drama progresses, these are increasingly accompanied by anxiety. By putting plurality on display, they also trouble the question of stable national and cultural identities. We can, nevertheless, read these disguises in terms of a carnivalesque counterrule because they allow the Jenningses to explore, albeit in an often troubling manner, what it means to be someone else. They do so, furthermore, on the clandestine stage that has come to be forged by espionage, juxtaposed on top of the everyday urban life of all the ordinary citizens who remain uninvolved. They are repeatedly shown to be playing a part in this counterworld, while they can only admit that they are not what they seem to be to those who are part of their spy jest. Oscillating between their costumes and their core disguise – the all-American 1980s couple, living in Falls Church with their two children and running a travel agency in Dupont Circle – Elizabeth/Nadezhda and Philip/Mischa actually perform not only a plethora of disguises. Their core role itself is contradictory, overlapping committed parents with ruthless, unrepentant killers, even while they embrace the very ideology of suburban domestic life which they also subvert.[17] Although their manifest intent is merely to dupe their targets, they implicitly render visible the instability of the designation 'American' as such.

As in *Twelfth Night*, performing an assumed identity not only allows the spy couple to charm those they seek to entangle in their missions and, like Viola, to comment on the effect their dupery has. They are also successful in getting others to fall for them because they tap into the self-deluding desires of those they enthral. Indeed, Elizabeth plays to fantasies of ambition as well as erotic daydreams on the part of those she cons into becoming her accomplices, compelling them to follow the script she has devised for them, much as Maria does Malvolio. Furthermore, in their case also, self-concealment brings with it the issue of how to read their bodies. Repeatedly, their adversary in the FBI, Stan Beeman, studies the faces which his sketch artist is able to draw based on the testimony of witnesses. Although he recognises early on that these may well be the illegals he is chasing, he is never sure whether they are all the same or all different. The 'one face … two persons', as the twins in *Twelfth Night* appear to Orsino in the final act of the play, has transformed into one couple and many faces. Yet Stan is not able to correlate this uncanny resemblance with the neighbours he has befriended because his own self-delusive desire compels him to misreading.

There is yet a further line of association worth noting. Like *Twelfth Night*, Washington in the 1980s is conceived as a topsy-turvy spy world with the last holiday in mind. To re-enact this turning point in Cold War politics as a theatre of carnivalesque transgression involves what Mieke Bal calls a preposterous engagement with the past.[18] As is the case with all historical period drama, we know that this decade will end in Gorbachev's *perestroika* and *glasnost*, making the type of spy work the Jenningses are involved in obsolete. Or, put another way, the entire historical re-imagination is undertaken under the auspices of our belated knowledge that this was a transitional moment in the history of the Cold War, whose outcome was everything but a necessity. In contrast to Shakespeare's festive comedy, the confessions and discoveries that bring about dramatic closure in the final season of *The Americans* are not made in public. Instead, they are relegated to the offices of the FBI or to nocturnal streets. Yet the carnival of spies this TV drama stages is also conceived as a collective dream from which, along the logic of contingency on which comedy is predicated, all the key players, together with the superpowers for whom they are doing battle on the ground, will have to wake up. All those entangled in this Cold War game of disguises and exchanges of clandestine information understand that their participation in this theatricalised world beyond the ordinary everyday was always temporary. From the first season onward, the Jenningses along with their handlers are aware that this is not something they will do forever. Their options are always clearly before them: to die, to disappear, or ultimately, to go home.[19]

## Shaping fantasies

One of Shakespeare's sustained explorations in his comedies is the way that fantasies shape our perception of the world, making ocular proof uncertain. When, in the beginning of the fourth act of *Twelfth Night*, Feste first meets Sebastian, his resemblance to his twin sister compels Olivia's jester to assume that he is Cesario. Annoyed that the latter claims not to recognise him, Feste negates all proof of what appears to be certain – 'No, I do not know you, nor I am not sent to you by my lady to bid you come speak with her' – only to finish by falling back on the assurance his own body affords as the measure of what can be known, 'nor this is not my nose neither. Nothing that is so is so.'[20] This concern with the way we encounter and make sense of the world through the lens of preconceptions is taken up by the credit sequence of *The Americans*. While, in Shakespeare's comedy, these imaginations pertain primarily to the foolery a love-inflected vision produces, in *The Americans* this claim pertains to political fantasies that intercede in and mediate our understanding of how we are emplaced and act in our world, such that nothing that is so, is, indeed, so.

Following upon an American and a Soviet state emblem that launch the credit sequence, we are shown binoculars, drawn in white lines, superimposed over the front door façades on a street in Washington, DC. A red map of the Soviet Union is spread across both glasses. Of the figure holding the binoculars we only see the free-floating hands. The elegantly filed fingernails, however, indicate that it is a woman, whose spectral gaze is aimed at an unknown target. It remains unclear whether she is focusing her gaze on the far-off country, mirrored on the surface of the glasses, or whether her fantasy of the Soviet Union mediates whatever she is gazing at. We are prompted to ask further: Is she looking out at the Soviet Union with her back to the American capital? Or is she looking at an American target through the lens of her training as a Soviet spy? In each episode, the scenes that follow can, in any case, be taken as a dramatised rendition of what this spectral secret agent is seeing through her spy glass.

It is, thus, fruitful to think of this gaze as a form of envisioning in terms of Louis Althusser's claim that ideology represents the imaginary relationship of individuals to their real conditions of existence. Not only are the Jenningses not what they seem to be. The world in which they engage their accomplices and their adversaries is also overlaid by the political fantasies that each side harbours. The characters are inhabiting an imaginary geography of espionage together, and while the ideological lens through which they view it is different, what they share is their investment in this fantasy.

At the same time, the red map on the surface of the binocular glasses does not cover up our view of the house façades that are behind the free-floating hands. Instead, the doors, windows, and walls shine through

Figure 17 The double vision of ideology

the spectral hands as though both the sketched image and the filmed house façade were dissolving into each other. As a reference to the American capital, this architecture shares the two round visual fields of the glasses with the Soviet Union. At issue is, thus, a complex bifocal vision. Not only are the two superpowers present simultaneously in the field of vision. While the binoculars draw something into focus which is far away, the gaze of the female spy is implicitly straddling two places – a street in Washington and her imaginary relation to it, negotiated through a place that is nothing other than a drawn red map. Given that both are visually present within the frame of the two round glasses, proximity and distance, the actual and what is conjured up, blend into each other. Furthermore, while the binoculars are initially at a vertical slant, within seconds they move into a perfectly horizontal position. This can be read as a further reference to the topsy-turvy world of carnival. To move seamlessly from an oblique gaze to a levelled one taps into the uncertainty of orientation regarding the vision that this spy glass affords, rendering unclear what is top and what is bottom, what is left and what is right.[21]

The destabilisation of identities so typical for Shakespeare's festive comedies is what the subsequent image montage puts on display. While the credits run in Russian and in English, we are shown a series of diptychs, foregrounding a double vision. Two propaganda posters, the Soviet 'Don't Blab' and the US 'Silence Means Safety', use the same pathos formula, an index finger on the lips, to warn the viewer that secrecy is of the essence. They are followed by two monuments, one of the raising of the Stars and Stripes in Iwo Jima during the Second World War (WWII), the other of a worker and a collective farm woman raising the hammer and sickle. As the credit sequence proceeds, characters from *The Americans* share the visual space with public insignia typical for the propaganda of both superpowers. Elizabeth's passport photograph is placed next to the face of Lilya Brik in Rodchenko's literacy promotion poster. Philip's passport picture is juxtaposed with a WWII War Bonds poster. A snapshot of their daughter Paige, patting an American eagle statue, is first placed next to a photograph of an astronaut, only to be replaced within seconds by the drawn image of a Soviet cosmonaut.

Then, as the credit sequence moves towards its end, we are given a parade of faces of past and current paternal figures of political authority on both sides, each pair giving way to the next one: George Washington (whose monument is repeatedly used as a backdrop) and Vladimir Lenin (whose painting hangs in the Rezidentura) segue into the cold warriors Nikita Khrushchev, John F. Kennedy, Jimmy Carter, Yuri Andropov, and finally Leonid Brezhnev with Ronald Reagan. A different kind of juxtaposition, in turn, serves as the visual climax. The faces in a photograph of a typical American nuclear family, sitting on the porch steps in front of their home, are pasted over with snapshots of the Jennings family. Even though the original faces are obliterated, the bifocal vision is maintained. The pictures of the Soviet spies and their children, who have replaced these Americans, do not blend into the grain of the photograph. Instead they are presented as visual foreign bodies, which both do and do not fit into the picture frame. After a last double vision of the Stars and Stripes next to the Red Star, the credit sequence ends with the title of the show in white letters against a black background. The letter 'c', however, has been exchanged for a red hammer and sickle.

What is drawn into focus by this visual montage is not only how the imaginary relation which those embroiled in the spy game entertain towards their real conditions of existence are materialised in political iconography. The serial doubling and replacement of these iconic visual emblems also draws attention to a salient instability at the heart of the pervasive paranoia that dominated Cold War culture. Because the entire nation was called upon to participate in a collective suspicion that what appeared to be so was not in actuality so, the line of demarcation between friend and enemy had become increasingly porous. Fear of a Soviet nuclear attack was accompanied by a far more intangible anxiety that a clandestine intervention in American politics was already well under way. Nervousness regarding those citizens who, owing to their political convictions, were deemed untrustworthy had soon transformed into the conviction that America was inhabited by internal enemies, threatening the American way of life. This fostered conspiracy fantasies in which it became difficult to tell a real American from a false one. Everyone could potentially be the enemy, having skilfully assumed the guise of a friend. As a result, a clear distinction between 'us v. them', so characteristic for the actual theatres of war in Korea, Vietnam, and Afghanistan, had steadily come to be replaced by a far more ambiguous opposition between 'us v. ourselves'.[22]

The rich array of disguises which Elizabeth and Philip put on display speak to precisely this anxiety regarding internal political enmity. When Soviet spies are able to play Americans to perfection, what is above all destabilised is the certainty that we know to whom this designation refers. To the Jenningses, the Americans are representatives of the government against which their subterfuge is aimed. But they are also all the people they emulate without being fully identical to them. The Americans is what they keep reassuring each other they are not, but one might also say what they delude themselves into believing they have not become. *The Americans* thus not only shares with *Twelfth Night* a preoccupation with a carnivalesque undermining of certainty, fostering instead the suspicion – whether mirthful or ominous – that nothing that is so is so. Theseus's sober comment at the beginning of the fifth act of *A Midsummer Night's Dream* also suggests, as has already been noted, a further crossmapping between Shakespeare's festive comedies and this serial TV drama. Conferring with his bride Hippolyta about the strange nocturnal events the lovers spoke of upon awakening, he calls these 'shaping fantasies', in the sense of images planted in the mind to create fantastical creatures. In a manner applicable to the visual distortion political ideology affords, he warns against the tricks that strong imagination can play, reminding her, 'in the night, imagining some fear,/ How easy is a bush supposed a bear!'[23]

At the end of this earlier comedy, four couples will share a wedding night. After a sustained quarrel that threatens to bring with it disastrous climatic aberrations, the fairy king Oberon is reunited with his queen, Titania, and together they have come to the Athenian court to bless the chambers throughout the palace. This includes not only the bride-bed of the Amazon queen Hippolyta, but also that of the two Athenian women, Hermia and Helena. With this magic consecration, Oberon hopes to procure the safety of all those who are sharing their bed with a spouse that night. Yet while his promise of peace and healthy propagation issuing from these marriages is something we are meant to expect, this remains a prediction. Furthermore, the blessing, of which Oberon is the stage director, occurs off stage. All the fairies disappear, leaving the Puck, Robin Goodfellow, alone on stage.

The epilogue he addresses directly to the audience, in which he compares the players to shadows and the action to a vision 'no more yielding than a dream', comprises an anti-theatrical gesture. In that he ends by wishing 'good night unto you all', a distinction is made between all those who have disappeared into their respective bedchambers to perform their intimate rites, and the audience.[24] We are called upon to wake up, not, however, into a new day, but rather into our ordinary night. The closure offered at the end of *A Midsummer Night's Dream* is, thus, open-ended on two levels. On the one hand, the consecration of the bridal beds promises that something is to come, although the outcome is as yet uncertain. On the other hand, as we awake from all the turmoil, but also all the magical charm that was the object of this play, we recognise that this dramatic traffic was, from the start, provisional.

Before looking closer at how *The Americans* repurposes this double resolution to the thematic preoccupations that it shares with this comedy, namely the charm but also the danger of an enchanted vision, it is worth exploring what Shakespeare's dramatic closure is predicated on. Furthermore, I propose working through the play backwards, to draw into focus what prompts the discoveries that this resolution affords. As already noted, Theseus maintains that what the lovers have recounted about their nocturnal adventures are the shaping fantasies of seething brains 'of imagination all compact', giving a visible shape to a fear that is itself imaginary.[25] Hippolyta, in turn, is more attuned to their story, maintaining that because 'all their minds transfigured so together,/more witnesseth than fancy's images'. However strange their testimony may be, she feels it 'grows to something of great constancy'.[26] The uncertain status of what happened in the forest during the previous night is what the lovers, lying together on the edge of the forest, themselves address upon waking up. Unsure whether he is awake or asleep, Lysander only vaguely remembers that he had intended to flee with Hermia to his aunt's home. Demetrius, who also cannot tell for sure whether they are not still dreaming, remembers that he followed his rival after Helena had told him of this plan, yet has no idea why he now desires the woman he had previously spurned, his love for Hermia having mysteriously vanished.

Hermia is the one to find a fitting name for the shaping fantasies which anticipate, as the following crossmapping will show, the shared dream of spy work in *The Americans*. 'Methinks I see these things with parted eye', she explains, 'When everything seems double'.[27] By appending to the difficulty of distinguishing between dreaming and waking the notion of a bifocal vision, Hermia speaks not only to an entanglement between seeing the ordinary world and seeing a fancied image. Whether this pertains to fear or desire, fancy is reshaping something that is already an imaginary relation. Indeed, what Shakespeare's lovers and Joe Weisberg's spies share is a degree of doubt regarding the shaping fantasies they are drawn in by. They understand them to be an imaginary relationship they maintain, with self-recognition a form of waking from them, even if only intermittently.

Given my suggestion that *The Americans* should be read with the awakening from the charmed counterworld of espionage in mind, it is useful to address the other two moments of waking up in Shakespeare's festive comedy. One involves the weaver Nick Bottom, who, with his head transformed into that of an ass, spent the previous night consorting with the fairy queen. Although, upon waking, he is aware that he has had a most rare vision, he is forced to admit that he would be a patched fool were he to offer to say what he had been. All he can do is ask his friend, Peter Quince, to write a ballad of this dream, to be called '"Bottom's Dream", because it hath no bottom'.[28] With a correspondence to *The Americans* in mind, this gesture of self-censorship proves significant. The dream experience is relegated to the realm of encrypted information, which can only be transmitted if re-encoded in another shape, which the intended audience, in turn, can decipher.

The other seminal moment of waking up in Shakespeare's comedy is the one that relates a charmed vision to the struggle over sovereignty, casting the fairy king and his queen in the position of two quarrelling superpowers. Oberon had previously enchanted Titania's eye so as to steal from her a changeling child. He makes sure to undo 'the hateful imperfection of her eyes' only after he claims to have 'had his pleasure taunting her' for her folly of having fallen in love with an ass-headed mortal.[29] Yet his Puck is not allowed to relieve Bottom of this mask until after Titania has woken from her enchantment to look with parted eye at her strange lover and take note of the consequence her folly has had. It is necessary for the queen, who had opposed her king's supreme sovereignty, to be given ocular proof of what she had been enamoured with, for Oberon to regain his position of superiority.[30] Amazed, and shamed, she will ask him to explain the visions she has seen, given that faced with the still disfigured Bottom, her disenthralled eyes 'do loathe his visage now'.[31] The remarriage of this couple not only requires Titania seeing the past night with parted eye. She also needs to be aware that her husband knows that she is now cognisant of the folly that this love had been predicated on.

What all the players wake up from – and therein lies the decisive correspondence to the imaginary geography of the world of late twentieth-century espionage – are carnivalesque scenes that have taken place in a nocturnal forest which was conceived as the anamorphic mirror of the demos; as what Michel Foucault calls a heterotopia reflecting and contesting the Athenian court.[32] The mistaken identities, resulting in abuse and violence, along with the enjoyment of sexual licence, can be seen as acting out problems on the level of an imaginary fairy world which are posed by the actual political struggle set up in the first scene of the play. This entails two parallel storylines, the first of which pertains to the military campaign which Theseus has won against the Amazon queen. He wooed Hippolyta on the battlefield, doing her injuries, but now hopes to wed her in another key. The second entails the struggle between Hermia and her stern father, Egeus, who says that if she does not take Demetrius as her husband, her only choices are the nunnery or death. Hermia, however, comes up with an alternative more in line with her own desire. Together with Lysander, the husband she has chosen for herself, she flees into the woods. Their goal is to reach the home of his widowed aunt, which is to say a place that is not only outside the jurisdiction of Athenian law but also a place of feminine rule.

Helena, who has been spying on her girlhood friend, betrays this plan to Demetrius, so that they, too, end up in the forest, where these two parallel storylines, revolving as they do around subduing the combative spirit of women, are continued, even while the royal couple in Athens are replaced with their fairy counterparts. As the duke's proxy, Oberon, along with his Puck, deploys a magic juice that charms the eye and makes the target fall in love with what they see first upon awakening. The misrule this produces does not, however, merely serve to re-establish his sovereignty over all the fairies, including his headstrong queen. The result is also the performance of internal enmity, in which – and therein lies another correspondence to *The Americans* – the line of demarcation between friend and foe becomes fluid. Not only does Helena continue to stalk her former friend, Hermia, until they confront each other in a *mano-a-mano* fight. The two young men, driven by mistrust and a desire to betray the other, abandon both women and end up instead chasing after each other through the night, each seeking the death of their rival. Before any killing can occur, however, all four collapse in exhaustion at the edge of the forest.

Reading the Athenian lovers' enjoyment of a violent desire in conjunction with the storyline that revolves around Titania's humiliation also brings into focus the other royal power who is introduced in the first act. While, throughout the play, Hippolyta is mostly silent, she seems not only to have inspired disobedience in Hermia. Now that she has been vanquished, the Amazon queen has her own proxy in Titania. While the young lovers, whose eyes have been enchanted with the love juice, can no longer tell who is a friend and who an enemy, a second line of demarcation emerges. This one runs between a set of figures of paternal authority, namely the duke, the fairy king, and his Puck on the one side, and, on the other, the Amazon queen, the fairy queen, and her court of fairies, as well as a votaress in India. The changeling child whom Oberon wants as his page is her issue. For Titania, to win the struggle over this child would mean establishing the legacy of a feminine sovereignty, and with it a rule that is different from the paternal one. At the end of the play, it will have proven to be nothing but a dream. The ambivalence inscribed in the resolution of *A Midsummer Night's Dream* thus consists in the fact that while both warrior queens – Hippolyta and Titania – lose their battles, Oberon's spy work and subterfuge ultimately works in favour of the two young Athenian women. Only because he has his love juice administered to the eyes of the two rivalling young men are Hermia and Helena able to get the husbands they have chosen for themselves. The marriages celebrated in the final act attest to Oberon's sovereignty in a contradictory relation to feminine desire, curtailing some of the female players while empowering others.

## The love juice of patriotism

The following crossmapping proposes to conceive the Cold War enmity between the two superpowers in *The Americans* in terms comparable to the battle between the Athenian duke and his Amazon queen. The Jenningses, and all whom they involve in their clandestine operations, are shown to perform – as transgressive revelry – the Cold War fantasies devised in the capitals of both these nations. Although, in this case, the Soviet Union has not been vanquished from the start, in hindsight we know the Americans to have won the arms race and the struggle for global capitalism. To think of the secret service handlers, investigators, and spies as fairy-like proxies and confused lovers means positing a narrative frame for this TV drama which, in its dramaturgic function, is similar to the nuptial celebrations that bookend Shakespeare's comedy, signalling the restoration of peace. In *The Americans*, détente stands for an end to the military conflict. The spy world of a charmed, bifocal vision, which takes as its stage primarily (though not exclusively) the nocturnal streets of Washington and Moscow, has, as its context, the Cold War negotiations that will culminate in the Washington Summit of 1987.[33] The nocturnal misrule that the Jenningses undertake serves to work through the preoccupations of ordinary politics in the form of clandestine operations, which are aimed at either subverting the Americans or putting the Soviets in a privileged position, even while discussions of easing the hostilities between the two superpowers are underway.

Reading the fairy world of espionage in terms of a heterotopic refiguration of ordinary politics also, however, thrives on two significant variations on Shakespeare's comedy. First, this serial TV drama conceives those who act out the spy fantasies of the superpowers in relation to architectural locations of power that are conceived as doubles of each other. While we never see the inside of the White House or the Kremlin, the buildings that house the FBI and the Soviet Rezidentura serve as the two official stages for the Cold War waged in Washington, with both in opposition to but also infiltrated by each other. Once Stan Beeman, working for counter-intelligence at the FBI, moves in across the street from the Jenningses, the murky entanglement of the two superpowers is given a second, more private location. While the intelligence agencies have information leaks because there are moles and double agents, the line of demarcation regarding the two homes in suburban Falls Church becomes blurred because Stan unwittingly befriends the very people he is chasing. Ironically, he suspends the suspicion that his work with the FBI requires, while the Jenningses socialise unconditionally with the neighbour they know to be their designated enemy.

Secondly, the quarrel between the master of surveillance, Oberon, and his fairy queen is not only reconfigured primarily in terms of a struggle among the Jenningses, as they act out the commands given to them by the KGB Center in Moscow – a spat that reflects as much on an internal discord within Soviet intelligence as it does on the legitimation of their marriage. Until the last season of *The Americans*, Elizabeth is also cast as a splice between Titania and her fairy king, as unremitting as Oberon in her deception and manipulation of others, while unwavering in her conviction in the righteousness of her cause. She is introduced in the opening sequence of the pilot as a blonde femme fatale, sitting at a bar at night, seducing a man. Using her sexual allure, she will successfully extort information from him about a Russian defector, so that she and Philip can kidnap him a few days later. Soon after, we see her in her car, taking off her wig, as though in disgust, not at the role-playing as such but at this particular part. There are, however, more layers to her serial performance of disguises. As already mentioned, the one role she plays consistently is that of the caring mother, who, after each nocturnal adventure, returns home and, having made breakfast for her children the next morning, sends them off to school. This tension between femme fatale and domestic queen is dramaturgically enhanced in the opening sequences of the pilot by virtue of the fact that even while she is performing her maternal role, the abducted man is lying gagged in the trunk of the Oldsmobile parked in their garage, She is considering stabbing him with a kitchen knife.

In Philip's case, the double life his disguises allow him to live also involves using sexual charm to inveigle his target while performing the attentive father, protecting his children. From the start, however, he is less stalwart in his support of their spy work, and while he is never as deceived by his wife as Titania is by Oberon, he, like her, is in the more vulnerable position. The cowboy boots that Philip buys at the mall early on in the first season (and which he will still be wearing while square dancing in the final one) renders visible how he is juggling two allegiances, one to Soviet espionage, the other to the American home story he has come to embrace. When, early in the first season, he clandestinely listens to the tape recording of Elizabeth's sexual act with the man she picked up at the bar, the distress that flickers across his face indicates the humiliation he feels in regard to the damage her exploit poses to his self-esteem as a husband. While he is, thus, shown to be far more aware of the emotional costs of their political enthralment, what both have in common is that they see everything with parted eyes – in terms of the country they left more than fifteen years ago and the country they will never be part of completely. This ingrained bifocal vision simply has different effects on them.

A charmed double vision is also what characterises Stan, who constantly gazes at the house of his new neighbours on the other side of the street. His suspicion is initially roused not least of all because he often sees the Jenningses going in and out of their home at odd hours. He fancies that they could be the illegals he is chasing and even breaks into their garage one night because the Oldsmobile they drive is the same make as the one a witness reported from the scene where the defector was abducted. The fact that he finds no clues is, however, only part of the reason why he abandons his professional impulse to mistrust all appearances. The relief he feels also speaks to a self-deluding desire that is at cross purposes with his professional intuition. Unaware that Philip has been hiding in the garage throughout the scene, his gun poised to shoot, Stan wants to believe that the neighbours he has befriended are not the enemies he thinks they might be.

In this constellation, Stan can be aligned with Nick Bottom. What makes him particularly susceptible to the Jennings' charm is that since he went undercover with a group of white supremacists, his own marriage has begun to fail. Comparable to the ass-headed artisan, he, too, does not resist what in their case is the offer of a charmed friendship – playing squash with Philip, coming over for family dinners, and watching out for their kids whenever work prevents the Jenningses from coming home. He is taken in by the all-American domesticity that his neighbours perform, given that sentimentality clouds his vision. He, like Bottom, does not resist this seduction because, especially once his wife has left him, sharing their family life is a compensation for the one he is in the process of losing. Ironically, then, while his work with counter-intelligence encourages him to see the ordinary everyday through the lens of Cold War paranoia, his predisposition to suspicion is also what nurtures his suspension of disbelief regarding these neighbours.

Like the enchanted nocturnal woods in *A Midsummer Night's Dream*, the Washington in which the Jenningses perform their infinite variety of Americans is, thus, not only part *of* yet distinct *from* the ordinary Washington, DC. It is also a heterotopic site of transgression that suspends the rules of the everyday. In contrast to Shakespeare's comedy, the revelling that is undertaken here entails excessive erotic activity enmeshed with equally excessive violence, and is, thus, more aggressive than playful. Nevertheless, all those who find themselves involved in the missions undertaken by the Jenningses are comparable to the Athenian lovers, with whose vision the fairies toy. Whether as willing accomplices or as unfortunate victims, once they have drawn the attention of the spy couple to themselves, they cannot help but play the parts for which they have been designated.

At the same time, the fact that the Jenningses run a travel agency also opens up a line of association to Oberon's Puck, who travels around the world in search of the magic flower. The tricks that Robin Goodfellow plays on those whose eyes he enchants re-surface in the erotic confusion that lies at the very heart of the Jennings' game of espionage. Furthermore, throughout this TV drama, Elizabeth and Philip are themselves compelled to perform the script their handlers dictate to them, much as Stan, though often at odds with his superiors, must abide by their dictates. The political leaders whose spirit rules over the entire carnival of spies are, in turn, merely a spectral presence throughout *The Americans*. Ronald Reagan and his Soviet counterparts in the Communist Party are only seen on TV news broadcasts or in photographs hanging on the walls in the offices of the FBI and the Rezidentura.

The patriotism that colours the vision of all those we are shown to be acting and acted upon by these higher powers can, therefore, be likened to the magic juice dispersed by Oberon in *A Midsummer Night's Dream*. What is being administered in this case is an unconditional love for one's country that resembles an equally all-embracing enthralment. This not only requires violence against those designated as enemies to this ideology but, equally disturbing, the destruction of family ties and humiliation in the case of many who are in complicity with spy missions on both sides.[34] While Elizabeth and Philip have fallen in love with the idea of fighting against the corrupt and destructive forces of global capitalism, their children are shown to be indoctrinated in school into falling in love with the idea of being an American. In a telling scene in the pilot, Philip accompanies his son, Henry, to an event at the Falls Church Middle School, where the astronaut Thomas P. Stafford has been invited to speak to the students and their parents as the epitome of a 'true American hero'. The role of sight is significant for the ideological manipulation being performed.[35] While the audience sings the national anthem, a select group of students are on stage with the speaker and the principal, facing the American flag, their right hands also placed over their hearts. The backdrop for this celebration are two enormous student paintings of the Apollo-Soyuz test project. The administering of the love juice consists in placing before the eyes of the audience this visual composite of American children of all ethnicities, a living icon of patriotism, and images pertaining to his political celebrity.

At the same time, attachment to a communal identity is debunked as a form of mesmerism. The expression on the faces of the audience close to Philip and his son is one of unequivocal rapture as they clap and wave little American flags. Henry, himself beaming with pride, keeps checking to see how his father is taking in this spectacle. Philip smiles and winks back at his son to reassure him, yet, when he feels unobserved, he allows himself to exhibit discomfort at the duplicitous role he is playing. The point is not only that he is merely feigning the patriotism that all the others are partaking in uncritically. He is the odd man out, whose eyes have not been enchanted by this particular love juice, and, as such, the one who signals to us that it is pure ideology.[36]

If *The Americans* is invested in such gestures of political disillusioning, this, however, pertains not only to the individual players on the ground, to whom this love juice is administered. Rather, the government leaders using their political power to sustain a crazy arms race in space are also accused of being enthralled by fantasy. Along with their subjects, they, too, are revealed as being caught up in a dream, which has grown 'to something of great constancy' precisely because their minds are so transfigured together.[37] The fact that some are aware of the illusory aspect of this communal belief recalls those moments in Shakespeare's festive comedies when one of the players wakes up and, by virtue of briefly standing apart, takes note of the foolery of the others around him. Such a moment of recognition comes in 'The Colonel' when, during a clandestine meeting with Philip, a man who has classified information about a secret defence programme gives his account of President Reagan's antiballistic missile programme.[38] The technology, he assures him, is *incredibilis* in the original Latin sense: 'At best, it's 50 years from being remotely operational. The damn thing's a fantasy.' His sobering assessment is that if the current administration is committed to it, then it is because the president 'only hears what he wants to hear. Some say it's all one big psy-op, a way of getting the Soviets to spend themselves into oblivion trying to keep up with a technology that will never pan out.'

However, in the first season of *The Americans*, two competing dreams involving the Jenningses are set up, entangling international politics with domestic happiness. Like the quarrel between Titania and her fairy king, so, too, the status of the marriage between Elizabeth and Philip is as much at issue as is the threat of discovery by the FBI and thus a failure of their entire mission. As the flashbacks from their arrival in America reveal, at the beginning, their marital covenant was nothing more than a convenient cover for their life as spies in their new home. The abduction with which the pilot opens reveals a change in both their attitudes. The defector they are holding hostage was formerly a KGB officer, who had raped Elizabeth while she was in training. Philip's rage at discovering this, culminating in his ruthless execution of their prisoner, reveals the depth of his attachment to his wife, even while, in Elizabeth, it awakens a new passion for her husband. She now wants their marriage to be real.

At the same time, their sustained quarrel over Philip's suggestion of defecting once again raises doubts about their loyalty to each other. His growing enchantment with the American way of life, which her unwavering enthralment with the communist cause forbids her, influences their marriage as well. Not sharing the same political dream puts the fantasy of a shared family bond into jeopardy. As the series creator, Joe Weisberg, has explained, *The Americans* is 'at its core a marriage story. International relations is just an allegory of the human relations. Sometimes, when you're struggling in your marriage or with your kid, it feels like life or death. For Philip and Elizabeth, it often is.'[39]

The uncertainty whether their life as a couple is merely another one of their disguises or an expression of mutual acknowledgement is at play in Philip's impromptu decision to marry Martha. He proposes to the secretary who works in the counter-intelligence department of the FBI not only because he wants to make sure that she will continue to supply him with information. He also does this to retaliate against his wife's wavering commitment to him as a husband. Elizabeth is never jealous of this second wife because she sees this union as nothing other than spy business as usual. Astonished at how much the wedding ceremony has moved her, she does, however, reflect on the legitimacy of their own marriage. She asks Philip whether things might have been different for them if, rather than simply having been assigned to each other, they, too, had exchanged marriage vows. What, in turn, does cause a temporary separation of the couple is actual deception on Philip's part. His attempt to keep secret the amorous night he spends with Irina, the woman he was in love with while training with the KGB, prompts Elizabeth, once she discovers their renewed involvement, to ask him to move out of their home.

In other words, while their performance of Americanness is successful because it is based on a clear distinction between what is a role and what is real, the legitimacy of their marriage is, from the very beginning of this TV drama, in crisis because this clear distinction does not hold. To underscore that this is a bond that requires a serial renegotiation, the first season of *The Americans* also explores the possibility of a romantic alternative open to Elizabeth. In contrast to her arranged marriage with Philip, who, when they arrived together in America, was a complete stranger, Elizabeth early on in her new life had a passionate relationship with an African American activist whom she enlisted in her cause. Now, fifteen years later, she again involves Gregory in one of her operations. When, in the process, she also confides to him her conflicted feelings about her husband, he tries to convince her to give up this marriage. He accuses her of foolishly insisting on living what to him was never anything other than a lie. Although Elizabeth can admit to Gregory that they share a history of real intimacy in a way she does not with her husband, she, nevertheless, cannot comply with his demand.

If, though promising happiness, their union is conceived by the screenplay as an impossibility, this also gestures towards that which is averted in Shakespeare's comedy, namely the star-crossed lovers from *Romeo and Juliet*. In the case of Elizabeth and Gregory, their passion for each other is also part of the war between the two houses, both in dignity alike, in which they are entangled. Like Romeo, who is banished from Verona for the death of his kinsman, Gregory, too, must be extradited to the Soviet Union for a murder that Elizabeth involved him in. Also, like Shakespeare's tragic lover, he refuses to leave Washington, choosing to remain in a situation that can end only in death, because this is the only city where he feels at home. In what her handler will subsequently call 'your act of street theater', Elizabeth devises for him a heroic self-sacrifice.[40] Gregory allows the police to corner him so that, rather than being taken alive, he can die in a shoot-out that is both brutal and pointless. On the manifest level of the dramatic plot, his death is a tragic necessity because it allows Elizabeth to return to Philip and, under the cover of domesticity, once more resume her spy work without the temptation of a different romantic solution. In deviation from Shakespeare's tragedy, however, only Gregory must be sacrificed, while, in contrast to Juliet, Elizabeth is not allowed to inhabit the role of star-crossed lover for long. Instead, she must return to the script offered by the comedy Shakespeare composed at the same time, and with it the possibility of remarriage that *A Midsummer Night's Dream* proposes for Titania and her fairy king.[41]

The first season of *The Americans* culminates in a shoot-out with the FBI, in which the Jenningses are themselves involved. Stan Beeman and his team, having discovered the car which the spy couple has been using as a drop-off point, are ready to arrest whoever opens the trunk. Philip, having sent Elizabeth to pick up a tape, realises this to be a set-up and arrives just in time to prevent her from being seized. During the car chase that ensues, she is, however, critically wounded, and they are forced to retreat to a safe house so that the bullet in her stomach can successfully be removed. When Elizabeth finally wakes up from the operation, her husband is waiting at her bedside. The first words she speaks to him are in Russian, asking him to 'come home'.[42] Looking intensely into her eyes, he kisses the hand she has reached out towards him.

## A long good-bye

In the following seasons, a serial pattern emerges regarding both the patriotic and the marital dream the Jenningses remain enthralled with. In the charmed counterworld of espionage, they continue to react to and act upon the daily politics of the Cold War. While Philip's doubt in the validity of their cause continues to grow, Elizabeth becomes ever more belligerent. In a refiguration of the two queens in *A Midsummer Night's Dream*, she performs Titania's sexual allure in a splice with the prowess of an Amazon queen. What changes, however, is the object of their quarrel, once Paige discovers who her parents really are. As if Titania had never given up the changeling child whom Oberon wants for his henchman, Elizabeth is able to undo her daughter's initial enchantment with Pastor Tim's religious instruction and, instead, administer her own love juice of patriotism. Her daughter subsequently becomes the page in the entourage of spies that accompanies Elizabeth during her clandestine assignments. Drawn more and more into these, Paige also begins to see the world with parted eyes. She slowly discovers a secret world, hidden from the eyes of ordinary citizens, even while this bifocality is often at cross purposes with her filial affection. Despite the fact the she, too, begins to don disguises, for Paige, the family life she grew up in is never anything other than real. Discovering the depth of her parents' duplicity instead serves as a source of intense suffering. Despite the fact that she comes to fully ascribe to Elizabeth's patriotic furore, she grows ever more estranged from her. The instability regarding who she is, which will plague Paige throughout the TV drama, is that she is identical with her role of daughter, even after she has also joined the spy game. What she comes to realise instead is that she never could nor ever will be able to trust Elizabeth's performance of her role as mother.

Philip, in turn, wants to disengage his daughter from what he perceives to be an unhealthy involvement in the work he has come to be disenchanted with, causing the rift within the couple to intensify. Having woken up with his eyes no longer charmed, he feels humiliation at seeing the monstrous psychic injury they have unwittingly inflicted on their children. Elizabeth, exhausted by her performance of disguises that are becoming ever more disagreeable, herself begins to harbour doubts – not about the cause itself but about who she has become. As the serial repetition of violence progresses, what also increases is the sense that something must change. As though to find refuge in their domestic bond where none can be found in the political one, Elizabeth and Philip decide to celebrate their marital vows belatedly. Once Martha has been extradited to Moscow because the FBI discovered her involvement with the illegals, they undergo a secret Russian Orthodox wedding. This performance is meant to reconfirm that their marital covenant is real and, for that reason, they appear before the priest without any disguise. This will subsequently prove to have not only authorised their remarriage but ultimately also to be the undoing of their double life. Their priest, to protect himself while being interrogated by the FBI, will offer a perfect description of them.

Until this final dramatic twist, however, as in *A Midsummer Night's Dream*, where, at the height of all nocturnal confusion, the lovers could turn their weapons on each other but are prevented from doing so owing to the mischievous intervention of Robin Goodfellow, fatality is always averted. As dangerous as their assignments are and as close as the FBI comes to discovering their identity, the Jenningses always manage to navigate a tragic outcome. Instead, the correspondence between their political and their domestic quarrels is rather such that, as the Cold War spy game starts to unravel, their family life also falls apart more and more. By the beginning of the last season, they are living separate lives, a silent war going on between them. Elizabeth is now working alone, donning ever new disguises, while Philip has decided to dedicate himself exclusively to their failing travel agency. Though more exhausted than ever, Elizabeth, sworn to secrecy by her superiors, is unable to share any of her exploits with him, so that there is no conversation between them of any kind. While Philip tries to convince her that this life of duplicity is finally getting to her as well, she cannot admit to him that she, too, is beginning to get disenthralled. Instead, she is repeatedly shown smoking alone in their backyard.[43]

This domestic enmity also reflects on the internal divide within the KGB regarding the vision of a post-nuclear world that Gorbachev is about to propose at the 1987 Washington Summit, the backdrop for the final season. While the old guard seeks to preserve the political antagonism, others in Moscow envision a future beyond an arms race that is crippling their economy. The way *The Americans* stages this struggle makes use of a gender division, pitting the women in the counter-world of espionage against the men. At the Rezidentura in Washington, Tatiana, a mid-level KGB intelligence officer, is a vehement supporter of those who want to get rid of her country's head of state. For this reason, she embraces a political complot, whose aim is to have one of the official envoys, Nestorenko, assassinated. She intends to tamper with his report and make it seem as though Gorbachev had asked him to trade away military secrets. Claudia, who is engaged as Elizabeth's handler, is herself aligned with those in the KGB seeking to undermine the summit to topple the current government. She has remained a hardliner cold warrior because her experience of WWII has made her wary of political compromises with the Americans. As her most cherished agent, Elizabeth is assigned with this treacherous task, with Paige in her wake.

This matrilineal troop is held together by an affective bond. When they are not on the street, sabotaging their male adversaries, they meet at a safe house, where Claudia deftly administers her love juice of patriotism. She cooks forbidden Russian dishes for the two women, evoking Elizabeth's nostalgia and Paige's curiosity for the culture on the other side of the ocean. Showing them listening to recordings of Tchaikovsky, watching Soviet films, or drinking vodka together, what is staged is a charmed world of solidarity between three generations of Russian women, reminiscent of Titania's revelry with her fairies. It is the only moment in the last season in which Elizabeth is shown as high-spirited, enjoying herself rather than assuming one of her many exhausting poses.

On the other side of the gender divide, the man who used to be the KGB Rezident asks one of his former colleagues to return to Washington. Now running the Directorate S programme in Moscow, Arkady belongs to those who support Gorbachev, and he needs someone to intervene in the complot against the divisive head of state. Oleg is willing to undertake this secret mission, having already previously undermined the hardliners in his party. Upon arriving, he draws Philip back into the spy game the latter had hoped to have left forever. Meeting with him in a park at night, Oleg is able to convince him to spy on his wife and report back to him. The ploy recalls Shakespeare's Oberon, who disenchants his queen's eyes to humiliate her into recognising the folly of her previous enthralment. When Philip finally confesses to Elizabeth that he has been working against her, he hopes this will make her acknowledge her own folly, and, in so doing, take responsibility for the despair they have caused. His attempt to undo the love juice of Cold War ideology they once both shared finally has its effect when she listens to a tape of one of the meetings Nestorenko conducted and discovers that he does not sound at all like a traitor. She will subsequently not only confront Claudia regarding her treachery and thwart her complot by refusing to undertake the assassination; she will also kill Tatiana, preventing her from murdering Gorbachev's envoy in her stead, but in so doing, will also disclose the fragility of this feminine alliance.

Once united again in their spy work, the Jenningses also come together again as a couple. This reunion, however, is predicated on a mistake Elizabeth makes unwittingly, which, once more following comedy's logic of contingency, will finally get them to leave the carnival of spies.[44] Because the Center needs her to rescue a fellow illegal, she does not attend the Thanksgiving dinner at Stan's house, arousing his original suspicion. So blinded is she by her spy mission that she has forgotten the importance of this holiday, and, for the first time ever, blunders in her otherwise perfect embodiment of an American mother. As though returning to the mindset he had in the first season of this TV drama, Stan again breaks into the Jennings home while they are out. Looking at the family photographs, he suddenly remembers the testimony of one of the illegals he had interrogated. On his deathbed, the man had told him about a couple, saying the husband was lucky and his wife pretty. It is this spectral voice which accompanies Stan as he checks through all the rooms for evidence, including the garage. Although he finds nothing there, Stan finally realises what a patched fool he has been once the sketch artist shows him the pictures he was able to make based on the confession of the priest.

The last episode of *The Americans* is entitled 'START'. Although this is the acronym for the bilateral Strategic Arms Reduction Treaty that was signed on 31 July 1991, it implicitly also gestures towards the fact that while this particular carnivalesque spy theatre is about to end, for both the superpowers and their proxies something new is about to begin. If, in hindsight, we know that Gorbachev's *glasnost* will have won out in the end, we have also come to recognise that the game is up for the Jenningses. Realising that Stan is finally closing in on them, Philip makes his distress call to Elizabeth, and she, prepared for this contingency, takes from their secret vault everything they need for their escape, including the wedding rings they exchanged during their clandestine marriage ceremony. They will leave their son, Henry, at the boarding school he is attending, because, still ignorant of their true identity, he can claim in good conscience to belong in America. When they go to the college apartment where Paige now lives, Stan is waiting for them, with his spy glass aimed at her window. He follows them to the garage, and, as they are about to get into their car, he confronts them at gunpoint, telling them 'it's all over'.[45]

Downplaying the gravity of the situation, Philip begins by explaining, 'we had a job to do', to which Stan, utterly bemused, responds, 'You were my best friend.' At the beginning of the long monologue of self-defence that follows, Philip appeals to precisely this mutual attachment. He tries to persuade Stan that he had been his only friend in a life that he has now come to see as a horrible jest. When Paige chimes in, assuring him that Henry knows nothing, Stan finally wakes up from the enchanted vision they had offered him all this time. Devastated at the degree not only of their deception but of his own foolishness, he admits, 'I would have done anything for you, Philip, for all of you.' Although Stan eventually lowers his gun, he remains mesmerised by a narrative that Philip continues to spin, in which the line between authentic feeling and adept performance is constantly blurred. Philip speaks to a patriotism that no longer makes sense to him, to his confusion at leaving the country they have lived in for such a long time, to his distress at having to abandon one of his children, and, finally, to the urgency that, in the interest of global peace, they get the message about the secret plot against Gorbachev to his defenders in Moscow.

Paige is the one to break the standoff, imploring Stan to take care of the brother who knows nothing about them. Utterly daunted, and overwhelmed by the emotions this discovery has provoked in him, Stan remains frozen in his pose of disenthralment, unable to speak as he watches the three people whom he now, for the first time, sees for what they really are, warily walk to their car and get in. As they drive towards him, he steps aside and lets them pass. He is left standing alone in the garage. He has had his epiphany.[46] He will keep what happened to himself, now fully awake to his own inadvertent complicity, but also accepting the parental mandate he has been given. In exchange for his silence, he gets his changeling child. He will become the foster father to the son who has been left behind.

For the Jenningses, in turn, the end of carnival means putting on one last disguise. That night, they bury everything that belonged to their American life in a park far outside Washington, DC. This is also the moment when, after the couple have taken off the wedding bands they had worn when they first arrived in America, Elizabeth once more offers to Philip the ring she had given him during their secret marriage ceremony, while slipping hers on as well. The remarriage that is now fully confirmed is also one in which they are once more alone as a couple. The most sobering discovery at the end of the carnival that was their

American life is that their children prove to be part of the theatrical props which they are compelled to shed as they leave this stage. Just before they cross into Canada, Paige, in a final defiance of her mother, will get off the train again, compelling them to finish their journey home without her.

The discovery, so prominent in *A Midsummer Night's Dream*, that to wake from a rare vision also entails realising that certain discoveries made in the night cannot be taken over into the new day, finds an encoded representation in the dream Elizabeth has on the plane to Europe.[47] In it, she wakes up in an unfamiliar room, her former lover, Gregory, in bed with her. After sharing a cigarette with him, she begins scrutinising the paintings on the wall and, once she looks at the bed again, she finds that he is gone. Her gaze then wanders to the bedside table where her attention is drawn to an eerie portrait, painted in black and white, of the two children which she, along with her first lover, has now forever lost. More awed than terrified, she looks at it for a while before waking up in her airplane seat. For the final part of their journey, the Jenningses, having crossed the border into Russia, meet up with their new handler, Arkady. He drives them through the day while they are fast asleep in the back seat of his car so that it is again night when they arrive in Moscow. Philip is the first to wake up and, seeing the city lights, asks Arkady to pull over in front of the Lomonosov University, before waking up Elizabeth.

In a celebration of the possibility of beginning anew befitting the genre of comedy, they are where they started out, now truly married to each other.[48] Awed, in a land that is both familiar and mysterious, they get out of the car and slowly walk to the stone railing. The camera catches them from behind, standing next to each other, as they look out at a panorama of the city, glittering in the darkness beneath them. The camera then moves to a medium shot of their faces as they begin to speak, still entranced by the vision before them. Elizabeth begins to wonder what would have happened had they remained here. Slightly wistful, they assure each other that their children will remember them, that they will be able to fend for themselves. Paige and Henry are no longer their concern. After Philip confides in his wife that this new world feels strange, she turns to him, reassuring him in Russian, 'we'll get used to it'. Then he, too, looks at her, and, smiling at each other, they silently affirm their bond before they once more turn to look at the new world opening up before them.

The camera again captures them from behind, standing at the edge of this stony threshold. Then it slowly begins to pan above their heads, allowing them to pass out of the visual frame. This is a moment of waking up, together, then, into a night harbouring utter potentiality. The

Figure 18 Moving from disenchantment to re-enchantment

serial repetition of their quarrels, incessantly leading to momentary reunions and new separations, is now over. They have returned to the place that used to haunt them in their flashbacks from the past, while America has become a site of memory. They are looking into an open future. It is certain that something is about to happen, yet utterly unclear what this might be.

As in *A Midsummer Night's Dream*, we, too, are left with the question, 'what next?' There is no Puck to remind us that we, too, have slumbered while visions appeared before us on our screens; that we, too, have partaken in this shared dream of espionage. Instead, the camera, passing over the solitary couple only to leave them behind, offers us a final panorama shot of nocturnal Moscow. Then, as the screen goes completely dark, we, too, are released from this stage. For us, this is a moment of sobriety, bringing together nostalgia for our involvement in a serial drama that has ended with the anticipation of a new enchantment still to come. The characters in whom we have invested our conflicted sympathy have vanished into a storyline we are no longer part of. Yet we, too, are on a threshold, called upon to realise that the resolution *The Americans* offers up with this last shot is itself provisional.

If, following the logic of serial drama, the story had always already begun, for us this ending, though necessary, is as contingent as it is unsettling. We, too, are called upon to ask what we are moving towards. The claim throughout this book has been that to look for Shakespeare's resilient legacy in contemporary TV drama means taking seriously the open-endedness of the dramatic resolutions he offers, when, returning to the point of departure, his plays re-pose the problems that set the dramatic action into motion, though doing so in a different key. Condensed in this final shot is the conundrum of closure his own plays, read as a series, re-pose. The solitary couple, disappearing from our sight, overlaps our knowledge about what happened previously with our anticipation of the effect this will subsequently have, with what will invariably ensue.

## Notes

1. William Shakespeare, *Twelfth Night*, Keir Elam (ed.), *The Arden Shakespeare*, third series (London: Bloomsbury, 2008), 3.1.34–5, 3.1.37–40.
2. Shakespeare, *Twelfth Night*, 3.1.59.
3. Shakespeare, *Twelfth Night*, 3.1.60–1.
4. Shakespeare, *Twelfth Night*, 1.3.105.
5. Shakespeare, *Twelfth Night*, 3.1.137, 3.1.139.
6. In his introduction to *Twelfth Night*, p. 18, Elam notes that this association was first suggested by the French critic É. Montégut in 1867, only to culminate in C.L Barber's famous *Shakespeare's Festive Comedies* (Princeton: Princeton University Press, 1959).
7. Shakespeare, *Twelfth Night*, 2.3.172. The reference also draws an implicit connection to Hippolyta, the Amazon queen in *A Midsummer Night's Dream*, and the warrior queen, Elizabeth I, who overshadows all the bellicose female rulers and headstrong heroines in the comedies.
8. Shakespeare, *Twelfth Night*, 3.4.53.
9. Shakespeare, *Twelfth Night*, 5.1.212.
10. Shakespeare, *Twelfth Night*, 'Introduction', p. 24.
11. Shakespeare, *Twelfth Night*, 5.1.367.
12. Shakespeare, *Twelfth Night*, 5.1.378.
13. *The Americans*, 'Duty and Honor', season 1, episode 7, dir. Alex Chapple, writ. Joshua Brand, m14.14 (FX 2013).
14. *The Americans*, 'Duty and Honor', m32.13.
15. *The Americans*, 'The Oath', season 1, episode 12, dir. John Dahl, writ. Joshua Brand and Melissa James Gibson, m45 (FX 2013).
16. David LaRocca suggests that this serial drama raises two seminal questions regarding the philosophical consequences of sustained role-playing. On the one hand, we are fascinated with the way Philip and Elizabeth are successful 'at seeming to be Americans, "passing" for authentic', while, on the other, their inability to be faithful to both their marriage and their mission undermines this illusion, raising questions such as 'Do I know who I am? If the marriage and the job and the self is surface, what lies beneath?', in Robert Arp and Kevin Guilfoy (eds), *The Americans and Philosophy. Reds in the Bed* (Chicago: Open Court, 2018), p. 60. In the same volume, Andrea Zanin suggests that the philosophical difference between 'identity' and 'self' is at issue not only whenever Elizabeth puts on her disguises, but already when Nadezhda dons her Elizabeth mask. None of these is the same as the self that embodies and informs them, 'We're Only What We Remember', p. 121.

17 See Esther Munoz-Gonzalez, '*The Americans*: Domesticity and Regendering of Classical Spy Narratives', *Brno Studies in English*, 44:1 (2018), pp. 119–36.
18 See Mieke Bal's introduction to *Quoting Caravaggio. Contemporary Art, Preposterous History* (Chicago: University of Chicago Press, 1999).
19 For a discussion of the way *The Americans* draws into focus the hypocrisy, corruption, and illegal tactics of contemporary political life while never questioning US supremacy when it comes to global influence and power, see Betty Kaklamanidou, 'The Cold War (re-)visited in *House of Cards* and *The Americans*', in Betty Kaklamanidou and Margaret J. Tally (eds), *Politics and Politicians in Contemporary US Television. Washington as Fiction* (London: Routledge, 2017), pp. 105–20.
20 Shakespeare, *Twelfth Night*, 4.1.5–8.
21 I want to thank Benno Wirz for pointing this minuscule but potent detail out to me.
22 For a discussion of the shift from a clearly demarcated external enemy to the far more ambiguous anxiety regarding domestic enmity, see Elisabeth Bronfen, 'Internal Enmity: Hollywood's Fragile Home Stories in the 1950s and 1960s', in Homer B. Pettey (ed.), *Cold War Film Genres* (Edinburgh: Edinburgh University Press, 2018), pp. 123–43. See also Alan Nadel, *Containment Culture. American Narratives, Postmodernism, and the Atomic Age* (Durham, NC: Duke University Press, 1995).
23 William Shakespeare, *A Midsummer Night's Dream*, Sukanta Chaudhuri (ed.), *The Arden Shakespeare*, third series (London: Bloomsbury, 2017), 5.1.5 and 5.1.21–2. As Chaudhuri notes, Shakespeare understands imagination to relate to 'the faculty of recalling and reordering visual impressions or images planted in the mind, perhaps to create unreal creatures and objects', p. 247.
24 Shakespeare, *A Midsummer Night's Dream*, 5.1.419 and 5.1.425.
25 Shakespeare, *A Midsummer Night's Dream*, 5.1.8.
26 Shakespeare, *A Midsummer Night's Dream*, 5.1.24–26 and 5.1.27.
27 Shakespeare, *A Midsummer Night's Dream*, 4.1.187–8.
28 Shakespeare, *A Midsummer Night's Dream*, 4.1.212–4.
29 Shakespeare, *A Midsummer Night's Dream*, 4.1.62 and 4.1.56.
30 The thwarted attempt at undermining Gorbachev at the 1987 summit in Washington, DC, around which the final episode of *The Americans* revolves, involves a similar gesture of disenthralment. Those who support his proposal for disarmament have come to recognise the folly in continuing a nuclear arms race that draws its legitimacy from remembering the suffering of WWII. They are fighting against those who persist in preserving this enchanted vision at all costs.
31 Shakespeare, *A Midsummer Night's Dream*, 4.1.78.
32 See Michel Foucault, 'Different Spaces', in James Faubion (ed.), *Aesthetics, Method, and Epistemology* (London: Penguin, 1998), pp. 175–85.
33 For a discussion of how this serial drama undermines the notion of the nuclear family by transforming it into the cover for an attack on American democratic liberal capitalism, see René Dietrich, 'Secret Spheres from *Breaking Bad* to *The Americans*: The Politics of Secrecy, Masculinity, and Transgression in 21st Century U.S. Television Drama', in Birgit Däwes, Alexandra Ganser, and Nicole Poppenhagen (eds), *Transgressive Television* (Heidelberg: Universitätsverlag Winter, 2015), pp. 195–216.

34 Taking the question of self-delusion in a slightly different direction, Talia Morag detects in this serial drama the structure of fetishism which Octave Manoni has labelled as 'I know very well ... but still', noting for *The Americans* 'a particular kind of self-deception, that is the prioritization of what we think over what we do, or our ideals and self-image over our embodied habits of action', *The Americans and Philosophy*, p. 58.
35 *The Americans*, 'Pilot', season 1, episode 1, dir. Gavin O'Connor, writ. Joe Weisberg, m59 (FX 2013).
36 I want to thank Emily Sun and her undergraduate students for pointing out the importance of this scene to me.
37 Shakespeare, *A Midsummer Night's Dream*, 5.1.26.
38 *The Americans*, 'The Colonel', season 1, episode 13, dir. Adam Arkin, writ. Joel Fields and Joe Weisberg, m32.48 (FX 2013).
39 Quoted in Darcie Rives-East, *Surveillance and Terror in Post-9/11 British and American Television* (London: Palgrave Macmillan, 2019), p. 216.
40 *The Americans*, 'Covert War', season 1, episode 11, dir. Nicole Kassell, writ. Joshua Brand and Melissa James Gibson, m9.43 (FX 2013).
41 For a discussion of how these two plays, both written around 1595, can be conceived of as a diptych, and their exploration of an amorous enchantment of vision which both blurs but also reasserts the distinction between comedy and tragedy, see the chapter 'Shakespeare's Night World' in Elisabeth Bronfen, *Night Passages. Philosophy, Literature, and Film* (New York: Columbia University Press, 2013), pp. 109–35.
42 *The Americans*, 'The Colonel', m44.38.
43 This could be seen as an intermedial reference to the marriage crisis in *House of Cards*, discussed in Chapter 3. There, smoking together was the ritual that marked the bond between Claire and Francis Underwood.
44 Stanley Cavell's discussion of remarriage in *Pursuits of Happiness. The Hollywood Comedy of Remarriage* (Cambridge, MA: Harvard University Press, 1981) is applicable here, given that it is also the case here that the heroine holds the key to a successful reunion of the couple. Elizabeth's transformation, tantamount as it is to turning away from her handler and accepting her husband's interpretation of this political conflict, is what, by getting them back together again, allows them to start over again. That this should involve the contingency of their being caught is once more part of the logic of comedy. It also reflects on an equally contingent moment in history that, given the failure of this coup, will culminate in the end of the Cold War with the fall of the Berlin Wall.
45 *The Americans*, 'START', season 6, episode 10, dir. Chris Long, writ. Joel Fields and Joe Weisberg, m24.45 (FX 2018).
46 As Smita A. Rahman 'Honor among Spies: The Cold War "Mom", Family, and Identity in *The Americans*', *Theory & Event*, 21:3 (2018), argues, this serial drama debunks the image of the honourable cold warrior by rejecting the patriotic narratives of honour and duty. The show's creator, Joe Weisberg, a former CIA operative, admits that having initially bought into the narrative of evil-empire rhetorics, he 'instead ended up seeing the world in a much more complex way – not so black and white', p. 604.
47 *The Americans*, 'START', m55.10.

48 *The Americans*, 'START', m1.04. We are reminded of the last lines of John Milton's *Paradise Lost*. There, Adam and Eve, expelled from the garden, find 'The World was all before them, where to choose/Their place of rest, and Providence their guide:/They hand in hand with wandring steps and slow,/Through Eden took their solitaire way', Book XII, 646–9 (New York: Dutton, 1956), p. 388. We might also recall the final shot of David Simon's TV drama, *The Wire*, where the camera lingers with a panorama shot of the Baltimore skyline even after the former detective Jimmy McNulty has got into his car and driven off.

# Bibliography

Aebischer, Pascale, Edward J. Esche, and Nigel Wheale. *Remaking Shakespeare. Performance across Media, Genres and Cultures*. London: Palgrave Macmillan, 2003.

Adelman, Janet. *The Common Liar. An Essay on Antony and Cleopatra*. New Haven, CT: Yale University Press, 1973.

———. *Suffocating Mothers. Fantasies of Maternal Origin in Shakespeare's Plays, Hamlet to The Tempest*. New York: Routledge, 1992.

Altenbernd, Erik and Alex Trimble Young. 'A Terrible Beauty: Settler Sovereignty and the State of Exception in Home Box Office's Deadwood'. *Settler Colonial Studies*, 3:1 (2013), pp. 27–48.

Alvarez, Rafael. *The Wire. Truth be Told*. New York: Grove Press, 2009.

Anker, Elisabeth R. *Orgies of Feeling. Melodrama and the Politics of Freedom*. Durham, NC: Duke University Press, 2014.

Arp, Robert and Kevin Guilfoy. *The Americans and Philosophy. Reds in the Bed*. Chicago: Open Court, 2018.

Auxier, Randall. 'Have You No Decency? Who is Worse, Claire or Frank'. *House of Cards and Philosophy. Underwood's Republic*. J. Edward Hackett (ed.). Chichester: Wiley Blackwell, 2016, pp. 265–81.

Babiak, Peter E.S. 'Introduction'. *Shakespeare Films. A Re-evaluation of 100 Years of Adaptations*. Jefferson, NC: McFarland & Company, 2016.

Baines, Barbara J. 'Girard's Doubles and Antony and Cleopatra'. *Antony and Cleopatra*. Nigel Wood (ed.). Buckingham: Open University Press, 1996, pp. 9–39.

Bal, Mieke. *Quoting Caravaggio. Contemporary Art, Preposterous History*. Chicago: University of Chicago Press, 1999.

Barker, Francis. *The Culture of Violence. Essays on Tragedy and History*. Manchester: Manchester University Press, 1993.

Barthes, Roland (1957). *Mythologies*. trans. Annette Lavers. New York: Hill and Wang, 1972.

———. *S/Z*. New York: Hill and Wang, 1974.

Beard, Mary. *Women & Power. A Manifesto*. London: Profile Books, 2017.

Benjamin, Walter. 'The Task of the Translator'. *Selected Writings Volume 1 1913–1926*. Marcus Bullock and Michael W. Jennings (eds). Cambridge, MA: Harvard University Press, 1996.
Benz, Brad. 'Deadwood and the English Language'. *Great Plains Quarterly*, 27:4 (Fall 2007), pp. 239–51.
Berrettini, Mark L. 'No Law: *Deadwood* and the State'. *Great Plains Quarterly*, 27:4 (Fall 2007), pp. 253–65.
Boose, Lynda E. and Richard Burt (eds). *Shakespeare The Movie. Popularizing the Plays on Film, TV, and Video*. London/New York: Routledge, 1997.
Bourdieu, Pierre. *Habitus and Field. General Sociology. Volume 2. Lectures at the collège de France 1982–1983*. London: Polity Press, 2019.
Boutet, Marjolaine. 'The Politics of Time in House of Cards'. *Transgressive Television. Politics, Crime and Citizenship in 21st-Century American TV Series*. Birgit Däwes, Alexandra Ganser, and Nicole Poppenhagen (eds). Heidelberg: Universitätsverlag Winter, 2015, pp. 83–102.
Bristol, Michael D. *Shakespeare's America, America's Shakespeares*. London/New York: Routledge, 1990.
Brittnacher, Hans Richard. 'Western als Drama und Theater: Deadwood'. *Fernsehserie und Literatur. Facetten einer Medienbeziehung*. Vincent Fröhlich, Lisa Gotto, and Jens Ruchatz (eds). München: Edition Text + Kritik, 2019, pp. 83–110.
Bronfen, Elisabeth. *Home in Hollywood. The Imaginary Geography of Cinema*. New York: Columbia University Press, 2004.
———. *Night Passages. Philosophy, Literature and Film*. New York/London: Columbia University Press, 2013.
———. *Crossmappings. On Visual Culture*. London: I.B. Tauris, 2018.
———. 'Internal Enmity: Hollywood's Fragile Home Stories in the 1950s and 1960s'. *Cold War Film Genres*. Homer B. Pettey (ed.). Edinburgh: Edinburgh University Press, 2018, pp. 123–43.
———. 'Rethinking Genre Memory'. *The Anthem Handbook of Screen Theory*. Hunter Vaughan and Tom Conley (eds). London: Anthem Press, 2018, pp. 193–208.
———. 'Seriality'. *Critical Terms in Futures Studies*. Heike Paul (ed.). London: Palgrave Macmillan, 2019, pp. 273–80.
Bronfen, Elisabeth and Barbara Straumann, 'Elizabeth I: The Cinematic Afterlife of an Early Modern Political Diva'. *The British Monarchy on Screen*. Mandy Merck (ed.). Manchester: Manchester University Press, 2016, pp. 132–54.
Burdeau, Emmanuel and Nicolas Vieillescazes. *The Wire. Reconstitution Collective*. Paris: Capricci, 2011.
Burnett, Mark Thornton and Ramona Wray (eds). *Screening Shakespeare in the Twenty-First Century*. Edinburgh: Edinburgh University Press, 2006.
Burt, Richard. *Shakespeares after Shakespeare. An Encyclopedia of the Bard in Mass Media and Popular Culture*. Westport, CT: Greenwood Press, 2007.

Burt, Richard and Lynda E. Boose (eds). *Shakespeare The Movie II. Popularizing the Plays on Film, TV, Video and DVD*. London/New York: Routledge. 2003.
Calbi, Maurizio. *Spectral Shakespeares. Media Adaptations in the Twenty-First Century*. New York: Palgrave Macmillan, 2013.
Callaghan, Dympna and Suzanne Gossett. *Shakespeare in Our Time. A Shakespeare Association of America Collection*. London: Bloomsbury, 2016.
Castonguay, James. 'Fictions of Terror: Complexity, Complicity and Insecurity in Homeland'. *Cinema Journal*, 54:4 (2015), pp. 132–8.
Cavanagh, Dermot, Stuart Hampton-Reeves, and Stephen Longstaffe (eds). *Shakespeare's Histories and Counter-histories*. Manchester: Manchester University Press, 2006.
Cavell, Stanley. *Pursuits of Happiness. The Hollywood Comedy of Remarriage*. Cambridge, MA: Harvard University Press, 1981.
———. *Disowning Knowledge in Seven Plays of Shakespeare*. Cambridge: Cambridge University Press, 1987.
Charnes, Linda. *Notorious Identity. Materializing the Subject in Shakespeare*. Cambridge, MA: Harvard University Press, 1993.
———. 'We Were Never Early Modern'. *Philosophical Shakespeare*, John Joughlin (ed.). London: Routledge, 2000, pp. 51–67.
———. *Hamlet's Heirs. Shakespeare and the Politics of a New Millennium*. New York/London: Routledge, 2006.
Cimitile, Anna Maria and Katherine Rowe. 'Introduction: Overlapping Mediascapes in the Mind'. *Anglistica*, 15:2 (2011), pp. i–iii.
Conway, Joe. 'After Politics/After Television: *Veep*, Digimodernism, and the Running Gag of Government'. *Studies in American Humor*, 2 (2016), pp. 182–207.
Cook, Diane. 'Moral Relativism in David Milch's *Deadwood*'. *Dark Reflections, Monstrous Reflections. Essays on the Monster in Culture*. Sorcha Ni Fhlainn (ed.). Oxford: Inter-Disciplinary Press, 2006, pp. 1–19.
Däwes, Birgit, Alexandra Ganser, and Nicole Poppenhagen (eds). *Transgressive Television. Politics and Crime in 21st-Century American TV Series*. Heidelberg: Universitätsverlag Winter, 2015.
De Certeau, Michel. *The Practice of Everyday Life*. Berkeley: University of California Press, 1984.
Deleuze, Gilles. *Difference and Repetition*. Revised edition. New York: Columbia University Press, 1995.
Denslow, Kristin N. 'Guest Starring Hamlet: The Proliferation of the Shakespeare Meme on American Television'. *Shakespeare/Not Shakespeare. Reproducing Shakespeare*. Christy Desmet (ed.). London: Palgrave Macmillan, 2017, pp. 97–110.
Derrida, Jacques. *Specters of Marx. The State of the Debt, the Work of Mourning, and the New International*. London/New York: Routledge, 1994.
———. *Rogues. Two Essays on Reason*. Stanford: Stanford University Press, 2005.

Desmet, Christy. 'Teaching Shakespeare with YouTube'. *The English Journal*, 99:1 (2009), pp. 65–70.
Desmet, Christy and Robert Sawyer. *Shakespeare and Appropriation*. London: Routledge, 1999.
Dessem, Matthew. 'Hillary Clinton Talks with Trevor Noah About Trump, Weinstein, and People Who Wish She'd Go Away'. *Slate*, 2 November 2017.
Dietrich, René. 'Secret Spheres from Breaking Bad to The Americans: The Politics of Secrecy, Masculinity, and Transgression in 21st Century U.S. Television Drama'. *Transgressive Television. Politics, Crime and Citizenship in 21st-Century American TV Series*. Birgit Däwes, Alexandra Ganser, and Nicole Poppenhagen (eds). Heidelberg: Universitätsverlag Winter, 2015, pp. 195–216.
Dollimore, Jonathan. *Radical Tragedy*. Reissued third edition. London: Palgrave Macmillan, 2010.
Drakakis, John (ed.). *New Casebooks Antony and Cleopatra*. Houndmills: Palgrave Macmillan, 1994.
Edgerton, Gary R. and Jeffrey P. Jones (eds). *The Essential HBO Reader*. Lexington, KY: University Press of Kentucky, 2008, pp. 23–41.
Eggert, Katherine. *Showing Like a Queen. Female Authority and Literary Experiment in Spenser, Shakespeare, and Milton*. Philadelphia: University of Pennsylvania Press, 2000.
Eschkötter, Daniel. *The Wire*. Zürich: Diaphanes, 2012.
Faragher, John Mack. 'HBO's *Deadwood*: Not Your Typical Western'. *Montana: The Magazine of Western History*, 57:3 (2007), pp. 60–5, 96.
Fazel, Valerie M. and Louise Geddes (eds). *The Shakespeare User. Critical and Creative Appropriations in a Networked Culture*. New York/London: Palgrave Macmillan, 2017.
Fernie, Ewan. 'Shakespeare and the Prospect of Presentism'. *Shakespeare Survey*, 58 (2005), pp. 169–84.
Fischlin, Daniel (ed.). *OuterSpeares. Shakespeare, Intermedia, and the Limits of Adaptation*. Toronto: University of Toronto Press, 2014.
Foucault, Michel. 'Different Spaces'. *Aesthetics, Method, and Epistemology*. James Faubion (ed.). London: Penguin, 1998, pp. 175–85.
Frame, George. 'The Leader of the Free World? Representing the Declining Presidency in Television Drama'. *Politics and Politicians in Contemporary US Television. Washington as Fiction*. Betty Kaklamanidou and Margaret J. Tally (eds). London/New York: Routledge, 2017, pp. 61–74.
Freud, Sigmund. *Beyond the Pleasure Principle* (1920). *The Standard Edition*. Volume XVIII. London: Hogarth Press, 1955, pp. 3–64.
Fröhlich, Vincent, Lisa Gotto, and Jens Rucharz. *Fernsehserie und Literatur*. München: Edition text + kritik, 2019.
Frye, Susan. 'Spectres of Female Sovereignty in Shakespeare's Plays'. *The Oxford Handbook of Shakespeare and Embodiment. Gender, Sexuality, and Race*. Valerie Traub (ed.). www.oxfordhandbooks.com, September 2016.

Garber, Marjorie. *Shakespeare's Ghost Writers. Literature as Uncanny Causality*. New York/London: Methuen, 1987.
———. *Quotation Marks*. New York: Routledge, 2003.
———. *Shakespeare After All*. New York: Pantheon Books, 2004.
———. *Shakespeare and Modern Culture*. New York: Pantheon Books, 2008.
———. *Profiling Shakespeare*. New York: Routledge, 2008.
Gilbert, Christopher J. 'Return of the Ridiculous, or Caricature as Political Cliché'. *Communication, Culture & Critique*, 7 (2014), pp. 390–5.
Glover, Allen and David Bushman. 'Lights Out in the Wasteland: The TV Noir'. *Television Quarterly*, 37:1 (2006), pp. 67–75.
Gombrich, E.H. *Aby Warburg, An Intellectual Biography*. Oxford: Phaidon, 1986.
Grady, Hugh and Terence Hawkes (eds). *Presentist Shakespeares*. London/New York: Routledge, 2007.
Gramsci, Antonio. *Prison Notebooks*. Joseph Buttigieg (ed.), trans. Joseph Buttigieg. New York: Columbia University Press, 2011.
Graulich, Melody and S. Witschi Nicolas. *Dirty Words in Deadwood. Literature and the Postwestern*. Lincoln, NE: University of Nebraska Press, 2013.
Greenblatt, Stephen. *Shakespearean Negotiations. The Circulation of Social Energy in Renaissance England*. Berkeley: University of California Press, 1988.
———. *Tyrant. Shakespeare on Power*. London: The Bodley Head, 2018.
Green, Richard and Joshua Heter. *Westworld and Philosophy. Mind Equals Blown*. Chicago: Open Court, 2019.
Grene, Nicholas. *Shakespeare's Serial History Plays*. Cambridge: Cambridge University Press, 2002.
Hackett, J. Edward. *House of Cards and Philosophy. Underwood's Republic*. Chichester: Wiley Blackwell, 2016.
Hatchuel, Sarah. '"What a piece of work is your machine, Harold": Shakespeare et la réinvention de l'humanité dans les séries américaines d'anticipation'. *TV/Serie*, 14 (2018), pp. 1–16.
Hodgdon, Barbara. *The Shakespeare Trade. Performances & Appropriations*. Philadelphia: University of Pennsylvania Press, 1998.
Holderness, Graham (ed). *Shakespeare's History Plays. Richard II to Henry V*. New Casebooks. London: Macmillan Palgrave, 1992.
———. *Tales from Shakespare. Creative Collisions*. Cambridge: Cambridge University Press, 2014.
Howard, Jean E. and Phyllis Rackin. *Engendering a Nation. A Feminist Account of Shakespeare's English Histories*. London/New York: Routledge, 1997.
Huang, Alexa and Elizabeth Rivlin (eds). *Shakespeare and the Ethics of Appropriation*. New York/London: Palgrave Macmillan, 2014.
Jackson, Russell. *Shakespeare and the English-speaking Cinema*. Oxford: Oxford University Press, 2014.

Jacobs, Jason. *Deadwood*. London: Palgrave Macmillan, 2012.
Jagoda, Patrick. 'Wired'. *Critical Inquiry*, 38:1 (2011), pp. 189–99.
Jess-Cooke, Carolyn. *Shakespeare on Film. Such Things as Dreams Are Made of*. London: Wallflower, 2007.
Jones, Patrick and Gretchen Soderlund. 'The Conspiratorial Mode in American Television: Politics, Public Relations, and Journalism in House *of Cards* and *Scandal*'. *American Quarterly*, 69:4 (2017), pp. 333–56.
Joughin, John (ed). *Philosophical Shakespeare*. London: Routledge, 2000.
Kaklamanidou, Betty and Margaret J. Tally. *Politics and Politicians in Contemporary US Television. Washington as Fiction*. London/New York: Routledge, 2017.
Kantorowicz, Ernst H., *The King's Two Bodies. A Study in Medieval Political Theology*. Second edition. Princeton, NJ: Princeton University Press, 1998.
Keller, James. R. 'The Vice in Vice President: *House of Cards* and the Morality Tradition'. *Journal of Popular Film and Television*, 43:3 (2015), pp. 111–20.
Kelleter, Frank. *Serial Agencies. The Wire and Its Readers*. Alresford: Zero, 2014.
Kennedy, Liam and Stephen Shapiro. *The Wire. Race, Class and Genre*. Ann Arbor: University of Michigan Press, 2012.
Klarer, Mario. 'Putting Television "Aside": Novel Narration in House *of Cards*'. *New Review of Film and Television Studies*, 12:2 (2014), pp. 203–20.
Knapp, Jeffrey. *Pleasing Everyone. Mass Entertainment in Renaissance London and Golden-Age Hollywood*. Oxford: Oxford University Press, 2017.
Kott, Jan. *Shakespeare Our Contemporary*. London: Methuen, 1965.
Landsberg, Alison. 'Waking the *Deadwood* of History: Listening, Language, and the "Aural Visceral"'. *Rethinking History*, 14:4 (2010), pp. 531–49.
Lanier, Douglas. *Shakespeare and Modern Popular Culture*. Oxford: Oxford University Press, 2002.
———. 'Shakespearean Rhizomatics. Adaption, Ethics, Value'. *Shakespeare and the Ethics of Appropriation*. Alexa Huang and Elizabeth Rivlin (eds). New York/London: Palgrave Macmillan, 2014.
———. '#Bard: "And noble offices though mayst effect of mediation"'. *Shakespeare Quarterly*, 67: 4 (2016), pp. 401–7.
Lavery, David (ed.). *Reading Deadwood. A Western to Swear By*. London: I.B. Tauris, 2006.
Lee, Patricia-Ann. 'Reflections of Power: Margaret of Anjou and the Dark Side of Queenship'. *Renaissance Quarterly*, 39: 2 (1986), pp. 183–217.
Lehmann, Courtney. *Shakespeare Remains. Theater to Film, Early Modern to Postmodern*. Ithaca: Cornell University Press, 2002.
Lehmann, Courtney and Lisa S. Starks (eds). *Spectacular Shakespeare. Critical Theory and Popular Cinema*. Madison, NJ: Fairleigh Dickinson University Press, 2002.
Leverette, Marc, Brian L. Ott, and Cara Louise Buckley (eds). *It's Not TV. Watching HBO in the Post-Television Era*. New York/London: Routledge, 2008.

Levine, Caroline. *Forms. Whole, Rhythm, Hierarchy, Network*. Princeton: Princeton University Press, 2015.

Levine, Nina S. *Women's Matters. Politics, Gender, and Nation in Shakespeare's Early History Plays*. Newark, DE: University of Delaware Press, 1998.

Loomba, Anita. 'Theatre and the Space of the Other'. *Antony and Cleopatra. New Casebooks*. John Drakakis (ed.). London: Palgrave Macmillan, 1994, pp. 279–307.

———. *Shakespeare, Race, & Colonialism*. Oxford: Oxford University Press, 2002.

Lyons, Tara L. 'Serial, Spinoffs, and Histories: Selling "'Shakespeare'" in Collection before the Folio'. *Philological Quarterly*, 91:2 (2012), pp. 185–220.

Marcus, Leah S. *Puzzling Shakespeare. Local Reading and Its Discontents*. Berkeley: University of California Press, 1988.

Maxwell, Julie and Kate Rumbold (eds). *Shakespeare and Quotation*. Cambridge: Cambridge University Press, 2018.

Milton, John. *Paradise Lost. Book XII*. New York: Dutton, 1956.

Moore, Lorrie. 'In the Life of *The Wire*'. *New York Review of Books*, 14 (2010), pp. 23–5.

Mueller, Stefanie. 'National and Economic Incorporation in HBO's *Deadwood*'. Christl Buschendorf, Stefanie Mueller, and Katja Sarkowsky (eds). *Violence and Open Spaces: The Subversion of Boundaries and the Transformation of the Western Genre*. Heidelberg: Universitätsverlag Winter, 2017, pp. 167–86.

Munoz-Gonzales, Esther. '*The Americans*: Domesticity and Regendering of Classical Spy Narratives'. *Brno Studies in English*, 44:1 (2008), pp. 119–36.

Naremore, James (ed.). *Film Adaptation*. New Brunswick, NJ: Rutgers University Press, 2000.

Negra, Diane and Jorie Lagerwey (eds). 'Analyzing *Homeland*'. *Cinema Journal*, 54: 4 (2015).

Newman, Michael Z. and Elana Levine (eds). *Legitimating Television. Media Convergence and Cultural Studies*. New York/London: Routledge, 2012.

Novak, Michael. *Choosing Presidents. Symbols of Political Leadership*. Second edition. New Brunswick, NJ: Transaction Publishers, 1992.

Nussbaum, Emily. '"*Homeland*": An Antidote for "24"'. *New Yorker*, 29 November 2011.

O'Neill, Stephen. 'Uploading *Hamlet*: Agency, Convergence and YouTube Shakespeare'. *Anglistica*, 15:2 (2011), pp. 63–75.

———. *Shakespeare and YouTube. New Media Forms of the Bard*. London: Bloomsbury, 2014.

——— (ed.). *Broadcast Your Shakespeare. Continuity and Change Across Media*. London: Bloomsbury, 2018.

Osborne, Laurie E. 'Speculations on Shakespearean Cinematic Liveness'. *Shakespeare Bulletin*, 24:3 (2006), pp. 49–65.

Palfrey, Simon and Emma Smith. *Shakespeare's Dead*. Oxford: Bodleian Library of the University of Oxford, 2016.

Peretti, Burton W. *The Leading Man. Hollywood and the Presidential Image*. New Brunswick, NJ: Rutgers University Press, 2012.

Perlman, Allison. '*Deadwood*, Generic Transformation, and Televisual History'. *Journal of Popular Film & Television*, 30:2 (2011), pp. 102–12.

Permagent, Alan. 'Milch Breathes Life into Characters on Deadwood'. *Buffalo News*, 21 July 2005, C7.

Petersen, Anne Helen. 'Whores and Other Feminists': Recovering *Deadwood*'s Unlikely Feminisms'. *Great Plains Quarterly*, 27:4 (2007), pp. 267–82.

Pilipets, Elena and Rainer Winter. '*House of Cards* – House of Power: Political Narratives and the Cult of Serial Sociopaths in Narrative Politics in American Quality Dramas in the Digital Age'. *Politics and Politicians in Contemporary US Television. Washington as Fiction*. Betty Kaklamanidou and Margaret J. Tally (eds). London/New York: Routledge, 2017, pp. 91–104.

Potter, Tiffany and C.W. Marshall (eds). *The Wire. Urban Decay and American Television*. New York: Continuum, 2009.

Press, Joy. '*The Good Fight* Showrunners Are (Not) Impeaching Trump and the Nature of Evil'. *Vanity Fair*, 12 May 2019.

Puff, Simone. 'Another Scandal in Washington: How a Transgressive, Black Anti-Heroine Makes for New "Quality TV"'. *Transgressive Television: Politics, Crime and Citizenship in 21st-Century American TV Series*. Birgit Däwes, Alexandra Ganser, and Nicole Poppenhagen (eds). Heidelberg: Universitätsverlag Winter, 2015, pp. 103–26.

Rahman, Smita A. 'Honor Among Spies: The Cold War "Mom", Family, and Identity in *The Americans*'. *Theory & Event*, 21:3 (2018), pp. 590–606.

Rimmon-Kenan, Shlomith. 'The Paradoxical Status of Repetition'. *Poetics Today*, 1:4 (1980), pp. 151–9.

Rives-East, Darcie. *Surveillance and Terror in Post-9/11 British and American Television*. London: Palgrave Macmillan, 2019.

Ronnenberg, Susan Cosby. *Deadwood and Shakespeare. The Henriad in the Old West*. Jefferson, NC: McFarland & Co, 2018.

Salerno, Daniel. '"I Will Have You Bend"': Language and the Discourses of Power in Deadwood'. *Literary Imagination*, 12:2 (2010), pp. 239–53.

Salkeld, Duncan. 'Shakespeare Studies, Presentism, and Micro-History'. *Cahiers Elisabethains*, 76 (2009), pp. 35–43.

Shakespeare, William. *Measure for Measure. The Arden Shakespeare*. Third series. A.R. Braunmuller and Robert N. Watson (eds). London: Methuen, 1965.

———. *Antony and Cleopatra. The Arden Shakespeare*. Third series. John Wilders (ed.). London: Bloomsbury, 1995.

———. *King Lear. The Arden Shakespeare*. Third series. R.A. Foakes (ed.). London: Bloomsbury, 1997.

———. *King Henry VI. Part 1. The Arden Shakespeare*. Third series. Edward Burns (ed.). London: Bloomsbury, 2000.

———. *King Henry VI. Part 3. The Arden Shakespeare.* Third series. John D. Cox and Eric Rasmussen (eds). London: Bloomsbury, 2001.
———. *King Henry VI. Part 2. The Arden Shakespeare.* Third series. Ronald Knowles (ed.). London: Bloomsbury, 2004.
———. *As You Like It. The Arden Shakespeare.* Third series. Juliet Dusinberre (ed.). London: Bloomsbury, 2006.
———. *Hamlet. The Arden Shakespeare.* Third series. Ann Thompson and Neil Taylor (ed.). London: Bloomsbury, 2006.
———. *Much Ado About Nothing. The Arden Shakespeare.* Third series. Claire McEachern (ed.). London: Bloomsbury, 2006.
———. *Twelfth Night. The Arden Shakespeare.* Third series. Keir Elam (ed.). London: Bloomsbury, 2008.
———. *Richard III. The Arden Shakespeare.* Third series. James R. Siemon (eds). London: Bloomsbury, 2010.
———. *The Winter's Tale. The Arden Shakespeare.* Third series. John Pitcher (ed.). London: Bloomsbury, 2010.
———. *Julius Caesar. The Arden Shakespeare.* Third series. David Daniell (ed.). London: Bloomsbury, 2011.
———. *Romeo and Juliet. The Arden Shakespeare.* Third series. René Weis (ed.). London: Bloomsbury, 2011.
———. *The Tempest. The Arden Shakespeare.* Third series. Virginia Mason Vaughan and Alden T. Vaughan (eds). London: Bloomsbury, 2011.
———. *Macbeth. The Arden Shakespeare.* Third series. Sandra Clark and Pamela Mason (eds). London: Bloomsbury, 2015.
———. *King Henry IV. Part 2. The Arden Shakespeare.* Third series. James C. Bulman (ed.). London: Bloomsbury, 2016.
———. *A Midsummer Night's Dream. The Arden Shakespeare.* Third series. Sukanta Chaudhur (ed.). London: Bloomsbury, 2017.
Shapiro, Michael J. 'HBO's Two Frontiers: *Deadwood* and *The Wire*'. *Geopolitics*, 20:1 (2015), pp. 193–213.
Shaughnessy, Robert (ed.). *Shakespeare on Film. New Casebooks.* London: MacMillan, 1998.
——— (ed.). *The Cambridge Companion to Shakespeare and Popular Culture.* Cambridge: Cambridge University Press, 2007.
Simkin, Stevie. *Early Modern Tragedy and the Cinema of Violence.* London: Palgrave Macmillan, 2006.
Singer, Mark. 'The Misfit: How David Milch Got from *NYPD Blue* to *Deadwood* By Way of an Epistle of St. Paul'. *New Yorker*, 14 February 2005, pp. 192–205.
Singh, Jyotsyna. 'Renaissance Anti-theatricality, Anti-feminism, and Shakespeare's "Antony and Cleopatra"'. *New Casebooks Antony and Cleopatra.* John Drakakis (ed.). Houndmills, Palgrave Macmillan, 1994, pp. 308–29.
Slotkin, Richard. *Regeneration through Violence. The Mythology of the American Frontier 1600–1860.* Norman, OK: University of Oklahoma, 1973.

———. *Gunfighter Nation. Myth of the Frontier in Twentieth-Century America*. Norman, OK: University of Oklahoma Press, 1998.

Smith, Emma. 'Shakespeare Serialized: *An Age of Kings*'. *The Cambridge Companion to Shakespeare and Popular Culture*. Robert Shaughnessy (ed.). Cambridge: Cambridge University Press, 2007, pp. 134–49.

South, James B. and Kimberly S. Engels. *Westworld and Philosophy. If You Go Looking For the Truth, Get the Whole Thing*. Oxford: Wiley Blackwell, 2018.

Stasi, Paul and Jennifer Greiman. *The Last Western. Deadwood and the End of American Empire*. New York: Bloomsbury, 2013.

Steenberg, Lindsay and Yvonne Tasker, '"Pledge Allegiance": Gendered Surveillance, Crime Television, and Homeland'. *Cinema Journal*, 54:4 (2015), pp. 132–8.

Takacs, Stacy. 'The Contemporary Politics of the Western Form: Bush, Saving Jessica Lynch, and Deadwood'. *Reframing 9/11. Film, Popular Culture and the War on Terror*. Jeff Birkenstein, Anna Froula, and Karen Randell (eds). New York: Continuum, 2010, pp. 153–63.

Tally, Margaret, '"Call it the Hillary-effect": Charting the Imaginary of "Hillary-esque" Fictional Narratives'. *Politics and Politicians in Contemporary US Television. Washington as Fiction*. Betty Kaklamanidou and Margaret J. Tally (eds). London/New York: Routledge, 2017, pp. 61–74.

Tennenhouse, Leonard. *Power on Display. The Politics of Shakespeare's Genres*. London: Methuen, 1986.

Wajcman, Gérard. *Les séries, le monde, la crise, les femmes*. Paris: Verdier, 2018.

Walzer, Judith B. 'Yes, Ms. President?' *Dissent*, 56:1 (2009), pp. 101–4.

Westerfelhaus, Robert and Celeste Lacroix. 'Waiting for the Barbarians: HBO's *Deadwood* as a Post-9/11 Ritual of Disquiet'. *Southern Communication Journal*, 74:1 (2009), pp. 18–39.

Wiggins, Kyle and David Holmberg. '"Gold is Every Man's Opportunity": Castration Anxiety and the Economic Venture in *Deadwood*'. *Great Plains Quarterly*, 27:4 (2007), pp. 282–95.

Winkler, Reto. 'This Great Stage of Androids: *Westworld*, Shakespeare and the World as Stage'. *Journal of Adaptation in Film & Performance*, 10:2 (2017), pp. 169–88.

Wood, Michael. 'This is America, Man'. *London Review of Books*, 27 May 2010, pp. 20–2.

Wood, Nigel (ed.). *Antony and Cleopatra*. Buckingham: Open University Press, 1996.

Zanin, Andrea. 'We're Only What We Remember'. *The Americans and Philosophy. Reds in the Bed*. Robert Arp and Kevin Guilfoy (eds). Chicago: Open Court, 2018.

# Bibliography

## *Film and Television Drama*

*Billions*. 'The Punch', season 1, episode 7, dir. Stephen Gyllenhaal, writ. Brian Koppelman and David Levien (Showtime 2016).

*Commander in Chief*. 'Pilot', season 1, episode 1, dir. Rod Lurie, writ. Rod Lurie (ABC 2005).

*Commander in Chief*. 'Unfinished Business', season 1, episode 18, dir. Rick Wallace, writ. Steven A. Cohen, Cynthia J. Cohen, and Dee Johnson (ABC 2006).

*Deadwood*. 'The Trial of Jack McCall', season 1, episode 5, dir. John Belluso, writ. Ed Bianchi (HBO 2004).

*Deadwood*. 'Plague', season 1, episode 6, dir. Davis Guggenheim, writ. Malcolm MacRury (HBO 2004).

*Deadwood*. 'Jewel's Boot is Made for Walking', season 1, episode 11, dir. Steve Shill, writ. Ricky Jay (HBO 2004).

*Deadwood*. 'A Lie Agreed Upon (Part 1)', season 2, episode 1, dir. Ed Bianchi, writ. David Milch (HBA 2005).

*Deadwood*. 'E.B. Was Left Out', season 2, episode 7, dir. Michael Almereyda, writ. Jody Worth (HBS 2005).

*Deadwood*. 'Childish Things', season 2, episode 8, dir. Tim Van Patten, writ. Regina Corrado (HBO 2005).

*Deadwood*. 'Boy-the-Earth-Talks-To', season 2, episode 12, dir. Ed Bianchi, writ. Ted Mann (HBO 2005).

*Deadwood*. 'True Colors', season 3, episode 3, dir. Gregg Fienberg, writ. Regina Corrado and Ted Mann (HBO 2006).

*Deadwood*. 'Unauthorized Cinemon', season 3, episode 7, dir. Mark Tinker, writ. Regina Corrado (HBO 2006).

*Deadwood*. 'Leviathan Smiles', season 3, episode 8, dir. Ed Bianchi, writ. Kem Nunn (HBO 2006).

*Deadwood*. 'A Constant Throb', season 3, episode 10, dir. Mark Tinker, writ. W. Earl Brown (HBO 2006).

*Deadwood*. 'The Catbird Seat', season 3, episode 11, dir. Gregg Fienberg, writ. Bernadette McNavara (HBO 2006).

*Deadwood*. 'Tell Him Something Pretty', season 3, episode 12, dir. Mark Tinker, writ. Ted Mann (HBO 2006).

*Deadwood. The Movie*. Dir. Daniel Minahan, writ. David Milch (HBO 2019).

*Godless*. 'The Ladies of La Belle', season 1, episode 2, dir. Scott Frank, writ. Scott Frank (Netflix 2017).

*Homeland*. 'America First', season 6, episode 12, dir. Lesli Linka Glatter, writ. Alex Gansa and Ron Nyswaner (Showtime 2017).

*Homeland*. 'Paean to the People', season 7, episode 12, dir. Lesli Linka Glatter, writ. Alex Gansa (Showtime 2018).

*House of Cards*. 'Chapter 1', season 2, episode 1, dir. David Fincher, writ. Beau Willimon (Netflix 2013).

*House of Cards*. 'Chapter 63', season 5, episode 11, dir. Agnieszka Holland, writ. Laura Eason (Netflix 2017).
*House of Cards*. 'Chapter 65', season 6, episode 5, dir. Robin Wright, writ. Melissa James Gibson and Frank Pugliese (Netflix 2018).
*House of Cards*. 'Chapter 67', season 6, episode 2, dir. Ami Canaan Mann, writ. Frank Pugliese and Melissa James Gibson (Netflix 2018).
*House of Cards*. 'Chapter 70', season 6, episode 5, dir. Thomas Schlamme, writ. Jason Horwitch and Charlotte Stoudt (Netflix 2018).
*House of Cards*. 'Chapter 73', season 6, episode 8, dir. Robin Wright, writ. Frank Pugliese and Melissa James Gibson (Netflix 2018).
*My Darling Clementine*. dir. John Ford, 20th Century Fox, 1946.
*Political Animals*. 'Resignation Day', season 1, episode 6, dir. David Petrarca, writ. Molly Newman and Speed Weed (ABC 2012).
*Prison Break*. 'By the Skin and the Teeth', season 1, episode 15, dir. Fred Gerber, writ. Nick Santora (Fox 2005).
*Prison Break*. 'Sweet Caroline', season 2, episode 19, dir. Dwight H. Little, writ. Karyn Usher (Fox 2007).
*Scandal*. 'Get Out of Jail, Free', season 5, episode 6, dir. Chandra Wilson, writ. Chris Van Dusen (ABC 2015).
*Scandal*. 'The Belt', season 6, episode 4, dir. Tom Verica, writ. Paul William Davies (ABC 2017).
*Scandal*. 'Trojan Horse', season 6, episode 11, dir. Jann Turner, writ. Jess Brownell and Nicholas Nardini (ABC 2017).
*Scandal*. 'Transfer of Power', season 6, episode 16, dir. Tony Goldwyn, writ. Matt Byrne and Mark Fish (ABC 2017).
*Scandal*. 'Army of One', season 7, episode 11, dir. Allison Liddi-Brown, writ. Austin Guzman (ABC 2018).
*Scandal*. 'People Like Me', season 7, episode 16, dir. Joe Morton, writ. Chris Van Dusen (ABC 2018).
*Scandal*. 'Over a Cliff', season 7, episode 18, dir. Tom Verica, writ. Shonda Rhimes (ABC 2018).
*The Americans*. 'Pilot', season 1, episode 1, dir. Gavin O'Connor, writ. Joe Weisberg (FX 2013).
*The Americans*. 'Duty and Honor', season 1, season 7, dir. Alex Chapple, writ. Joshua Brand (FX 2013).
*The Americans*. 'Covert War', season 1, episode 11, dir. Nicole Kassell, writ. Joshua Brand and Melissa James Gibson (FX 2013).
*The Americans*. 'The Oath', season 1, episode 12, dir. John Dahl, writ. Joshua Brand and Melissa James Gibson (FX 2013).
*The Americans*. 'The Colonel', season 1, episode 13, dir. Adam Arkin, writ. Joel Fields and Joe Weisberg (FX 2013).
*The Americans*. 'START', season 6, episode 10, dir. Chris Long, writ. Joel Fields and Joe Weisberg (FX 2018).

*The Deuce.* 'Our Raison d'Etre', season 2, episode 1, dir. Alex Hall, writ. David Simon and George Pelecanos (HBO 2018).

*The Good Fight*, 'The One Where the Sun Come Out', season 3, episode 9, dir. Brooke Kennedy, writ. Eric Holmes (CBS 2019).

*The West Wing.* 'Pilot', season 1, episode 1, dir. Thomas Schlamme, writ. Aaron Sorkin (NBC 1999).

*The Wire.* 'The Buys', season 1, episode 3, dir. Peter Medak, writ. by David Simon (HBO, 2002).

*The Wire.* 'Straight and True', season 3, episode 5, dir. Dan Attias, writ. Ed Burns (HBO 2004).

*The Wire.* 'Homecoming', season 3, episode 6, dir. Leslie Libman, writ. Rafael Alvarez (HBO 2004).

*The Wire.* 'Moral Midgetry', season 3, episode 8, dir. Agnieszka Holland, writ. Richard Price (HBO 2004).

*The Wire.* 'Reformation', season 3, episode 10, dir. Christine Moore, writ. Ed Burns (HBO 2004).

*The Wire.* 'Middle Ground', season 3, episode 11, dir. Joe Chappelle, writ. George Pelecanos (HBO 2004).

*The Wire.* 'Mission Accomplished', season 3, episode 12, dir. Ernest Dickerson, writ. David Simon (HBO 2004).

*The Wire.* 'Transitions', season 5, episode 4, dir. Dan Attias, writ. Ed Burns (HBO 2008).

*The Wire.* 'Late Editions', season 5, episode 9, dir. Joe Chappelle, writ. George Pelecanos (HBO 2008).

*The Wire.* '-30-', season 5, episode 10, dir. Clark Johnson, writ. David Simon (HBO 2008).

*24.* 'Day 8: 9.00am–10.00am', season 8, episode 18, dir. Milan Cheylov, writ. Chip Johannessen and Patrick Harbinson (Fox 2010).

*24.* 'Day 8: 3.00 p.m.–4.00 p.m.', season 8, episode 24, dir. Brad Turner, writ. Howard Gordon (Fox 2010).

*Veep.* 'Frozen Yoghurt', season 1, episode 2, dir. Armando Iannucci, writ. Armando Iannucci and Simon Blackwell (HBO 2012).

*Veep.* 'Inauguration', season 5, episode 10, dir. Becky Martin, writ. Jim Margolis (HBO 2016).

*Veep.* 'Veep', season 7, episode 7, dir. David Mandel, writ. David Mandel (HBO 2019).

*Westworld.* 'The Original', season 1, episode 1, dir. Jonathan Nolan, writ. Jonathan Nolan and Lisa Joy (HBO 2016).

*Westworld.* 'Chestnut', season 1, episode 2, dir. Richard J. Lewis, writ. Jonathan Nolan and Lisa Joy (HBO 2016).

*Westworld.* 'The Stray', season 1, episode 3, dir. Neil Marshall, writ. Daniel T. Thomsen and Lisa Joy (HBO 2016).

*Westworld.* 'Trompe L'Oeil', season 1, episode 7, dir. Frederick E.O. Toye, writ. Halley Gross and Jonathan Nolan (HBO 2016).

*Westworld*. 'Trace Decay', season 1, episode 8, dir. Stephen Williams, writ. Charles Yu and Lisa Joy (HBO 2016).
*Westworld*. 'The Bicameral Mind', season 1, episode 10, dir. Jonathan Nolan, writ. Lisa Joy and Jonathan Nolan (HBO 2016).
*Westworld*. 'Journey into Night', season 2, episode 1, dir. Richard J. Lewis, writ. Lisa Joy and Roberto Patino (HBO 2018).
*Westworld*. 'Virtù e Fortuna', season 2, episode 3, dir. Richard J. Lewis, writ. Roberto Patino and Ron Fitzgerald (HBO 2018).
*Westworld*. 'Les Écorchés', season 2, episode 7, dir. Nicole Kassell, writ. Jordan Goldberg and Ron Fitzgerald (HBO 2018).

# Index

*Note*: 'n.' after a page reference indicates the number of a note on that page
*Note*: page numbers in *italic* refer to illustrations.

abdication 5, 39–42, 53, 58–65, 70, 74, 93–4, 103, 137–8, 185
adaptation 5–10, 29, 38, 58–9, 160
   adaptability 4, 16
Adelman, Janet 24n.32, 143
Aebischer, Pascale 7
aesthetic form 13–17, 20–1, 37, 149–50
   *see also* Warburg, Aby
afterlife 40
   cultural *see* Benjamin, Walter, cultural afterlife
   spectral 13, 15, 27, 30, 33
allegory 61, 75, 82n.5, 191n.24, 213
Althusser, Louis 201
American civil religion 18, 99–100, 104, 117n.31, 150n.4
American Dream 62, 68, 72
*Americans, The* (TV series) 194–222
   credit sequence 201–4
Anderegg, Michael 54
Anderson, Paul Allen 82n.5
Anker, Elisabeth R. 137
*Anthony and Cleopatra* (William Shakespeare) 122, 140–4, 149
*Apocalypse Now* (Francis Ford Coppola) 158
appropriation 1–38, 49–53, 59, 85, 88, 158–60, 177–80
   media 3, 9, 11
   of power 65, 69, 71, 75, 95
   process of 7, 15, 24n.25, 37
*As You Like It* (William Shakespeare) 180–4
Auxier, Randall 116n.4

Babiak, Peter E.S. 159
Baines, Barbara J. 141

Bakhtin, Mikhail 113
Bal, Mieke 9, 200
Banks, Carol 117n.20
Barker, Francis 53
Barthes, Roland 5, 27–8
Beard, Mary 98
Benjamin, Walter 8–14, 55n.14
   cultural afterlife (*Fortleben*) 8–10, 13, 16, 28
   cultural survival (*Überleben*) 8, 10, 13–14, 29, 30
   post-ripening (*Nachreife*) 8–10, 13, 15, 30–1, 123
   translatability 8, 12–13, 16, 30
   *see also* translation
Benz, Brad 189n.9
bifocal vision 202–15
   *see also* double vision
*Billions* (TV series) 2
*Birth of a Nation, The* (D.W. Griffith) 79
black intelligencer 66, 71–3, 135
   *see also* Richard III (William Shakespeare)
body 100, 133, 140, 180
   dead 57n.48, 77, 91, 156, 174, 187
   female 99, 146, 173, 201
   host 27, 32, 34
   maternal 24n.32, 137
   natural 99–101, 107
   politic 99–103, 106, 109, 112, 122, 138
   symbolic 100, 109–13, 134, 137
Brittnacher, Hans Richard 190n.14
Bronfen, Elisabeth 24n.27, 118n.33, 151n.6, 193n.53
Bush, George W. (president) 18, 150n.4, 152n.25

# Index

Calbi, Maurizio 15, 29, 38
  *see also* survivance
capitalism 63, 65, 172, 208, 212, 223n.33
carnival 196–9, 202, 219
  of spies 20, 194, 200, 211, 218
carnivalesque 19, 127, 159, 163, 196–206, 218
Castonguay, James 152n.25
Cavell, Stanley 16, 46–7, 54, 130, 139
  'meet and happy conversation' 112, 180
  remarriage 97, 112, 122, 140, 147, 149, 206, 215–16, 219, 224n.44
Certeau, Michel de 61
Charnes, Linda 4, 8, 25n.42, 154n.51
chess 146–7
  in *The Tempest* 41, 75
  in *The Wire* 59–65, 75, 80, 82n.5, 84n.42
Christian (religion) 32, 172
  purgatory 2, 27, 32, 40
Cimitile, Anna Maria 24n.30
civil war 94–5, 132–4, 157
  American 19, 79
  in Wars of the Roses 62–6, 71, 74, 133–4
  in *Westworld* 43, 48, 52
  in *The Wire* 64, 66–8, 74, 76
Cleopatra (queen) 18, 140–3, 146–7, 153n.46
Cold War 19, 194–222
collage 160, 186
comedy 106, 122, 129, 143, 163–4, 177–8, 184, 187, 218, 220
  Shakespeare's 19, 93, 102–5, 129–31, 140, 175, 180–1, 195–214
  subversive spirit of 176
  and tragedy 155, 160–4, 175, 177, 182
  *see also* tragedy
*Commander in Chief* (TV series) 104–6, 108, 114, 118n.39, 153n.33
consciousness 26, 31–2, 36, 42–7, 115, 180
conspiracy 18, 101–3, 109, 121, 132–5, 143–6, 204

constellations 5, 15, 17, 20, 97, 160, 186
  character 6–7, 12, 158
  dramaturgic 160, 186
contingency 9–10, 47, 53–4, 79, 102, 200, 218
corpse 28, 53, 57n.48, 77–9, 93, 102, 140, 149, 156, 175, 180
  *see also* body, dead
Cosby Ronnenberg, Susan 164, 190n.18–19
counter-intelligence 198, 209–13
countersovereignty 120
  female 121–30, 140–8
  *see also* female sovereignty; sovereign; sovereignty
creative reading 9–11, 20
crime 70–2, 77–9, 86, 89, 109, 145, 181
crossdressing 19, 181, 194–9
  *see also Twelfth Night* (William Shakespeare)
crossmapping 9–18, 38, 59, 62–5, 99, 122–3, 141, 198, 204–8
  *see also* Bronfen, Elisabeth
cultural authority 4, 7–8, 27, 29
cultural capital 3, 12, 22n.8, 24n.26
cultural imaginary 14–18, 29–30, 123, 163
cultural ventriloquism 12, 17, 24n.35, 28, 30, 36
culture 13, 15–16, 23n.21, 149, 217
  American 17, 80, 118n.32
  Cold War 203
  contemporary 7, 37, 91, 150
  media 3, 12
  political 64
  popular 4, 7–8, 16, 99, 117n.29
*Cymbeline* (William Shakespeare) 186

daughter 27–42, 49–53, 91–7, 107–9, 127–9, 186, 203, 215–16
*Deadwood* (TV series) 155–86, *188*
*Deadwood. The Film* 186–9
Deleuze, Gilles 7
democracy 18, 120–3, 129, 134, 138–9, 144–8
Denslow, Kristin N. 14
Derrida, Jacques 29, 120–1, 144

# Index

*Specters of Marx* 29
  *see also* rogue
desire 13–15, 20, 31, 35, 93, 127–8,
    141, 179, 195–200, 208
  erotic 181
  intimate 195
  for power 28, 39, 86, 122, 142
  for revenge 2, 4
  for self-assertion 91, 94
  transgressive 169–74
  for violent ends 44–51, 54, 57n.48,
    161, 207
Desmet, Christy 7–8, 25n.38, 28, 36
*Deuce, The* (TV series) 1–2
disenchantment 20, 216–17, 221
dislocation 3, 7, 10, 14–16
displacement 13, 96, 195
Dollimore, Jonathan 140
domestic strife 41, 62–6
double vision 10, 51–2, 79,
    202–10, 215
  *see also* bifocal vision
double-voiced 28, 35–6, 103, 139
dream 26, 32, 38–43, 49–54, 69–75,
    80–1, 142, 182, 208,
    212–15, 220
  American *see* American Dream
  Bottom's 206
  collective 13, 20, 200, 221
duplicity 89, 101, 108, 112, 169, 171,
    194, 197, 215

Edward IV (king) 65–70, 133, 137
Eggert, Katherine 153n.41
Eleanor of Aquitaine 97–8, 117n.20
Elizabeth I (queen) 58, 65–6, 71, 97–8,
    110, 152n.26
Eschkötter, Daniel 82n.14, 83n.25
espionage 20, 195–221
  counterworld of 199, 206, 215, 217
Estill, Laura 22n.8
excess 75, 129, 164, 211

fantastic 175–6
fantasy 39, 96, 150, 176, 195–9, 208–9,
    212–13
  hateful 128–31
  political 200–1

serial 43
shaping 204–6
Faragher, John Mack 189n.9
father 5, 27–38, 41–53, 93–5, 128, 133,
    143, 156, 164–5, 207–12, 219
  of the nation 101
  *see also* paternal sovereignty
Federal Bureau of Investigation (FBI)
    66, 107–8, 131, 198–200,
    209–16
female president 85–119
  first wave of 18, 101, 106, 122
  second wave of 18, 113, 121–2
female ruler 18, 122, 141, 222n.7
  *see also* female president; female
    sovereignty; sovereign; warrior
    queens
female sovereignty 18, 91–8, 111,
    117n.21, 133–9, 151n.5
  black 141
femme fatale 209
Fernie, Ewan 11, 30, 164
Folio 58–9
Ford, John 84n.45, 158–9
Foucault, Michel 39, 207
  heterotopia 39, 43, 54, 207, 209, 211
founding 17, 68
fourth wall break 85, 88, 166, 191n.24
Freud, Sigmund 123
frontier 155–93
  literature 158
  town 161, 177
  *see also Deadwood* (TV series)
Frye, Susan 117n.21

Garber, Marjorie 3, 13, 16, 32, 37
gaze 80, 136, 139, 183–8, 201, 220
  oblique 202
  preposterous 19
  spectral 201
Geddes, Louise 23n.20
Gilbert, Christopher J. 154n.55
ghosts 13, 187
  in Shakespeare 26–57, 90, 98, 131,
    165, 187
  *see also* haunting; spectrality
*Godless* (TV series) 1–2
*Good Fight, The* (TV series) 2, 114

243

Gorbachev, Mikhail 216–19, 223n.30
Greenblatt, Stephen 13, 189n.8
Greiman, Jennifer 157, 190n.12, 191n.24
Grene, Nicholas 66, 81n.3

*Hamlet* (William Shakespeare) 2, 26–32, 64, 158–60, 163–9, 182, 197
haunting 3, 13–15, 21, 29–33, 45–50, 131, 188
hauntological *see* Calbi, Maurizio
Hawkes, Terence 8
*Henry IV Part 1* (William Shakespeare) 58
*Henry IV Part 2* (William Shakespeare) 35, 58, 63, 70
*Henry V* (William Shakespeare) 58, 97
*Henry VI* (William Shakespeare) 18, 58–74, 81nn.2–3, 97, 132–7
Henry VII (king) 62, 74, 139
*Henry VIII* (William Shakespeare) 58, 98
historical difference 11, 30
histories *see* history plays
history plays 5, 12–18, 35, 58–77, 97–8, 110, 132–6, 144, 152n.26
  *see also* Henry IV; Henry V; Henry VIII; King John; Richard II; Richard III
Holderness, Graham 9, 64
*Hollow Crown, The* 5
*Homeland* (TV series) 113, 121–2, 131–9, 147, 150, 152n.25
*Hope Leslie* 158
horror 6, 36, 39
*House of Cards* (TV series) 85–93, 98–100, 113–16, 121–7, 131, 153n.32
Howard, Jean E. 98
Huang, Alexa 23n.22, 24n.25, 158
Hundred Years' War 62

identity 7, 17–19, 28, 41, 77, 120, 199, 212, 216–18, 222n.16
  destabilisation of 195, 199, 202
  mistaken 19, 195, 198–9, 207

  rogue 123
  sexual 194
ideology 4, 10, 20, 64, 199, 201, 204, 211–12
image formula *see* pathos formula
impeachment 85–7, 114, 146–7
inheritance 14, 20–1, 65
intermediary 165, 172, 197
interregnum 157, 164, 172, 180, 183, 189n.5

Jess-Cooke, Carolyn 6
Joy, Lisa 17
  *see also* *Westworld* (TV series)
*Julius Caesar* (William Shakespeare) 29, 32, 143

Kaklamanidou, Betty 99, 150n.4
Kantorowicz, Ernst 100
Keir, Elam 196–7, 222n.6
KGB 197–8, 209, 213–17
Kinder, Marsha 64
*King John* (William Shakespeare) 58, 97
*King Lear* (William Shakespeare) 2, 5, 17, 19, 33–8, 51–5, 85, 93–4, 155–8, 163
*Kisses for My President* (Curtis Bernhardt) 118n.39
Klarer, Mario 85
Knapp, Jeffrey 6
Kott, Jan 12, 18

Lanier, Douglas 3–4, 23n.22, 160
Lanier, Stephen 7, 10
  *see also* Shakespop
LaRocca, David 222n.16
*Leatherstocking Tales* (James Fenimore Cooper) 158
Lee, Patricia-Ann 152n.26
legitimacy 4, 65, 68–71, 133
  of female sovereignty 97–136, 144
  of marriage 213, 214
  royal 62–9, 97, 110, 223n.30
legitimation 65, 68, 74–7, 127, 209
  political 59
  self- 62–8, 73–7
Lehmann, Courtney 4
lesbian desire 181

244

Levine, Caroline 25n.46, 178
Levine, Nina S. 117n.22
Looma, Ania 140
*Love's Labour's Lost* (William Shakespeare) 95, 105, 110, 114
Lyons, Tara 58

*Macbeth* (William Shakespeare) 18, 85–94, 98, 116n.4, 142, 187
*Madam Secretary* (TV series) 114, 150nn.4–5
Malone, Toby 27
Marcus, Lea 98, 117n.24
Margaret Reignier (Queen Margaret) 65–70, 97–8, 117n.20, 117n.22, 132–7, 152n.26
Marshall, C.W. 63
massacre 45, 48, 94, 182
Maxwell, Julie 22n.9
*Measure for Measure* (William Shakespeare) 169–75, 183
media 3–7, 12–16, 24n.30, 29–30, 131, 142
  appropriation 3, 9, 11
  culture 3, 12
  format 12–14, 149
  image 123–5
mediascape 15, 22n.9
medieval England 12, 59, 62
meme 14, 15, 22n.9, 37
*Merchant of Venice* (William Shakespeare) 102
*Midsummer Night's Dream, A* (William Shakespeare) 19, 81, 96, 122, 127–30, 163, 198, 204–22
  Puck (Robin Goodfellow) 81, 96, 204–8, 211, 216, 221
Milch, David 19, 155, 157–67, 175, 186
  *see also Deadwood* (TV series)
Mnemosyne atlas *see* Warburg, Aby
monologue 26, 29, 103, 115n.3, 147–8, 158–61, 191n.24, 219
Morag, Talia 224n.34
mother 5, 66, 91, 100–3, 123, 127, 209, 216–20
  of the nation 93, 137
*Much Ado About Nothing* (William Shakespeare) 164, 179–84

multiple perspectives 17, 177, 190n.18
*Music Man, The* (Morton DaCosta) 29
*My Darling Clementine* (John Ford) 158

narrative multiplicity 17
  *see also* multiple perspectives; parallel storylines
Negra, Diane 153n.36
new historicism 13
Nolan, Jonathan 17
  *see also Westworld* (TV series)
Nowak, Michael 100
Nussbaum, Emily 131

O'Neill, Stephen 3, 12, 25n.39, 37
*Othello* (William Shakespeare) 2, 24n.26

parallel editing 82n.3, 143, 163, 178
parallelism 9, 16
parallels 6, 7, 10, 44, 56n.42, 159, 164, 165
parallel storylines 16–17, 160, 163, 178, 196, 207
  *see also* multiple perspectives; narrative multiplicity
paternal sovereignty 38, 54, 93, 208
  *see also* sovereign; sovereignty
pathos formula 13–18, 25n.46, 37, 42–7, 54, 114, 123, 202
  *see also* pathos gesture; Warburg, Aby
pathos gesture 16, 42, 137, 153n.32
  *see also* pathos formula; Warburg, Aby
Paul, Heike 100, 117n.31
peace 50, 66–7, 71–5, 97, 134, 139, 182–5, 204, 208, 219
  treaty 108–9
Peretti, Burton W. 118n.32
period of interim 20, 122, 128
peripeteia 73, 109
Pilipets, Elena 85
*Political Animals* (TV series) 111–13
political power 18–19, 39, 62–3, 90–2, 97, 141–4, 188, 212
  *see also* power
potentiality 8–12, 21, 178, 189, 220

# Index

Potter, Tiffany 63
power 4–6, 14–18, 28, 33, 40–2, 47, 51, 61–80, 87–115, 120–50, 158–78, 207
  absolute 26, 62, 73, 86, 97, 102–3, 108, 134, 142–4, 178
  games 21, 103–7, 143
  relations 62–4, 68, 80, 144–6, 160, 176
  struggles 18, 54, 65, 97, 178, 183–5, 199
  theatricalisation of 78–9, 160, 169, 177
  vacuum 64–6, 144
  see also political power
Prison Break (TV series) 101–4
purgatory see Christian (religion), purgatory

queenship 18, 93–9, 106, 123, 152n.26
quotation 2–6, 11, 17, 28, 32–6, 52, 158–9

Rackin, Phyllis 98
Rahman, Smita A. 224n.46
re-articulation 7, 13
reassemblage 3–8, 16, 33–7, 160, 186
reciprocity 4, 8–9, 15–16
recycling 4, 8–9, 23n.21, 29, 186–7
Reed, Jason 66
re-making 28
remediation 4, 15, 30
repetition 5–18, 48, 58, 64, 114, 139, 143, 182–3
  compulsion 15, 43, 47, 113, 123, 139, 147
    see also Freud, Sigmund
  cycle of 18, 130
  with difference 7
  serial 12, 32, 124–9, 168, 184, 187–8, 216, 221
  with variation 6–7
resurgence 15, 93, 151n.5
resuscitation 5–16, 21, 32, 37, 40–8, 80, 86, 98, 142, 164, 175, 181, 190n.18
revenge tragedy 6, 43, 94, 143, 147
Rhimes, Shonda 18, 141, 143
  see also Scandal (TV series)
Richard II (William Shakespeare) 58
Richard III (William Shakespeare) 18, 58, 59, 62, 66, 71–4, 81n.3, 85, 97, 115n.3, 136–9
Ritt der Walküren (Richard Wagner) 79
Rivlin, Elizabeth 24n.25, 158
rogue 2, 45, 49, 61, 74, 107, 115
  queen 120–54
  see also Derrida, Jacques
Romeo and Juliet (William Shakespeare) 17, 33, 36–8, 43–57, 214
Rowe, Katherine 24n.30
Rumbold, Kate 22n.9

sacrifice 26, 64, 67, 130–7, 149, 174, 214
Salerno, Daniel 165, 190n.15
Scandal (TV series) 18, 113, 121–2, 141–50
Searchers, The (John Ford) 84n.45
self-creation 140, 149
self-meditation 136–7, 165–7
self-performance 19, 127, 147
sexual abuse 173–4
sexual act 169, 210
sexual allure 141, 147, 209, 215
Shakespearean aside 88, 151
  see also fourth wall break
Shakespearean western 158–60, 190n.12
Shakespop 7
  see also Lanier, Stephen
signifier 8, 27–8
Simkin, Stevie 6
Simon, David 18, 59, 62–5, 71–2, 78–9, 81, 225n.48
  see also Wire, The (TV series)
Singer, Mark 189n.9
Singh, Jyotsyna 140
Slotkin, Richard 193n.53, 56n.43
Smith, Emma 59
Sons of Anarchy (TV series) 5
sovereign 40, 51, 58, 64, 93–8, 100, 107–14, 161, 172, 175
  absolute 72–4, 92
  female 93, 137, 139
  see also sovereignty

sovereignty 26, 35–9, 43–7, 64, 72–4, 88, 95–7, 127, 142–4, 164–5, 170, 182, 192n.35, 206–7
  see also countersovereignty; female sovereignty; paternal sovereignty
spectacle 19, 36, 40, 168, 172–4, 184, 212
spectrality 17, 29, 98
  spectral afterlife 13, 27–33
  spectral double 31
  spectral presence 15, 38, 44–6, 53, 159, 211
  spectral voice 45, 218
  see also ghosts; haunting
spy 178, 195, 201
  couple 199, 211, 215
  game 203, 216–17
  glass 201–2, 219
  work 196–200, 205, 208–10, 213–14, 218
  see also espionage
stage within the stage 41, 78
Stanley, Alessandra 99
Starks, Lisa S. 4
Stasi, Paul 157, 191n.24
*State of Affairs* (TV series) 151n.5
Steenberg, Lindsay 152n.25
Stein, Gertrude 35, 57n.48
subaltern 27, 177
subversion 157–62, 178, 183, 194
succession 58, 61–5, 70–5, 98, 133
*Succession* (TV series) 5
superpower 199–209, 218
surveillance 19, 40, 70, 96, 147, 164, 176, 209
  drama of 165–6, 169, 176
  police 68, 80
survivance 25n.41, 29
  see also Calbi, Maurizio
symptom 77, 110, 149

Tally, Margaret 99, 116n.4, 119n.46
Tasker, Yvonne 152n.25
*Tempest, The* (William Shakespeare) 17, 33, 38–43, 51–7, 75
theatre within theatre 33, 41, 78
theatricality 4, 53, 75–9, 158–9, 161

Thirty Years' War 62–3
*Titus Andronicus* (William Shakespeare) 94, 103
tragedy 43–7, 53, 70, 122, 130, 139, 149, 182
  Greek 63
  revenge 43, 94, 143
  Shakespearean 17, 35, 53, 85–90, 155–6, 165, 214
  see also comedy
transgression 19, 151n.18, 163, 169–71, 190n.17, 199, 200, 211
transhistorical dialogue 6, 10, 27
transition 19, 104, 113, 130, 134
  historical 20–1, 157, 160, 164, 183, 200
  political 159
translation 8–16, 24n.25, 30, 100, 123
  see also Benjamin, Walter
trope 5–6, 13, 112, 157–8, 190n.14, 193n.53
*Twelfth Night* (William Shakespeare) 19, 163, 185, 194–204
*24* (TV series) 106–10
*24: Redemption* 106
*Two Noble Kinsmen* (William Shakespeare) 93–5

uncanny 25n.41, 28–30, 34, 45, 154n.55, 200

*Veep* (TV series) 121–31, 139, 150
violence 19–20, 31–4, 39–54, 64, 76, 79, 94–8, 134–9, 159–63, 174, 183–7, 211
  and creation 17
  foundational scene of 45–9
  serial 45–6, 54, 66, 147, 216
  systemic 71–2
voice control 40, 48–52, 56n.43

Wajcman, Gérard 17, 110, 149, 177, 192n.49
Walzer, Judith 105
Warburg, Aby 13–16, 37
  see also pathos formula; pathos gesture

war on drugs 18, 59, 63–5, 71, 79
war on terror 66, 152n.25
warrior queens 51, 69, 93–8, 102, 140, 208, 222n.7
   *see also* female president; female ruler; female sovereignty; sovereign
Wars of the Roses 18, 58, 62–6, 71, 81n.3, 97, 117n.24, 132, 139, 152n.26
western (genre) 17, 19, 84n.45, 158, 161, 189n.9
   *see also Deadwood* (TV series); frontier

*West Wing, The* (TV series) 99–100, 117n.31, 150n.4, 151n.12
*Westworld* (TV series) 17, 19, 26–57
Wheale, Nigel 23n.20
Winkler, Reto 57n.57
Winter, Rainer 85
*Winter's Tale, A* (William Shakespeare) 96–8, 111–13
*Wire, The* (TV series) 18, 58–84, 225n.48
Wood, Michael 80
world as theatre 32, 53, 156

Zanin, Andrea 222n.16